Francis Adams

The free school system of the United States

Francis Adams

The free school system of the United States

ISBN/EAN: 9783337278267

Printed in Europe, USA, Canada, Australia, Japan

Cover: Foto ©Paul-Georg Meister /pixelio.de

More available books at **www.hansebooks.com**

THE FREE SCHOOL SYSTEM

OF

THE UNITED STATES.

BY

FRANCIS ADAMS,

SECRETARY OF THE NATIONAL EDUCATION LEAGUE.

LONDON:
CHAPMAN AND HALL, 193, PICCADILLY.

1875.

NOTE.

The aim of the following pages is to supply for English Educational reformers the means of insight into the operation of the American system of Elementary Education. If it should be objected that the social conditions of England and the United States lie at extremes which render comparisons useless or fallacious, it may be replied, that successive Governments have recognised the policy of examining the educational systems of various countries, with the view of adopting for our own use the best methods found anywhere in practice. Moreover, international comparisons are now forced upon all countries by international competition.

That the experience of the United States furnishes valuable lessons for England the writer trusts will be made clear. Notwithstanding the differences which exist in the circumstances of the two countries, the type of the inhabitants is essentially the same. Nor are the ideas to which Americans attach the greatest importance in education foreign to England.

Local self-government is not the conception of American politicians. The people of the United States borrowed the principle from England, and making it the foundation of their Education system, demonstrated the advantages of its application in such a manner.

Neither is free education an exotic in England. Of all English schools the free schools have been the most popular. By making education universally free the Americans have made the common school the most popular and successful institution of that country.

Upon the subject of compulsion—an idea equally alien to the political philosophy of both nations—English and American proofs point to exactly the same conclusion,—that however popular a system may be, it cannot produce the highest results unless the school rights of children are placed under the protection of the law.

The absence of a dominant church has helped to protect the school system of the United States from the perils and the odium of religious strife. Yet the "religious difficulty" is not unknown. The attempt to find a common religious ground cannot be said to have succeeded. The question for the present remains unsettled—but it is a growing opinion that the common school, to be preserved, must be placed upon a distinctly secular basis.

One thing more. Bishop Fraser warns the readers of his report that in judging of American education an average is no safe guide. The same caution is still necessary. The key to the true comprehension of the development of the system in particular States will be found in an extract from the "Theory of Education," published by the National Bureau of Education. It is as follows :—

" As a consequence of the perpetual immigration from the older sections of the country to the unoccupied Territories, there are new States in all degrees of formation, and their institutions present earlier phases of realisation of the distinctive type than are presented in the mature growth of the system as it exists in the thickly settled and older States. Thus States are to be found with little or no provision for education, but they are rudimentary forms of the American State, and are adopting, as rapidly as immigration enables them to do so, the type of educational institutions already defined as the result of the American political and social ideas."

August 12th, 1875.

CONTENTS.

I.

GOVERNMENT.

	PAGE
(a) RELATION OF THE NATIONAL GOVERNMENT TO THE STATE	17
Representative character of system	17
Local self-government the mainspring	17
No federal education law	18
Powers of national government limited	18
Duty of State Legislatures	18
Success depends on enlightenment of people	19
Different views of popular education	19
Slavery hostile to the common school	19
Divergencies in social condition	19
Wealth and illiteracy in Massachusetts and South Carolina	19
Powers of central government	20
Dread of centralization	20
Establishment of National Bureau	21
Its functions and powers	21
Policy of American statesmen	21
Mr. Hoars' bill to establish a national system	22
Opinions of National Education Association	23
Mr. Perce's bill to establish an educational fund	23
Extent of federal jurisdiction	23
Work of the central department	24
(b) RELATION OF THE STATE GOVERNMENT TO THE MUNICIPALITY	24
Responsibility of States	24
Action of free States	24

	PAGE
Position of the South	25
Common school system in every State	25
State legislatures enact school laws...	25
Local management	26

PROVISION OF SCHOOLS 27
    Requirements of Massachusetts law... 27
    Law of Maryland 27
    School accommodation in New Jersey 28
    Supply of schools in Detroit and Cleveland ... 28
    Development of school expenditure... 28
    Provision of schools in Pennsylvania 29
    Powers of State over local corporations 29
    Laws in harmony with popular sympathy... ... 30
    Results of local government... 30

(c) SCHOOL DISTRICTS... 31
    Area of school districts 31
    The "district system" 32
    School districts in England... 32
    Multiplication of small schools 33
    Abolition of "district system" 33

(d) LOCAL SCHOOL BOARDS OR MANAGEMENT
        COMMITTEES 34
    How described in different States 34
    Constitution and powers of 34

(e) LOCAL SUPERVISION 35
    County superintendents 35
    Advantages of system 36

(f) STATE SUPERINTENDENCE 42
    Powers of boards of education 42
    Duties of State Superintendents 43
    Annual reports 43

II.

COST.

	PAGE
(a) THEORY OF FREE SCHOOLS	45
Introduction of free system	45
Element of rate-bills	46
Reasons for State provision of education	46
Policy of retaining school fees in England	49
Arguments against free schools considered	50
Free education not a charity	51
Responsibility of parents not lessened	52
Experience of Connecticut	52
Remission of fees in special cases degrading	53
The "odious rate bill"	53
Effects of rate bills in New York	54
Policy of educating at common cost children of improvident parents	54
Causes which operate against free schools in England	56
No financial difficulty involved	57
(b) PROVISION OF FUNDS FOR EDUCATION	57
Sources of school revenue	57
State school funds	58
Land appropriations	59
Amount of permanent funds	60
State taxes in different States	61
Reasons for advocating State taxation in Massachusetts	64
Local taxes	65
Expense chiefly met by local taxation	65
Table showing amount and source of income	67
Unparalleled taxation for education	68
Increase of expenditure	68
Voluntary taxes in Maine	69
School expenditure in New York and Massachusetts	69
School expenditure in the South	69
Expenditure per head of population	70
Comparison with English expenditure	72

		PAGE
	Donations	72
	The Peabody fund	73
(c)	TOTAL ABOLITION OF RATE BILLS...	75
	Its effect in New York State	75
	Increase of attendance	76
	Report of Rhode Island Commissioner	77
	Operation of free school law in New Jersey	77
	Michigan report	78
	Larger attendance and longer school terms	78
	Favourable effects of free school in Connecticut	79
	Large increase of attendance	79
(d)	FREE SCHOOLS—THE PEOPLE'S SYSTEM	80
	Unanimity of opinion	80
	Testimony of State superintendents	81
	Reports of county superintendents...	84
	Difference of opinion respecting free high schools	85
	The law of Michigan	85
	Mr. Dawson on opinion in Ohio	85
	Free school books	86
	Decrease of private schools...	87
	Schools attended by all classes	92
	Power of assimilation	94
	The work of the free school	95
	Roman Catholic parochial schools...	95

III.

ATTENDANCE.

(a)	ANNUAL ENROLMENT	96
	Per centage of enrolment in different States	97
	Comparison with England	98
	Extracts from State reports...	99

(b) AVERAGE ATTENDANCE ...	102
Degree of regularity the most important fact	102
Methods of arriving at averages confusing	103
Rivalry in School Statistics...	103
Evils of apportioning State-aid on average attendance	104
The experience of England ...	104
"Average number belonging"	105
Number enrolled, and average attendance compared	106
Comparison with England ...	107
Bishop Fraser's view fallacious	108
Average attendance compared with school population	109
The position of England	110
Average attendance and number belonging	110
American and English cities compared	111
Obstacles to regular attendance	113
Influx of Foreigners ...	113
Difficulties of climate	114
Demand for children's labour	115
Importance of the problem ...	115
(c) PERIOD OF ATTENDANCE	116
School-age in different States	116
Percentage of scholars over sixteen...	117
Age of leaving school	118
The school year	119
Length of school terms in different States	119
Not equal to English school term ...	120
Period of attendance in cities	121
(d) FAILURE OF INDIRECT COMPULSION	122
History of Factory Laws in Pennsylvania	122
Report of Mr. Woodruff	122
The law of Connecticut	124
Report of Mr. Cleveland	124
Co-operation of employers	125
Direct compulsion the only remedy	126
The law of Rhode Island ...	126
Favourable conditions for experiment	126

(e) TRIAL OF COMPULSION	127
Antagonism to compulsion	127
States having compulsory laws	127
Law of Massachusetts	128
Reasons for partial failure	129
Experience of Boston	129
Mr. Philbrick's reports on compulsion	129
The New Hampshire law	131
Satisfactory results of	131
The Connecticut law	132
The law of Michigan	133
Danger that it will prove ineffective	133
Weakness of the law	135
Compulsion in Nevada and New York	135
(f) DEMAND FOR COMPULSION	136
Reform urgently demanded	136
Action of State Legislatures	137
Reports of State Superintendents	138
Waste caused by irregularity in Iowa	139
Truancy and absenteeism in Ohio	140
Demand for compulsion in Indiana	140
Missouri, Louisiana, California, and Nebraska	141
Resolution of National Teachers' Association	142
Compulsion a question of time	143

IV.

RELIGION AND MORALS.

(a) LAW AS TO RELIGIOUS INSTRUCTION	144
Difference of legal opinions	144
Case of Minor *et als v.* Cincinnati Board of Education	144
Distinctive denominational teaching prohibited	146
Illegal to subsidise denominational schools	146

		PAGE
Christian and protestant instruction given...	...	146
Religious exercises in New England schools	...	147
Discretion of teachers	...	147
Statutory provisions in different States	...	147
Reading of Bible	...	148
Use of school buildings for religious purposes	...	150

(b) BIBLE READING—MORAL INSTRUCTION ... 150

Sectarian instruction not permitted... ...	...	150
Bible reading the rule	...	150
Exceptions in some States	...	151
Secular teaching at St. Louis and Cincinnati	...	151
Discretion as to use of Bible	...	154
Moral teaching in Maine	...	154
Instruction in Morals in Boston and St. Louis	...	155
Morality of common schools	...	155
Infidel tendencies do not exist	...	157
The Bishop of Manchester's view	...	158
Religious teaching in English schools ...	...	159

(c) THE RELIGIOUS DIFFICULTY 159

Majority favourable to Bible reading ...	...	159
Growing opinion in favour of secular schools	...	160
Two sections of community opposed to Bible reading		160
The Roman Catholic view	...	161
Conflict in New York State	...	162
Resolution of Chicago Board	...	163
Reports of the Superintendents of Iowa and Missouri	...	164
Opinions of Mr. Northrop of Connecticut...	...	166
The Struggle in Cincinnati...	...	167
Roman Catholic testimony in favour of common schools...	...	170
A contest apparently inevitable	...	172
The parochial system impossible	...	173

V.

TEACHERS.

	PAGE
(a) TRAINING	175
The conditions of teaching	175
Unfavourable effect of short school terms	176
Inadequate payment of teachers	177
Preponderance of female teachers	177
Necessity for training teachers of recent recognition	178
Dr. Hodgson's description of some English teachers	178
Action of London School Board	179
First Normal Schools in England and America	179
Reasons for Normal Training	180
The American problem	181
County Normal Schools	184
Number of Normal Schools in differrent States	185
Instruction in Normal Schools	185
Private Normal Schools	186
Teachers Institutes	187
Their objects and value	187
Normal institutes	189
The pupil teacher system has no advocates	189
(b) EXAMINATION—QUALIFICATIONS	190
Teachers must be certificated	190
The practice in different States	190
Grades of certificates	191
Methods and standards of examination	191
Want of uniformity	192
Reform required	193
Suggested reforms	193
Worth of American teachers	194
Bishop Fraser's opinions	194
(c) SALARIES AND SOCIAL STATUS	195
Low salaries	195
Table of salaries	195

		PAGE
Improvement in salaries	... ...	196
High social standing of teachers	... ...	197
Comparison with England ...	... ...	197

VI.

GRADES.—RESULTS.

(a) GRADING	199
Description of graded schools	199
Advantages of grading	200
Economy of time and money	201
Its effect upon the pupils	201
Disadvantages of too strict grading	202
Union schools	203
Plans of school houses	203
Grades in the chief cities	204
(b) COURSE OF STUDY	207
Practically only two courses — elementary and higher	207
Description of course in New York and Boston ...	208
Grades in Cincinnati, Chicago, St. Louis, and Cleveland	208
Comparison with English code	209
Materials for a close comparison wanted	210
No prescribed course in any State	210
Absence of uniformity	211
Connection between elementary and higher instruction	211
Subjects generally taught	212
Teaching of German	212
The schools of Boston	213
Gradation of scholars	214
Promotion of Pupils	214
Compared with England	215

	PAGE
Elementary schools of New York	217
Examination of scholars	217
Comparison with English standards	218
The Cleveland schools	220
Examination questions	221
Ages and status of pupils	223
St. Louis schools	223
The Cincinnati schools	224
Classification of scholars	225
The Chicago schools	226
Night schools	228

(c) PRACTICAL OUTCOME 229

General reputation	229
Opinions of visitors to the States	229
Census statistics of illiteracy	230
Decrease of native illiterates	231
Foreign illiteracy	232
Per centage of illiteracy in England	234
Native and foreign illiterates in the free school States	235
Nativity of foreign population	236
Adverse influences of slavery and immigration ...	237
Results of the system	237
Bishop Fraser's testimony	238

VII.
REVIEW.

GENERAL REVIEW OF THE SUBJECT 239

APPENDIX A.

EXAMINATION OF DR. RIGG'S CHARGES ... 255

APPENDIX B.

COURSE OF STUDY IN BOSTON, NEW YORK, AND CINCINNATI 275

STANDARDS OF EXAMINATION IN ENGLISH SCHOOLS 308

I.

GOVERNMENT.

(a) RELATION OF THE NATIONAL GOVERNMENT TO THE STATE
—*(b)* RELATION OF THE STATE GOVERNMENT TO THE
MUNICIPALITY—PROVISION OF SCHOOLS—*(c)* SCHOOL
DISTRICTS—*(d)* LOCAL SCHOOL BOARDS—*(e)* LOCAL
SUPERVISION—*(f)* STATE SUPERINTENDENCE.

(a) Relation of the National Government to the State.

The most conspicuous feature of the American school system is its representative character. The doctrine of the sovereignty of the people, pervading all American social and political organisations, is carried to its furthest limit in the schools of the country. The principle to which the inhabitants are most attached is thus fitly exhibited in the institution upon which they set the highest value. Bishop Fraser says: "Local self-government is the underlying principle of democratic institutions; local self-government is the mainspring of the American school system." [1] The Schools Enquiry Commissioners, in their report, ascribed chiefly to this characteristic of the system

---

[1] Fraser's Report, p. 14.

the excellent results which the common school has produced. "The schools are in the hands of the people, and from this fact they derive a force which seems to make up for all their deficiencies." (¹) In the United States they have actually that which Mr. Forster promised to give England by the Act of 1870, but which at present we are far from the realisation of—" an education of the people's children, by the people's officers chosen in their local assemblies, and controlled by the people's representatives in Parliament."

It is sometimes said, apparently in disparagement, that there is no national system of education in the United States. It is perfectly true that there is no federal education law embracing all the States. Such a law would be widely regarded as repugnant to one of the fundamental principles of government as generally accepted throughout the Union, the object of which is to secure the largest amount of local discretion consistent with the recognition of national obligations. The powers of the National Government over the States are limited by the Constitution. Certain limitations are also imposed upon the Legislatures of the States by their particular Constitutions. So far, however, from restricting educational facilities, the State Constitutions generally declare the duty of the Legislature to make ample provision for popular instruction; but it is in the municipal organisation of each school district that the motive power which supplies and administers the educational wants and machinery of the country lies. The principle of local self-government upon which the system is founded, presupposes a desire for education in the community. Its success, therefore, will always greatly depend upon the degree of enlightenment in the district where it is

---

[1] Report of Schools Enquiry Commission, p. 640.

applied. In a priest-ridden country a system of education depending chiefly upon popular suffrage would be, comparatively, a failure. That which Massachusetts regards as her chief blessing, New Mexico rejects with disdain. ([1]) While America was yet a dependency of Great Britain, a forcible illustration of the widely different lights in which popular education may be regarded was contained in two replies, sent from different colonies, to questions put by the English Commissioners for Foreign Plantations. The Governor of Virginia replied, "I thank God there are no free schools or printing presses, and I hope we shall not have, these hundred years." The Governor of Connecticut answered, "One fourth the annual revenue of the colony is laid out in maintaining free schools for the education of our children." So long as slavery existed it was impossible that the common school should find a home in the Southern States. This must always be remembered in estimating educational progress in the United States. To this cause must be ascribed the wide divergences which still exist in the social and educational conditions of the inhabitants of different States. Under the influence of slavery, and up to a recent period, without the free school system, the rate of native illiteracy in South Carolina is about 60 per cent., while the wealth of the State is less than three hundred dollars per head of the population. With conditions precisely reversed, native illiteracy in Massachusetts is under one per cent., and the wealth of the State averages nearly two thousand dollars per head of the inhabitants. It will be apparent, therefore, that the free school system must not be judged either by the errors or eccentricities of a single State, or by an average calculated upon the statistics of the whole country. If, upon an impartial examination of the experience

---

[1] Report of Commissioner of Education, 1870, p. 327.

and results of the system in the free school States, it is found to be a failure, then only can it be justly condemned.

The powers of the Central Government are summed up in "A Statement of the Theory of Education in the United States," recently issued by the Bureau of Education at Washington. "By the Constitution of the United States, no powers are vested in the Central Government of the nation, unless the same relate immediately to the support and defence of the whole people, to their intercourse with foreign Powers, or to the subordination of the several States composing the Union." [1] It was held by many of the earlier statesmen of the country, including Washington, that the authority given by the Constitution "to levy taxes and provide for the general welfare of the United States" included the power to make laws respecting education. This opinion is not, however, generally accepted, and the more correct view appears to be that the relation of the National Government to public education is limited. It is admitted that the National Government may use either the public domain or the money received from its sale for the purposes of education, and may call all persons or States to account for whatever has been entrusted to them by it for educational purposes. In various ways, but chiefly by making reservations and grants of land for the support of common schools and agricultural and scientific colleges, Congress has recognised its duty to promote education among the people. But the direct jurisdiction of the Central Government is confined to the military education of the army and navy, to the Territories and the district of Columbia. [2] The dread of "centralisation" which prevails throughout the States has had the effect of checking every movement for enlarging the powers of the

---

[1] Statement, p. 9. [2] Proceedings of National Teachers' Association, 1870. Paper by General Eaton, p. 122.

National Government. The whole tide of public sentiment in America is in favour of a perfectly unfettered working of the State systems. It was not until 1867 that any department taking cognisance of national education existed at Washington. In that year the National Bureau of Education was established. This department had its origin in "the need long felt by leading educators of some central agency, by which the general educational statistics of the country could be collected, preserved, condensed, and properly arranged for distribution." ([1]) Its function is not to direct the school affairs of States, but to co-operate with them in the work of administering systems of public instruction. The Act which creates it defines the work it shall perform, it being founded "for the purpose of collecting such statistics and facts as shall show the condition and progress of education in the several States and Territories, and of diffusing such information respecting the organisation and management of school systems and methods of teaching as shall aid the people of the United States in the establishment and maintenance of efficient school systems, and otherwise promote the cause of education."

It will be seen that this department has no control whatever over the school organisation of the States. Even in the Territories, where the legislative power of Congress is supreme, the authority of the Bureau is confined to the collection and diffusion of information.

Whatever opinion may be formed in this country respecting the advantages or disadvantages of the limitations imposed upon the Central Department of Education, it must be well understood that they do not arise from accident or neglect, but are the expression of the settled policy of American statesmen. Any invasion of the rights

---

[1] History of "The National Bureau of Education," p. 1.

and duties of the municipality, either in respect to education or other questions, is regarded with the greatest distrust. In the session of Congress for 1871, a bill was introduced by Mr. Hoar, of Massachusetts, "to compel by national authority the establishment of a thorough and efficient system of public instruction throughout the whole country." Although the discussion of the bill in Congress, and the comments of the press, revealed a public sentiment of considerable strength in favour of some such measure, the general feeling is thoroughly antagonistic to the proposal. At a meeting of the National Educational Association, held in St. Louis in 1871, Mr. Hoar's bill was discussed, and it was declared to be "in opposition to the uniform practice of the National Government," and to "the views of the founders of the Republic, and the leading statesmen of the nation"—"of doubtful constitutionality," and opposed to a sound Republican political philosophy. ([1]) The establishment of the National Bureau was advocated in Congress on the express ground that it would create no interference with State rights. General Garfield, by whom the bill for the formation of the Bureau was introduced, said, "The genius of our Government does not allow us to establish a compulsory system of education, as is done in some of the countries of Europe. There are States in this Union which have adopted a compulsory system, and perhaps that is well. It is for each State to determine." Mr. Boutwell said, "This measure is no invasion of State rights. It does not seek to control anybody. It does not interfere with the system of education anywhere. It only proposes to furnish the means by which, from a Bureau here, every citizen of every State in this Republic can be informed as to the means of education existing and applied in the most

---

[1] Proceedings of Educational Association, 1871, p. 18.

advanced sections of the country and the world." (¹) These extracts fairly represent the prevailing sentiment of the people at the time the Bureau was established, and there is ample proof that the feeling has not perceptibly changed. The annual meetings of the National Educational Association are attended by the most prominent educationists from all parts of the Union, and all topics affecting education are discussed. At the meeting of the Association held at Washington, January, 1874, it was resolved unanimously, "That this convention strongly approves the policy hitherto pursued by the Federal Government, of leaving the people and local Government of each State to manage their own educational affairs without interference, believing that the principle on which this policy is based is as sound educationally as it is politically."

Any measure which, however slightly or indirectly, encroaches, or seems to encroach, upon the absolute independence of the several States excites antagonism. In 1872, Mr. Perce brought before Congress a bill " to establish an educational fund, and to apply the proceeds of the public lands to the education of the people." The professed object of the bill was to dedicate the proceeds of the public lands to the education of all the people of all the States. The income arising from the fund to be thus formed was to be annually apportioned to the several States and Territories upon the basis of population; but it was required, as a condition of receiving a share of the apportionment, that each State should report certain specified statistics at certain fixed times in the year. This was sufficient to arouse the vigilance of the State officers, and the bill was resisted on the ground that it would encourage centralisation and be prejudicial to the cause of education. (²)

---

[1] History of National Bureau, p. 10.   [2] New York State Report, 1872, p. 63.

Enough has been said to show the extent of federal jurisdiction upon the question. Of the work of the Central Department of Education I shall have occasion from time to time to speak. At the outset, one is impressed by the vast field over which its enquiries extend. Thirty-seven States and eleven Territories are comprised within the area of its investigations. Besides the enormous number of common schools, which they contain, nearly 5,000 other institutions of instruction are in correspondence with the Department.

(b) Relation of the State Government to the Municipality.

Upon each State rests the responsibility of providing for the education of its citizens. "This responsibility has been generally recognised in the establishment, by legislative enactment, of a system of free common schools, supported in part by State school funds, accumulated from national grants of lands, and from appropriations made from the State revenue, and in part by local taxation or assessment made upon those directly benefited by the schools themselves." ([1]) In many States this duty is enjoined by the Constitution. How far the free States have fulfilled these obligations may be learned from the report of Bishop Fraser. "The common school system, which occupies so proud a position among American institutions, is almost exclusively a product of free soil. Into the Southern States, usually so called, it had scarcely penetrated before the civil war, with the exception, as I was informed, of a tolerably complete organisation for the city of Charleston, S. C., and another for

---

[1] Statement of Bureau, p. 10.

the State of Louisiana. In the border States, as Kentucky and Missouri, the system existed, but in very dwarfed dimensions. In the new State of Western Virginia it was being organised during the period of my visit. But over the Northern States, from the Atlantic to the Pacific, and from the Ohio to the St. Lawrence, it has covered the land with a vast network of schools." [1] In the ten years which have elapsed since Bishop Fraser visited America, the Southern States have made a vigorous, and in part a successful, effort to remove the disgrace of a defective provision for popular education. In considering what they have done it must always be kept in mind that they have had to deal with the legacy of ignorance and indifference left to them by slavery. They have had, also, to contend with the difficulties which followed the civil war, the chief of which was the impoverished condition of many parts of the country, and the consequent inability of the inhabitants to pay taxes for the support of schools. To surmount all the obstacles in the way of an efficient school system in a country with such antecedents must be a work of time; but it is satisfactory to know that the attempt is being made, and that the reports from the Southern States show that the system is gradually taking root in the soil.

In theory, at any rate, every State in the Union has now a system of common schools, fashioned mainly on the model of that which exists in New England, and which has been made familiar to English readers by the descriptions of Bishop Fraser and other visitors to the States.

It is, first, in obedience to the commands of the State Legislatures that provision is made for common school education; but the principle of self-government is applied much more closely than is indicated by the recognition of the

---

[1] Fraser, p. 11.

independence of the States. In no State—even where a State Board of Education exists—is any extensive intervention on the part of the State Government called for. The State issues the command, and the municipality, or local government, by whatever name it is known, carries it into execution. " The local direction and management of the schools are left to the municipalities or to the local corporate bodies organised for the special purpose, and a general supervision is reserved to itself by the State. In some States, compulsory educational laws have been passed; not, however, requiring those who are taught in other ways to resort to the public schools."

" The State arranges the school system, and designates the various kinds of schools to be supported and managed by the public authorities, and sometimes prescribes moreor less of the branches of knowledge to be taught; provides how districts may be created, divided, or consolidated with others, and how moneys may be raised by or for them; prescribes their organisation, officers, and their powers, and the time and manner of filling and vacating offices, and the functions of each officer; prescribes the school age and conditions of attendance, and provides, in some cases, for the investment and application of the school funds derived from the General Government. The local municipalities organise school districts under State laws, elect school officers, and levy and collect taxes for school purposes. The local school officers examine, appoint, and fix the salaries of teachers, when not otherwise done, build school-houses, procure school supplies, arrange courses of study, prescribe the rules and regulations for the government of the schools, and administer the schools." ([1])

---

[1] **Statement of Bureau, p. 10.**

Provision of Schools.

Bishop Fraser has set out at some length, in his valuable report, the laws of the State of Massachusetts respecting the supply of schools. The requirement of the law in that State is that every school district shall maintain schools enough for all the children of school age for the period of six months in each year. ([1]) In Dr. Rigg's superficial criticism of the American system, it is represented that the State has no power to enforce its regulations. Happily, the exercise of such a power in America is rarely called for, ample provision being generally made for schools by the spontaneous action of the people. Of the law of Massachusetts Bishop Fraser says: "The law is imperative, but the penalty attached to failure to comply with it might be difficult of infliction. Mr. Mann says that a township is indictable and punishable if it does not maintain one or more schools, and he refers, in proof of this assertion, to Revised Statutes, ch. 23, s. 60." ([2]) I know of no State but Maryland in which the provision of school accommodation is not compulsory. The Maryland report for 1873 (p. 10) says: "The law puts it in the power of the citizens of every county to have a good school in every district; it gives them advice, encouragement, and substantial aid, but it does not use compulsion." The Maryland Board of Education defend this policy on the express ground that the time has not arrived when it would be advisable to force the system on the inhabitants of the State. They are adopting it of their own accord; to attempt to force it would check its development. In regard to all the Southern States the true policy of American statesmen is to be patient. Throughout the Northern and Western States inadequate accommodation

---

[1] Mass. report, 1873, p. 19.   [2] Fraser's Report, p. 17.

is very exceptional. Here and there in the State reports, a complaint of the kind may be found. In an examination of the reports of more than thirty States, the only case which I discovered that had the appearance of culpable negligence was in the State of New Jersey. The report of that State for 1873 (p. 50) states that in Jersey city there were as many as 8,000 children for whom accommodation was needed. This was partly owing to a large influx into the schools; and it was a healthy sign that at the date of the report a very vigorous effort was being made by the school officers to secure the requisite accommodation. In many of the western towns, it is not always an easy matter to supply schools as fast as they are required. The report upon the schools of Detroit (1873) says: "The pressure for admission into our public schools still continues, and, notwithstanding the addition of 400 seats this year, hundreds have been denied admission. To partially relieve these urgent wants, we are operating a number of half-day schools. At the rate of increase of population, we ought to furnish about 1,000 new seats each year. With this in view, we recommend the purchase this year of six sites on which to erect school buildings." ([1])

The report for the city of Cleveland (Ohio), 1872, says: "The necessity for more new buildings, having seating capacity of from five hundred to eight hundred pupils each, is pressing. . . . . . A careful survey of the entire city will satisfy anyone at all familiar with its wants that, for some years to come, it will be necessary to erect one new building annually." ([2])

These extracts, while they show the kind of demands made upon the energy and liberality of American educationists, are

---

[1] Mich. Report, 1873, p. 325.   [2] Cleveland Report, 1872, p. 11.

a valuable index to the spirit in which they are met. If the remarkable development of American industry, population, and resources is taken into account, it is proof of the attachment of Americans to their system of education that the supply of schools keeps pace with national progress in other directions. The amount of expenditure for school purposes was doubled during the ten years from 1850 to 1860, and almost trebled between 1860 and 1870.

Previous to 1868 there were in the State of Pennsylvania some twenty-four districts which had refused or neglected to supply public schools. Some of them had private schools in operation, but in most the education of the children was greatly neglected. The energetic measures taken by the State authorities since 1868 have "accomplished the much-needed work of bringing in the recusant districts." ([1]) This will dispose of the suggestion that the State authorities have no means of compelling localities to do their duty. If, however, any doubt about it exists in the mind of any English reader, it may be set at rest by the authoritative statement of the National Bureau. "The general form of the National Government is largely copied in the civil organisation of the particular States, and no powers or functions of an administrative character are ordinarily exercised by the State as a whole, which concern only the particular interests and well-being of the subordinate organisations or corporations into which the State is divided for judicial and municipal purposes; but the State usually vests these local powers and functions in the corporations themselves, such as counties, townships, and cities. The power of the State over these local corporations is complete; but they are generally allowed large legislative and administrative powers of a purely local character, while the State ordinarily confines its action and

---

[1] Penn. Report, 1872, p. xii.

legislation to matters in which the people of the whole State are interested." (¹)

But it is highly fortunate for the United States that the school laws are in harmony with the sympathies of the people, and that the interposition of the Government to secure provision for education is unnecessary. Everywhere the school-house is "the unerring sign of civilisation." The report for Michigan (1873) refers to "the interest felt, and the sacrifices made, by the pioneers in the new counties, who sometimes organise districts and establish schools before there are voters enough to fill the district offices." (²)

The simple principle of the American school laws is that the people can be trusted to attend to their own business. In the preliminary matter of providing school buildings and machinery it leaves little to be desired. The doctrine of the supreme authority of each district over its own affairs may be pushed to inconvenience, and no doubt it has worked injuriously in some respects—notably in the multiplication of small school districts; but striking a balance between the good and evil, and judging from the results alone, it is difficult to understand what better system could have been devised. There are localities to be found in the United States, as in most other countries, where schools are unpopular; but they are, as one of their reports says, chiefly places "not favoured with convenience for speedy transmission of news, and where people are still voting for General Jackson."

---

[1] Statement of Bureau, p. 10.   [2] Mich. Report, 1873, p. 53.

(c) *School Districts.*

Massachusetts was the first State in which a common school law was enacted. Upon the model set up by this State all the New England States and many other States of the North and North-West have founded their school systems. In Massachusetts, and all the New England States, the township is the " political unit " upon which lies the obligation to make provision for education ; ([1]) and the township as the area of the school district has been adopted in Illinois, Indiana, Iowa, Ohio, Missouri, and some other States. ([2])

"Both the area and the population of a township vary indefinitely in the Eastern States. In the new States of the West the *area* of all townships is the same—thirty-six square miles—unless they lie on the borders of the State, in which case they may happen to be curtailed." ([3])

" In New York the ' township ' almost disappears as an element in the organisation of the school system, its only important constitutents being (*a*) the county, (*b*) the district."([4])

This remark applies to many other States and Territories, including Alabama, Arkansas, California, Florida, Georgia, Kansas, Kentucky, Maryland, Michigan, Nebraska, Nevada, New Jersey, North Carolina, Oregon, Pennsylvania, South Carolina, Tennessee, Texas, Virginia, West Virginia, Wisconsin, Arizona, Colorado, Dakota, Utah, Washington, Wyoming." ([5])

Although, at first sight, the area of a school district may appear to be an unimportant matter of detail, yet upon it, as the experience of the United States has proved, the efficiency of any school system largely depends. The most formidable

---

[1] Fraser's Report, p. 16.   [2] Report of Commissioner of Education, 1873, p. cxx.   [3] Fraser's Report, p. 16.   [4] Fraser's Report, p. 29.
[5] See Report of Commissioner of Education, 1873, p. cxx.

difficulty which the American system has encountered has arisen out of this question. This is what is known in the United States as "the district system." It had its origin in a law passed in Massachusetts in 1789, authorising the division of townships into districts for school purposes. The original object of the law, Fraser remarks, was innocent and praiseworthy; the result has been to create a most powerful impediment to the easy working of the system.

In our discussions in England since the passing of the Education Act it has been suggested that in adopting the parish as the school district we have selected, in many cases, too small a division. We have, however, happily steered clear of the extreme which, in the United States, has been very prejudicial to harmonious and efficient action. If every small hamlet in the English parishes had been created a separate school district, the error could hardly have occasioned greater difficulties than have resulted under the law of Massachusetts. Mr. Horace Mann said that this was "the most unfortunate law on the subject of common schools ever enacted by the State."[1] Unfortunately, it was not confined to Massachusetts. The spirit of the law was in harmony with the strong political predilection of Americans—the right of each locality to govern within its own limits; and the system was adopted in New York and many other States, before its action in Massachusetts had demonstrated the mischief it would occasion. In 1869 Massachusetts passed a law abolishing the system,[2] and, I believe, in nearly all of the States where the law was in operation, it has been repealed since Bishop Fraser made his report; but wherever it still exists it is the subject of the most bitter complaint and condemnation amongst school superintendents and officers. The State Superintendent of Maine, says: "Under the 'district system' these facts were

---

[1] Fraser's Report, p. 35.   [2] Mass. Report, 1873, p. 112.

patent—first, that the school moneys were inequably divided, some districts receiving much more than they could profitably expend, others much less than was absolutely needed; second, poor school-houses in remote and sparsely-settled sections; third, short schools, or poor ones, if the agent attempted to lengthen by hiring cheap teachers. Little money, poor school-houses, short schools, are the necessary attendants of this system." ([1]) In Maine an Act has been passed authorising the abolition of the system by a vote of the township.

The School Committee of Peru (Mass.) say: "In the report of the agent of the Board of Education, in illustration of the beauties of the district system, an instance is given where a school was taught some months for the benefit of one scholar, at an expense of sixty dollars." ([2])

The Pennsylvania report for 1873 gives an instance of a district in which the school was composed of members of one family. ([3])

Most of the States have, after an extended trial of the district system, reorganised under the township plan; and the complete abolition of the former system, if it can be secured by the almost unanimous condemnation of school officials of all grades, would appear to be a question of time only. I have alluded to the subject, partly because the information is necessary to a fair understanding of the previous working of the American system, and partly because the experience of the United States may have valuable lessons for England in any future development of our educational system. If the time should ever arrive to attempt in this country a gradation of schools, the area of the school districts will have to be reconsidered. In the meantime it

---

[1] Maine Report, 1872, p. 86.   [2] Mass. Report, 1873, p. 16.
[3] Penn. Report, 1873, p. 135.

will be seen that it is possible to push a healthy principle—that of local self-government—to an inconvenient extreme.

(d) *Local School Boards or Management Committees.*

The local Boards which have the control of schools are called School Committees in Massachusetts, Maine, New Hampshire, and Rhode Island; School Visitors in Connecticut; School Directors in Illinois, Indiana, Iowa, Louisiana, Oregon, Pennsylvania, Tennessee, Texas, and Washington; School Trustees in Arkansas, Kentucky, New Jersey, and South Carolina; School Commissioners in New York; School Boards in Michigan, Mississippi, Missouri, Nebraska, Nevada, and Ohio; and Prudential Committees in Vermont. ([1])

However named in the several States, these bodies are very similar in their constitution, powers, and duties, and directly represent the opinions and will of the people themselves in reference to the maintenance and condition of their schools. ([2])

In Massachusetts the Committees consist of any number divisible by three, elected by the township, one third of whom retire annually. In this and some other States they are paid a salary. Their duties consist in the employment of teachers, provision and maintenance of a sufficient number of school-houses, visitation of schools, and selection of text-books.

In Ohio the duties and powers of School Boards follow very much the line of the English Education Act. The Boards are bodies politic and corporate, and as such are

---

[1] See Report of Commissioner of Education, 1873, p. cxx.
[2] Proceedings of National Educational Association, 1872, p. 255.

capable of suing and being sued, making contracts, acquiring, holding, and disposing of property.

The Boards are empowered to appoint superintendents, and to fix their salaries. They are also required to make rules and regulations for the government of the schools under their control. They must publish annual reports of the condition of the schools and the management of school affairs. They are also required to report to the county auditor, and they are authorised to require teachers and superintendents to keep full and complete school records. The studies to be pursued, and the text-books to be used, are to be determined by the Boards in their respective districts. ([1])

In other States School Boards are invested with similar powers.

(c) Local Supervision.

Between the local School Board and the State Board, or Superintendent, a third office, charged with the duty of inspection and supervision, has been created in most of the States—that of "County Superintendent," which is now in use in twenty-eight States and six Territories. Upon the necessity for such an agency American educationalists are unanimous. In their school reports the motto of Holland, "As your inspection is, so is your school," is constantly quoted and enforced. When Bishop Fraser was in America he noticed the want of a Central Bureau of Education, and of the kind of control exercised by Her Majesty's Inspectors of Schools in England. As I have shown, the Central Bureau has since been established. With regard to supervision or inspection, Bishop Fraser appears to have been

---

[1] See Ohio Report, 1873, p. 38.

under the impression that it was in use only in the larger cities, such as New York, Boston, Newhaven, Cincinnati, and Chicago. During the last ten years there has been a very marked educational revival in America, and much has been done to supply adequate means for inspection; but I think Bishop Fraser is mistaken in supposing that this kind of supervision existed only in cities at the time of his visit to the States. It is true that the County Superintendents are not under the regulations of the National Government as in England, but they are responsible to the State Department of Education, whether that Department be under the control of a superintendent, as in some States, or a Board, as in other States. County Superintendents, or Inspectors, were appointed in Iowa in 1858, in New York State in 1856, in Pennsylvania, in 1854; and they now are employed in Alabama, Arkansas, California, Delaware, Florida, Georgia, Illinois, Indiana, Iowa, Kansas, Kentucky, Maryland, Michigan, Minnesota, Mississippi, Missouri, Nebraska, Nevada, New Jersey, New York (where they are called County Commissioners), Oregon, Pennsylvania, Tennessee, Texas, Virginia, West Virginia, Wisconsin, Arizona, Colorado, Dakota, District of Columbia, Idaho, Montana, Utah, Washington, and Wyoming.

On this subject General Eaton, the Commissioner of Education, in his last report, says: "The importance of intelligent oversight of schools finds continually increasing recognition with our people. In some form, almost every State and Territory in the Union has now both general and local superintendence. The system abides where it has already found a lodgment, and steadily makes its way to points beyond. Arkansas has, in 1873, exchanged its former circuit supervision for the closer inspection of county superintendency. Indiana has put County Superintendents in place of the County Examiners it had before. North Carolina is calling for a kindred change, and Maine desires the restoration of the superintendency it had. Tennessee, after abolishing it, has restored it. And although, from false ideas of economy, or from discontent with the imperfect work which small salaries secure, there have been mutterings against it in some quarters, good supervision abundantly justifies itself by its effects, wherever a judicious liberality provides salaries sufficient to secure the proper kind of men, and enable them to give their undivided time to the performance of the duties of their office. A universal adoption of the system on this liberal plan would probably do more than any other single thing to promote the interests of education in the States." [1]

The first qualification of a County Superintendent, in American opinion, is that he should be "a live man," having an eye like the Lady Blanche's—"a lidless watcher of the public weal."

The functions of County Superintendents vary to a considerable extent in the different States. Amongst the duties imposed upon them are: To visit, examine, and inspect schools; to give advice and direction to teachers; to adjust district boundaries; to give information and counsel to School Boards; to settle all disputes respecting school matters; to examine and license teachers; to apportion school moneys, and to issue orders for the payment of the same; to examine school accounts, and to prepare the annual county school reports.

While amongst school officers the County Superintendency is considered the right arm of the system, it is not always a popular office amongst the people. It checks too much, and grates upon the American notion of independence. The consequence is that in some States an effort has been made to keep the Superintendent in a subordinate

---

[1] Report of Commissioner of Education, 1873, p. cxvii.

position. By offering low salaries a class of incapable officers has been secured, and, as an inevitable result, the work has been badly done. In Iowa and Missouri a very considerable feeling exists against the continuance of the office. In the former State it has had a trial of over sixteen years—long enough, one would think, to demonstrate its utility, if it were really a useful agency—yet there exists a wide difference of opinion as to its value. The friends of the system claim that it has not had a fair trial. The officers have been chosen at political conventions, and all the vices of American politics have had a share in the contest. The salary, too, has always been insufficient to attract good officers. No wonder that the office has been but a partial success. "The greatest wonder is that the office has, under such circumstances, not become more unpopular than it actually has; and it doubtless would but for the fact that a large number of talented, earnest, superior men have been from time to time drawn into this office, and have devoted their best energies to the performance of its duties." [1]

In the State of New York the system was in operation previous to 1847. In that year it was abolished. The effect of the abolition is described by the Hon. S. S. Spencer, late Deputy Superintendent in the State, who says: "Its effect upon the prosperity and advancement of the common school system was, in many essential respects, most disastrous. During a period of nearly forty years the progress of that system had been uninterruptedly onward and upward; and a succession of wise enactments had strengthened and consolidated its foundation, and expanded its usefulness in every direction. The destruction of that feature, which, perhaps more than any other, had come to constitute its most distinctive charac-

---

[1] Iowa Report, 1872, p. 43.

teristic and crowning excellence, giving to its details their peculiar symmetry and power, was the first retrograde step in its history." (¹) After the lapse of nine years the office was restored in New York State in 1856, by providing for the election of a School Commissioner in each assembly district.

In his report for 1871, the Superintendent of Public Instruction, the Hon. A. B. Weaver, says: "There is no attribute of our school system which, when wisely and faithfully exercised, is productive of more direct and practical benefit than personal supervision by competent officers. Much of the success and improvement which has already been witnessed in many of the cities and rural districts of the State is due to this agency; and if ever our schools are brought to the highest condition of excellence, it will be through an efficient administration of this branch of educational service." (²) After referring to the plan of inspection in Holland, Mr. Weaver adds: "In our own State, and under our own system of public instruction, it is not less fundamental."

The Hon. J. P. Wickersham, Superintendent of Public Instruction in Pennsylvania, in a recent report says: "We have had superintendents of schools in our counties since 1854, a period of fifteen years, and nothing is risked in saying that wherever persons well qualified have filled the office, it has done great good, and is popular. It must be continued, either in its present or in some modified form that will render it more efficient. The work it does, I am satisfied, cannot be as well done by any other agency that can be substituted for it."

Dr. Newton Bateman, Superintendent of Public Instruction in the State of Illinois, in the course of a long review of the results in other States, says: " I am persuaded

---

[1] Iowa Report, 1872-3, p. 43. [2] New York State Report, 1871, p. 55.

that county supervision cannot be dispensed with without serious detriment to the free school interests of the State. I believe that its benefits are so obvious and manifold, that it ought to have, and will have, a permanent place in the final adjustment of the working forces in every State school law—that experience has abundantly demonstrated its claim to be regarded as an indispensable part of the true American system of school supervision. . . . . It can hardly be doubted that the model system of school supervision, the ultimate system of the future, will embrace as its essential parts the State, the county, and the town." [1]

The Massachusetts Board of Education have arrived at the conclusion that this office must be adopted in that State. Massachusetts having for years led the way in matters of education, has been slow to receive suggestions from her neighbours, or to accept reforms not initiated in the State. Horace Mann said: "The newer Western States enjoy one great advantage over the people of Massachusetts. They have been exempted from the immense labour of for ever boasting of their ancestors, and so have had more time to devote to their posterity." Now, however, the most prominent educators in the State are of opinion that the appointment of County Superintendents ought not to be longer delayed. The report of the Board issued in 1873 recommends the creation of an additional superintending and inspecting agency. "Many of our sister States," says the report, "in the organisation of their school systems, have incorporated what is best in our own, and not a few have superadded improvements of which our own system remains destitute. And in no particular have other States surpassed us more conspicuously than in the provisions they have made for the supervision of schools. In nearly all

---

[1] Illinois Report, 1871-2, p. 145.

the States of the Union there has been provided a class of educational officers, occupying an intermediate position between the Towns' Committees on the one hand, and the State system of supervision on the other. In most of these States, these supervisors or superintendents are county officers. With the existing evidence of the utility and importance of this agency of progress and improvement, which comes to us from a score of States, it would be the height of presumption in us to assume that Massachusetts can maintain her former prestige in educational matters without the adoption of this or some analogous instrumentality for the increase of the economy and efficiency of the management of her schools." [1]

(f) State Superintendence.

All the States and Territories, except Delaware and Alaska, have State Superintendents of Public Schools; and the following States have State Boards of Education for the general regulation of their public school systems:—Alabama, Arkansas, California, Connecticut, Florida, Georgia, Indiana, Kentucky, Louisiana, Maryland, Massachusetts, Michigan, Mississippi, Missouri, Nevada, New Hampshire, New Jersey, North Carolina, Oregon, Rhode Island, South Carolina, Vermont, and Virginia. A Territorial Board of Education exists in Arizona. Kansas has a State Board of Commissioners for the management and investment of the State school fund. [2]

---

[1] Massachusetts Report, 1873, p. 19.
[2] See Report of Commissioner of Education, 1873, p. cxxii.

These Boards are not entrusted with the extensive powers and prerogatives which are exercised by the Education Department in England. In this country, where the "insolence of office" is proverbial, we find it a difficult matter to submit at all times patiently to the humours of "my lords" at Whitehall, and it may be safely said that such extensive checks upon local freedom of action as they possess would not be tolerated for an instant in the United States. A School Board in England may not build a school, select a site, or prescribe the amount of a school fee, without the sanction of the Education Department. It is well understood that the policy of the Department is directed by its chief for the time being, whether he be President or Vice-President. This is what in America is known as the "one-man power," against which the ire of American speakers and writers is so frequently and so freely concentrated. As we know in England, this almost absolute sway of the Department has its inconveniences. But, on the other hand, it may be doubted whether the superintendence of the State School Boards in the Union is not of too restricted a character to secure the highest efficiency in the administration of the school systems.

The State Superintendent or the School Board in each State is required to issue an annual report.

Personal supervision of schools to any extent is not required of State Superintendents, and it is obvious that it would be impossible. The State Superintendent for Iowa says in his report for 1872: "The Superintendent of Public Instruction is charged with the general supervision of all the public schools of the State, but this must necessarily be of the most general character. In a State like Iowa, with ninety-nine organised counties, twenty-five hundred school districts, nine thousand schools, fifteen thousand school officers, and as many teachers, it is impossible, even if it were desirable, for this officer to exercise personal supervision to any considerable extent." ([1])

The State Superintendent is the executive head of the system of supervision. He is the official adviser and assistant of the County Superintendents, through whom he communicates with subordinate school officers, and sees that the school laws are understood and obeyed. The policy of school legislation in the United States depends to a very large degree upon the views taken by the State Superintendents. They are constantly addressing the people, either through educational conventions and associations, or by means of their annual reports. Those who have studied the latter, however much they may differ as to the value of American methods, will admit that in the State Superintendents the United States possess a class of school officers whose value it is impossible to estimate too highly. While their reports are marked throughout by the strongest feeling of patriotism, and of attachment to the American school idea, they never attempt to slur over the blemishes or defects of the system. Every detail of organisation is subjected to a microscopic examination, and every rotten place is discovered and exposed. The evidences of partial weakness and failure which are seized upon with such avidity by the enemies of the "free common school" in England, are precisely those which the State Superintendents have been the first to indicate, not as proofs of general inefficiency and unsoundness, but as imperfections of detail which demand a remedy.

Another feature of their reports worthy of notice is the candour and fairness with which new methods are discussed, weighed, and tried upon their merits. There is no "finality" party amongst them. They are actuated by

---

[1] Iowa Report, 1872, p. 40.

the belief that education is a progressive science, and while claiming for their methods a large measure of success, their almost universal opinion is that America, in common with other countries, has taken but the earliest steps towards the perfect school system of the future.

II.

COST.

(*a*) Theory of Free Schools—(*b*) Provision of Funds for Education—(*c*) Total Abolition of Rate Bills (School Fees)—(*d*) Free Schools, the People's System.

(*a*) *Theory of Free Schools.*

The idea of throwing the cost of public education upon the State is not of American origin. Free schools existed in Holland long before they were known in the United States.

Also, it is said that in 1526—more than 100 years before the Pilgrim Fathers landed in America—Luther propounded to the Elector of Saxony the proposition that "Government, as the natural guardian of all the young, has the right to compel the people to support schools. That which is necessary to the well-being of a State, should be supported by those who enjoy the privileges of the State. Now, nothing is more necessary than the training of those who are to come after us and bear rule." [1] From this reasoning sprang the Saxon free school system.

---

[1] Indiana Report, 1872, p. 12.

More than one of the United States claim the honour of having first introduced the free school in America. On behalf of New York, it is said that the Dutch who colonised that State, took it there from Holland. Hartford (Conn.) appears to be the first town which established a free school, but there can be little doubt that Massachusetts was the first State to make laws providing for a regular system of free schools. In 1642 an Act was passed by the Massachusetts Legislature enjoining upon the municipal authorities "the duty of seeing that every child within their respective jurisdictions should be educated."([1]) From this beginning, the free system, previously to the revolutionary war, had extended over the New England States. The element of school fees, or rate-bills, as they are called in America, was subsequently engrafted on the system in some of the States.

The morality of taxes for education is no longer considered a debatable subject. No one questions the moral right of a Government to levy taxes in order to repel a foreign enemy. Now, the moral right to tax property for educational purposes rests upon the ground that education laws have become more necessary than armies for the defence and preservation of the State; and especially this is true under a free Government like our own or that of the United States. "An ignorant people can be governed, but only an educated people can govern themselves." We cannot expect to have a wise Legislature unless we have an educated constituency. If this be true, it is impossible to attach too much importance to the education of voters, for upon their qualifications depend those of the law-makers. In a Government where every citizen has a voice, education must be co-extensive with universal suffrage. Thus the education of the people, considered purely by each nation as a home

---

[1] Fraser's Report, p. 12.

question, is in an important degree a police measure. Daniel Webster so described it. He said, "We regard it as a wise and liberal system of police, by which property, and life, and the peace of society are secured."

But when the foreign relations of the State are taken into account, education occupies even a more important place, as a means of national preservation. It is not so much to the wisdom of Legislatures, or an enlightened social organisation, as to skill in productive arts, that States in future must look for their supremacy. Education is the great instrument which determines this excellence. To secure these ends—wise laws at home, and dexterity in competitive industry—the justice and morality of taxes ceases to be canvassed.

To use a simile of Mr. Horace Mann, "In a wisely administered Government taxes are the fares which we pay on railroad cars, the price for being safely carried and well provided for through the journey of life." [1] Holding this view of educational taxes above all others, some of the most wealthy citizens of New York petitioned the Legislature for the passage of a law to tax their property for the support of the public schools, thereby making them free for all, both rich and poor. [2] They acted upon the conviction that it is unsafe to live in a community where children are suffered to grow up without education. The education of the people is regarded in the United States as the first and most important interest of society, and as a work "too gigantic for private capital, too momentous for the mischances of private judgment." It takes the first rank amongst the necessities of the nation, and, accordingly, it has been founded upon the most permanent and immovable basis, instead of being left to the shifting ground of private

---

[1] Randall's History of Free Schools, p. 220.
[2] Ibid, p. 218.

benevolence or caprice, or even to that self-interest which is so strong a motive power in modern society. That basis is the whole property of the nation. The rule, subject to a few exceptions, is that every man shall contribute to the support of the schools in his district, in proportion to his wealth. In the consideration of this question—the value of education to the child or to the family—the bare personal interest involved is allowed to sink very much out of sight. The relation of the individual to society, the necessities of the whole community and of succeeding generations, are the prime elements in the controversy. Taxes to support education are founded not upon " the idea that the individual wants it for his personal good, but that society requires it ;" and upon the further principle, that " the public has a proprietary interest in all property as well as the individual, and may use it as necessities demand." (¹)

" The poor man with a family of six children to be educated ought not to be obliged to pay six times as much as the rich man with one child, or even as much as the latter with six children. It is common intelligence we are endeavouring to secure, and the cost of the attempt, and all the instrumentalities connected therewith, in justice and equity should be paid by the common wealth, by all the property in the State. This is a principle long recognised in the school district, and in the town, since never the individual, but property, is assessed for educational and other purposes." (²)

In discussing this question as between poor and rich, or between property and labour, the important share exercised by the working classes in the production of wealth should not be overlooked. The rate of increase in wealth in all countries depends, in a large degree, upon the presence of the labourer, and this is pre-eminently

---

¹ Kentucky Report, 1872, p. 11.   ² Maine Report, 1872, p. 25.

the case in the United States. The value of real property augments constantly and rapidly, and the increment is owing directly and largely to the increase of settlers. The value of other kinds of property also depends, if not so directly, still chiefly, upon the same cause, for without the workman capital would remain idle and unproductive. It is admitted, also, that in proportion to the education of the labourer, the increase in the value of property is more or less rapid.. In a new country with the vast resources of America, the presence of sufficient educated labour is the greatest force in the accumulation of wealth. It is right, therefore, that the cost of education should be borne by the wealth which it is mainly instrumental in producing.

Upon such considerations as the foregoing, the policy of the American free school system has been established. By different ways, perhaps, England and most of the European States have arrived at the same conclusion—that it is the duty of the nation to provide for the education of the people. The following sentence from a New York report might have been written of England with equal truth : "Education is a matter of State concern. The popular sense has recognised it as such, and that conviction is the basis of all Governmental regulations upon the subject. Unless this be true, very much of our legislation in past years is unjustifiable, and all appropriations from the State Treasury for the support of schools are indefensible." ([1]) We have no longer in this country to contend about the principle of free education :· that has been admitted by all educational legislation during the present century. What remains for us to consider is the policy of retaining the small contribution now made by parents in the shape of school fees. Our legislators have swallowed the camel, and are now

---

[1] New York State Report, 1871, p. 19.

E

straining at the gnat, a process which it is to be hoped will be of short duration.

In this place it may be well to notice some of the familiar arguments which are used in England against free schools, and to examine them in the light of American experience. One of the most common assertions is that free education is a charity, and is calculated to undermine the sense of independence in those who receive it. It is strange that, in a country where free education for the middle classes has been so general, such an argument should ever be used, and still more so that it should be advanced by those who have themselves been educated in free schools. In Birmingham, I remember to have heard this weighty reason stated by the master of a free grammar school which was at one period of its history almost entirely appropriated to the use of the middle classes.

In the older States of America, where free schools have been long in operation, such a criticism is never heard ; but in some of those States where the system has been inaugurated during recent years objections of the kind have been made. The State Superintendent for Virginia thus replies to them in his second annual report : " According to current usage, public education means education provided by the community as a whole, in contradistinction from education provided by private means. It recognises the principle that the commonwealth has a stake in the pupils—the young people—and that she means to guarantee her own future by seeing that they do not lack the means of improvement. It is education by the people, of the people, for the people. In other words, it is education by the public for the public good ; and this education is free as well as public. It does not mean charitable, by free. To say that a community, in providing a benefit for itself, is doing an act of charity, is a solecism. A public school is no more a provision of charity than a town pump.

It is free as the public hydrant is free, or a street lamp is free. It is free to the individual, and to all individuals alike. The cost is borne by the community, like the cost of water, street lights, public roads, bridges, and such like public conveniences, all of which are free. Nobody stultifies himself by calling a free bridge a charity." ([1])

The State Superintendent for Kentucky says: "We claim that the common school is no charitable institution, erected outside of the State, to be abandoned or maintained as charitable wealth may elect to dole out its alms; but it is a needful part of the civil order, to dispense with which is to abrogate one of the legitimate functions for which the body politic is organised." ([2])

In the Northern and Western States no man dreams that in sending his children to a free school he becomes the recipient of charity, and no argument so absurd is ever advanced against the system.

In Connecticut, before the abolition of rate bills or school fees, it was said (as it is constantly alleged in England) that such a step would weaken the feeling of self-respect in parents, and lessen their interest in the work of education. How far it has done so the Secretary of the Connecticut Board of Education shall tell. "Experience has disproved the objection that free schools would lessen the interest and responsibility of parents. The argument was that men never value what costs them nothing; but the fact is that parents do pay, and all pay their fair and equal share for the support of this central public interest. This system not only enhances the interest of the parent, but dignifies the school in the esteem of the pupils, and quickens the educational spirit of the whole people. Every taxpayer, having contributed his share to the support of the schools, naturally looks after this investment.

---

[1] Virginia Report, 1872, Part II., p. 1.   [2] Kentucky Report, 1872, p. 13.

Such was our theory, and now we say such is the fact. Each school register has two blank pages for the record of visits of school officers, parents, and others. These records show a great increase in the number of visits to our schools. The united testimony of teachers and school officers affirms the quickened sympathy and zeal of parents. Their visits to the schoolroom are always welcome. Where all are partners in the concern, none need be debarred by fear of intrusion. Our best teachers are most cordial in welcoming the visits of even the humblest parents. The frequent conference of parents and teachers often prompts valuable suggestions as to the needs and characteristics of individual pupils. The details of public schools are better known to the parents than are the plans of private schools to their patrons." [1]

It is time that in England we heard the last of the assertion—and it is mere assertion—that the abolition of school fees will degrade either parents or scholars. It would be as wise to say that the abolition of turnpike tolls is calculated to degrade the travellers who use the highways. If this is so, debasement on an extensive scale has been going on of late years.

But, on the other hand, it has been abundantly proved that the custom of demanding school fees and remitting them in special cases does produce a sense of degradation.

Our public elementary schools of England have always been regarded as charitable schools. All the expensive and cumbersome machinery for regulating school fees in England —the .25th clause, the 17th clause, the Act substituted for Denison's Act, the bye-laws of School Boards—all these are contrivances for preserving the eleemosynary character of public education as it now exists; and that these do create a feeling of debasement there are proofs enough if men will look for them. The same effect was produced by the rate-

---

[1] Connecticut Report, 1870, p. 29.

bill in America, and it was this that earned for it, wherever it was in existence, the well-known name of "the odious rate-bill."

The power to remit school fees, which formerly existed in New York as it now exists in England, was ineffectual to secure attendance at school. A former Superintendent of that State says: "What proportion of the whole number of children in the State are excluded from all participation in the benefits of our common schools on account of the poverty of their parents, or of the refusal or neglect of the trustees to make the exemptions on this account required by law, cannot now be accurately ascertained, and probably never will be, however important these facts may be. The Superintendent believes that the number in the whole State, embracing our large cities, populous villages, and manufacturing towns, whose destitution entitles them to be placed on the list of free scholars, is much larger than has been generally supposed by accurate observers ; and the lowest probable estimate we can form of that number is over forty-six thousand. Among other obstacles to be encountered is the reluctance of many parents to participate in the benefits afforded by these exemptions, owing to the manner in which this bounty, as they call it, is bestowed. They will not send their children to the schools to be reproached for their poverty, and assailed with taunts that they are educated at the expense of their more fortunate neighbours." ([1])

As long ago as 1845, the County Superintendent of Genesee (N. Y.) presented a report on free schools, in which he says : "There are children in the State, and, we have reason to believe, in almost every county in the State, who do not attend any school, for the very obvious reason that their parents have not the means to pay their rate-bill ; and the

---

[1] Randall's History, p. 214.

self-respect and pride of those parents forbid that they should be exonerated from such payment by the trustees." (¹)

Again, the State Superintendent for New York reported: "Teachers complain of the rate-bill system, not only because it improperly withholds their wages, but because the trustees find great difficulty in exercising with fidelity, and at the same time satisfactorily, the power of exemption. While the cupidity of the taxpayer is excited, the pride of men of moderate means is aroused, and their sense of independence revolts at being certified and put upon the record as indigent persons." (²)

Governor Clark, in his message to the Legislature, in 1856, proved from the returns sent to the Superintendent's Department that a very large number of children were kept out of school on account of "the repugnance on the part of parents to avail themselves of their privilege to educate their children *in formâ pauperis*, as a district charge." (³) Bishop Fraser also refers to cases in which parents were too poor to pay rate-bills, and too proud to own it. (⁴)

Another argument often advanced in England is, that it is wrong to tax the thrifty and industrious citizen for the education of the children of the idle and improvident. This reasoning was admirably answered by Mr. Horace Greeley in an address read at a Free School State Convention in New York. He said: "But we are asked why a citizen who has worked, and saved, and thrived, should pay for schooling the children of his neighbour, who has drank, and frolicked, and squandered till he has little or nothing left. We answer, he should do it in order that these needy and disgraced children may not become what their father is, and so, very probably, in time a public burden, as criminals or paupers. The children of the drunkard and reprobate have a hard enough

---

¹ Randall's History, p. 217.   ² Randall's History, p. 252.
³ Randall's History, p. 330.   ⁴ Fraser's Report, p. 55.

lot without being surrendered to his judgment and self-denial for the measure of their education. If they are to have no more instruction than he shall see fit and feel able to pay for, a kind Heaven must regard them with a sad compassion, and men ought not utterly to leave them uncared for, and subjected to such moral and intellectual influences only as their desolate homes may afford. To stake the education of our State's future rulers and mothers on such parents' ideas of their own ability and their children's moral needs is madness, is treason to the common weal. They will be quite enough detained, even from free schools, by supposed inability to clothe or spare them; but to cast into the wrong scale a dead weight of paternal appetite and avarice, in the form of rate-bills, is to consign them heartlessly to intellectual darkness and moral perdition. And, in truth, the argument for taxing, in equal amounts, the improvidently destitute and the frugally affluent father of a family for school purposes is precisely as strong for taxing them in equal amounts to build court-houses, support paupers, dispense justice, or for any other purpose whatever. Nay, it is even stronger, for the drinking, thriftless, idle parent is far more likely to bring expense on the community in the shape of crime to be punished, or pauperism to be supported, than his thrifty and temperate neighbour; and, according to our adversaries' logic, he should pay more taxes on his log-cabin and patch of weedy garden than that neighbour on his spacious mansion and bounteous farm. The former will, probably, turn off two paupers to one of the latter, and should be assessed in a pauper rate-bill accordingly. And this argument, from parental misconduct against the justice of free schools, is of a piece with the rest."[1]

There is a large class in England who think that wise ends are served by keeping the people under restraints which

---

[1] Randall's History, p. 270.

they consider to be due, but which are in reality petty and vexatious. While it is from them that we hear most about preserving the independence of the poor, they have always been opposed to measures intended to enlarge popular freedom. They find a personal gratification in the exercise of petty charity, and the power to deal out to the working classes little doles such as are contemplated by the clauses of our Education Act, which provide for remission and payment of fees. They have a morbid curiosity which takes a delight in investigating the circumstances of families, and in probing the bitter experiences of poverty. Notwithstanding their eternal homilies about parental independence and responsibility, they possess the spirit of patronage, long fostered by the social conditions of the country, which has done much to keep so many of our people in a state of miserable dependence and subjection. When their system of alms-giving can be carried on at the public expense, their zest is no doubt greater, and they will not willingly surrender any power which still has force to pluck "the slavish hat from the villager's head." This class now stands in the way of the complete realisation of the free school system in England.

The amount of the school fees, which is steadily decreasing in proportion to the amount expended upon education, can no longer be taken into account either as an element in the preservation of self-respect, or as a fiscal question of great moment. It would not over-tax the ingenuity of even the present Chancellor of the Exchequer to provide a substitute, if the school revenue now derived from fees were entirely remitted, and the amount paid out of the Consolidated Fund. Mr. Salt, the Conservative member for Stafford, in a recent speech, expressed an opinion that the Government would have had no difficulty last year in making provision, by means of the education grant, for the school fees; and whereas the remission of local taxation made by them, amounting to about two millions sterling, has hardly been felt in the country, the abolition of fees would have been a direct boon to thousands of homes throughout the land.

If, on the other hand, the sum now realised by school fees were thrown upon the rates, it would not, taking the whole ratal of the country into the calculation, have amounted to an extra charge of $1\frac{1}{2}$d. in the pound. The net annual value of rateable property in England and Wales, in 1872, was £109,447,111. The poor-rate for the year was £12,100,490, or 2s. $2\frac{1}{2}$d. in the pound. The school fees for the same year amounted to £599,283. If the latter sum had been added to the poor-rate it would have amounted to an increase of only one and three tenths of a penny in the pound.

Judging by the experience of the United States, which will be again referred to when considering the abolition of rate-bills, there is every reason to believe that the advantages of abolishing school fees in England would be immediate, and, in proportion to the difficulty of the financial operation, immense.

(b) Provision of Funds for Education.

A fashionable way of accounting for the American free school system, and one that was gravely advanced at a meeting of the London School Board some time back, is to say that the Americans possessed vast tracts of national lands which, not knowing what else to do with them, they devoted to educational purposes. It is common, therefore, to speak of the schools of the United States as depending chiefly for their support on funds derived from public lands. An examination of the sources of revenue in almost any State will show that this is a popular error.

The school revenues of the different States are of various kinds, and as there is but little approach in this respect to uniformity of nomenclature, a good deal of confusion is possible in the investigation of the subject. There are what are known as School Funds, Surplus Revenue Funds, Saline Funds, State Taxes, District Taxes, Registry Taxes, Dog Taxes, Liquor Licences, State Appropriations, and State Apportionments, and in some States in the South there are the Capitation Tax and Poll Tax. It is not necessary to examine separately the nature of each of these sources of income. In American discussions they are generally classified under three heads—I, State School Funds, answering to Endowments in England; II, State Taxes, answering to our Government Grant; III, Local Taxes, or, as we should call them, Local Rates. To these divisions must be added another which occupies an important position in the school finances, that is—IV, Donations.

I. STATE SCHOOL FUNDS.

These are generally permanent funds, the income of which may be used for school purposes, the principal remaining intact. They have been accumulated, for the most part, from national grants of lands and from appropriations made from time to time by the State Legislatures.

The lands granted by Congress are known as the "16th Section Lands." Bishop Fraser explains the 16th section lands as follows :—" Out of the 3,250,000 square miles which constitute the territorial extent of the Union, the public lands embrace an area of 2,265,625 square miles, or 1,450,000,000 acres." "This immense extent of territory, as it is gradually surveyed, is laid off in townships six miles square, each divided into 36 sections or square miles, of which the 16th is specially appropriated for the support of schools, and is called the 'School Section.'" ([1])

This process of reservation began in the earliest days of the Union. In 1785 Congress enacted that there should " be reserved the lot No. 16 in every township for the maintenance of public schools." ([2]) In the Acts admitting Oregon and Minnesota to the Union, the 36th section in each township, as well as the 16th, was devoted to school purposes. ([3])

A section of a township is 640 acres—a square mile. Land of the same description is sold by the Government for one dollar twenty-five cents per acre; but in Indiana the 16th section lands remaining unsold are valued at five dollars twenty-five cents, and this is about their average market value in most Western States. In 1870 there had been altogether set apart by Congress for common schools, universities, agricultural and mechanical colleges in the States and Territories, 79,566,794 acres, or 124,322 square miles—a larger surface than that of Great Britain and Ireland.

In nearly all the States the greater portion of the land has been sold, and the proceeds invested for school purposes. The history of the proceeds of these 16th section lands in some of the States is a very melancholy one. In the South especially it is so. One of the first acts of secession in several instances was the perversion of the school funds for the purposes of war. ([4]) In Arkansas and Louisiana, the attempts to trace the devolution of the funds reveal the most deplorable state of affairs. All the records of transactions relating to them were lost or destroyed during the war.

Another contribution to the school funds was made by

---

[1] Fraser's Report, p. 42.   [2] Proceedings of National Teachers' Association, 1870. Paper by Gen. Eaton, p. 112.   [3] Ibid, p. 115.
[4] Commissioner's Report, 1870, p. 13.

Congress in 1836. Under the administration of President Jackson, the National Debt contracted by the revolutionary war and the purchase of Louisiana was discharged, and there remained a large surplus in the treasury. The Government distributed this money among the States in the ratio of their representation in Congress, and the income in a large number of States was set apart for school purposes. By the terms of the Act of Distribution, this money is liable to be recalled; but although nearly forty years have elapsed since the deposit with the States, not a dollar has ever been recalled, and the probability is that the fund will never be disturbed. This is known as the United States Deposit Fund, or the Surplus Revenue Fund, and it helps to make up the permanent State School Fund in many States.

The following table shows the amount of the permanent school fund in different States in 1872 ([1]):—

STATE.	$.
Indiana	8,437,593
Arkansas	2,000,000
Connecticut	2,809,770
Florida	216,335
Illinois	6,348,538
Iowa	4,274,581
Kansas	750,000
Kentucky	1,400,270
Maine	289,991
Massachusetts	2,210,864
Michigan	2,500,214
Minnesota	2,471,199
Missouri	2,525,252
Nevada	29,263

[1] Indiana Report, 1872, p. 20.

State.	$.
New Hampshire	336,745
New Jersey	556,483
New York	2,880,017
North Carolina	968,242
Ohio	6,614,816
Rhode Island	412,685
West Virginia	216,761
Wisconsin	2,237,414

The total revenue derived from Permanent School Funds throughout the Union, in 1873, amounted to 3,884,408 dollars; while that proceeding from State and local taxation was 63,324,293 dollars. ([1])

II. State Taxes.

In the majority of the States a State School Tax is raised and apportioned amongst the school districts—in a few instances on the basis of average attendance, but more frequently according to the population of school age as shown by the census.

In New York State the law provides that there shall be raised each year a tax of one mill and one-fourth of a mill (1¼ mills) for the support of the common schools. ([2]) This State tax was a part of the free school plan.

The free school law of New Jersey (1871) provides that for the purpose of maintaining free schools there shall be levied annually a State School Tax of two mills on each dollar of the valuation. The sum derived from this tax amounts to about three fourths of all the money needed to maintain the schools. The tax is uniform in all counties, and is apportioned for the use of schools on the basis of the school census. ([3])

---

[1] Report of Commissioner for Education, 1873, p. 512. [2] New York State Report, 1874, p. 63. [3] New Jersey Report, 1873, p. 11.

In Ohio a State School Tax of "one and three tenths mills on the dollar" was formerly raised. In the last two years, however (1872-3), the tax has been only one mill on the dollar. (¹)

The school law of Missouri provides that 25 per cent. of the State revenue shall be applied annually for the support of schools. (²)

In Pennsylvania an annual sum is appropriated from the State Treasury for the support of education. (³)

In Rhode Island, the State is required to appropriate at least 50,000 dollars for the support of the schools. In 1873 the State appropriation was 90,000 dollars. (⁴)

The State Board of Education and the Commissioner of Public Schools advocate a State tax of one mill on the dollar. "This amount, divided by the present system, would give relief, immediate and valuable, to all the poorer towns of the State, while it would be a small return from the richer for the benefits which have been and will be conferred by the constant contribution of population, labour, and capital to the growing centres of business." (⁵)

The Legislature of Indiana, by an Act passed in 1865, provided for the collection of a tax of sixteen cents on each 100 dollars of taxable property in the State, and 50 cents on each taxable poll, for the support of common schools. (⁶)

Under the school law of 1872, the State of Connecticut pays out of the State Treasury to each town one dollar and a half for each child enumerated. (⁷)

The Maine school law of 1872 provides for a tax of one mill per dollar on all the property in the State. This amounts to about one dollar per census scholar. (⁸)

---

[1] Ohio Report, 1873, p. 4.
[2] Missouri Report, 1873, p. 9.
[3] Pennsylvania Report, 1873, p. xlii.
[4] Rhode Island Report, 1874, p. 49.
[5] Rhode Island Report, 1874, p. 76.
[6] Indiana Report, 1872, p. 25.
[7] Connecticut Report, 1873, p. 9.
[8] Maine Report, 1872, p. 10.

The law of Illinois requires the State to levy a tax of two mills on each dollar's valuation of all the taxable property in the State. This sum, which in 1872 amounted to 900,000 dollars, is distributed amongst school districts in proportion to the number of children under twenty-one years of age. ([1])

The Constitution of Alabama, adopted in 1867, provides that one fifth of the aggregate annual revenue of the State shall be devoted to the maintenance of public schools. ([2])

The school law of Arkansas provides for a tax of "one dollar per capita on every male inhabitant over twenty-one years of age," for maintaining free schools. ([3])

The law of California requires that a tax of ten cents on each one hundred dollars shall be levied upon taxable property throughout the State. The report for 1873 advocates the raising of this tax to twelve cents.([4])

In Michigan a tax of two mills is levied in addition to district taxes, but the exact nature of this tax does not appear from the only report which I have seen—that for 1873.

State School Taxes, varying in amount and in the manner of assessment are collected in Florida, Georgia, Kansas, Kentucky, Louisiana, Maryland, North Carolina, South Carolina, Tennessee, Virginia, and West Virginia.

Massachusetts has no State School Tax, but the Board of Education, in the report issued in 1873, recommended its adoption. The following extract sets forth the reasons for which the tax is advocated:—" While the principle that underlies the American system of popular education—that it is the duty of the State to provide for the education of all the children of the State, by means derived

---

[1] Illinois Report, 1872, pp. 13, 18.   [2] Connecticut Report, 1871, p. 31.
[3] Connecticut Report, 1871, p. 31.   [4] California Report, 1873, p. 57.

from the taxation of every man in proportion to his property, whether he have children to educate or not—is nowhere more generally accepted than among the citizens of this commonwealth, yet, strange to say, the State has never voted a dollar from the general State revenues for the direct maintenance of her common schools. It has ever been her policy, from the time when schools were first required to be set up in the colony of Massachusetts Bay down to the present day, to require the towns to provide their own schools without any aid whatever from the public treasury. The effect of this policy has been, no doubt, to develop to a great extent the local interest in the public schools, and any change in the support of schools is to be deprecated which would release the municipalities from the responsibility of providing mainly for the support of their schools by raising an annual school tax. In the early periods of our history the plan of throwing the entire burden of the support of the schools upon the town worked satisfactorily, and it was, perhaps, as well adapted to the then existing circumstances of the population as any which could have been devised. While agriculture was almost the sole occupation of the people the taxable property was very equally distributed, and there was no marked disparity of the burdens imposed for the maintenance of education, nor any great inequality in the benefits which it conferred. But that state of things no longer exists: we have become a manufacturing people, there has been a rapid accumulation of wealth, and the taxable property of the State is concentrated to a remarkable extent in the cities and large towns. Certainly, two fifths, if not a half, of the property of the State is embraced in the limited territory which lies within five miles of the State House. The consequence is that, while in certain portions of the State a tax sufficient to maintain good schools during the period required by law is a serious burden, in other portions the tax adequate for the same purpose is comparatively light. This radical change in the state of things imperatively demands a corresponding change in the mode of providing for the support of schools. The object in view is to restore, to some extent at least, the ancient equality of educational burdens and equality of educational advantages."

"The proposed plan does not contemplate any increase in the aggregate taxes for schools; it does not propose to shift all the responsibility from the municipalities to the State. It proposes to appropriate a small share of the means of the whole State for the benefit of the whole State. The specific recommendation is, that provision be made for raising a half-mill State School Tax, to be distributed to the cities and towns, a part in proportion to the number of children of school age, and a part in proportion to the school attendance, a fraction being reserved for the education of teachers, and for other general educational purposes." [1]

III. LOCAL TAXES.

From what has gone before it will be seen that the school system of America must rest chiefly (indeed, in some States—such as Massachusetts, almost wholly) for support upon local taxation. This was so at the time of Bishop Fraser's visit, and although local taxation has since been relieved to some extent, his description, if we except Indiana and New Jersey, remains substantially true. "The amount of State aid, even when it is largest, as in Connecticut or Ohio, measured by dollars, is not, it is true,

---

[1] Massachusetts Report, 1873, p. 15.

very considerable—at least, not in proportion to the total cost of each child's education." (¹)

Again: "But a school's main reliance for support, even in Connecticut, where the State Fund is so disproportionately large, and the income from that source consequently so considerable, is upon funds either raised in or belonging to the township or district in which it lies." (²)

In the report of the Commissioner of Education, the items of State taxation and district taxation are not given separately.

In order, however, to enable English readers to form correct conclusions upon the subject, I have referred to the reports of some of the chief States for the items of local taxation. In the following table I have arranged the income derived from (1) permanent school funds; (2) taxation both general and local; (3) taxation purely local. It will be apparent from the table how large a proportion of the school revenues is raised by local levies. (³)

For the convenience of home readers, I have translated the American currency into English—taking the value of the dollar at 3s. 9d. :—

State.	Interest on Permanent Fund.	Total Revenue derived from Taxation, General (i.e., State) and Local.	Revenue separately derived from Local Taxation.	Year of Report.	Page of Report.
California	$81,795 £15,336 11 3	$1,423,719 £266,947 6 3	$1,541,597 (¹) £289,049 8 9	1873	9
Connecticut	$131,748 £24,702 15 0	$1,203,842 £225,720 7 6	$1,105,601 £207,300 3 9	1874	26
Illinois	$487,731 £91,449 11 3	$6,675,097 £1,251,580 13 9	$5,292,942 £992,426 12 6	1872	13

¹ Fraser's Report, p. 50. ² Ibid, p. 50.
³ NOTE.—For the amount of the State School Tax in proportion to the average attendance in certain States, see Appendix A., p. 258.

Table continued from preceding page :—

State.	Interest on Permanent Fund.	Total Revenue derived from Taxation, General (i.e., State) and Local.	Revenue separately derived from Local Taxation.	Year of Report.	Page of Report.
Indiana	$531,561 £99,667 13 9	$1,482,279 £277,927 6 3	$530,667 £99,500 1 3	1874	5
Iowa	$275,789 £51,710 8 9	$3,898,702 £731,006 12 6	$3,569,137 £669,213 3 9	1873	11
Louisiana	$44,884 £8,415 15 0	$493,845 £92,575 18 9	$204,995 £38,436 11 3	1873	12
Maine	$19,361 £3,630 3 9	$849,775 £159,332 16 3	$683,776 £128,208 0 0	1874	8
Massachusetts ..	$180,000 £33,750 0 0	$3,889,053 £729,197 8 9	$3,594,686 (²) £674,003 12 6	1873	150
Michigan.........	$196,176 £36,783 0 0	$2,561,133 £480,212 8 9	$2,095,220 £392,853 15 0	1873	59
Missouri	$291,817 £54,715 13 9	$1,145,384 £214,759 10 0	$1,145,384 £214,759 10 0	1872	6
New Jersey.....	$70,363 £13,193 1 3	$2,426,705 £455,007 3 9	$1,154,374 £216,445 2 6	1873	8
New York	$335,000 £62,812 10 0	$10,305,397 £1,932,261 18 9	$7,643,364 £1,433,130 15 0	1874	22
Ohio	$231,276 £43,364 5 0	$6,739,344 £1,263,627 0 0	$5,252,550 £984,853 2 6	1873	4
Pennsylvania ...	nil. ,,	$7,548,149 £1,415,277 18 9	$8,075,679 (¹) £1,514,189 16 3	1873	335
Rhode Island ...	$30,000 £5,625 0 0	$556,250 £104,296 17 6	$455,850 £85,471 17 6	1874	49
Virginia	$83,000 £15,562 10 0	$850,000 £159,375 0 0	$574,434 £107,706 7 6	1874	10

Note.—The first two columns of the above table are taken from the Commissioner's Report, 1873, p. 512. The figures in the third column are derived from the several State Reports for the year indicated.

Bishop Fraser says of the sums raised by taxation in the United States, that, " viewed as a burden pressing equally on

---

[1] These amounts are taken from later Reports than those in the second column. [2] This amount is raised for support of schools, including only wages, fuel, and care of school room.

the property of the whole community," they are "quite unparalleled. That they are borne so generally without complaint, and, indeed, that the amount appropriated to the public schools keeps growing so considerably year by year, is a proof, if proof were wanting, of the value the Americans attach to their system of education, and of their determination that it shall be efficiently maintained." (¹)

Since these words were written the progress of education in America, and the development of school revenue, has been more remarkable than at any former period.

In Iowa the aggregate annual expenditure rose from 761,537 dollars in 1863, to 4,229,455 dollars in 1873. "The significance of this fact is unmistakable. Such munificent expenditure can only be accounted for by the liberality and public spirit of our people, all of whom manifest their love of popular education and their faith in the public schools by the annual dedication to their support of more than one per cent. of their entire taxable property; this, too, uninterruptedly through a series of years commencing in the midst of a war which taxed our energies and resources to the extreme, and continuing through years of general depression in business, years of moderate yield of produce, of discouragingly low prices, and even amid the scanty surroundings and privations of pioneer life." (²)

Of other Western States the same story is true; and not only of the Western States.

In 1872, Connecticut raised $10.95 per child, while ten years before she raised only $3.54 per child. (³) The report for the same State for 1867 showed an increase of 37 per cent. in one year. (⁴)

In Maine, the purely voluntary taxes for the purpose of

---

[1] Fraser's Report, p. 55.
[2] Iowa Report, 1873, p. 16.
[3] Connecticut Report, 1873, p. 30.
[4] Connecticut Report, 1867, p. 25.

prolonging school terms, additional to the amount required by law, have generally been from 20 to 30 per cent. of that amount. (¹)

In New York State, the expenditure for the maintenance of public schools was 3,744,246 dollars in 1860, while in 1870 it amounted to 9,905,514 dollars. The proportion of the latter sum raised by taxation (State and local) was over nine and a half million dollars. In twenty-one years the people of New York State have expended, in support of public education, almost one hundred millions of dollars. (²)

In Massachusetts, the sum raised by taxation for the support of schools in 1871 showed an increase of 100 per cent. over the sum raised for the like purpose in 1864-5, a period of only six years. (³)

A word of recognition is due also to the manner in which some of the Southern States are carrying the burden of the public schools—doubly severe to them because of the impoverished and exhausted condition in which the war left them. In Virginia, the first two annual taxes (for 1870 and 1871) were both collected in rapid succession within the year 1871. Mr. W. H. Ruffner, the Superintendent of Public Instruction, says he trembled for the result; "but this sudden and severe strain on the popularity of the school system was borne astonishingly well, even by the opponents of the system, and abundant evidence was furnished that the people were ready for its general extension." (⁴)

Throughout the Union the expenditure for school purposes was doubled during the ten years from 1850 to 1860, and almost trebled between 1860 and 1870. The amount raised by taxation in 1860 was two and a half times the

---

¹ Maine Report, 1872, p. 31.   ² New York State Report, 1871, p. 24.
³ Massachusetts Report, 1873, p. 13.   ⁴ Virginia Report, 1873, p. 166.

amount raised by taxation in 1850; while the amount thus raised in 1870 was more than three times that of 1860. During the twenty years expiring in 1870 the population had increased about 70 per cent., and the aggregate amount expended for education had increased to six times the sum raised in 1850. The school income derived from taxation is more than eight times as large. In 1850, the amount raised by taxation was less than one half the entire amount, while in 1870 it was nearly two thirds. ([1])

The following table exhibits the amount of public school expenditure in the States referred to, *per capita* of population between six and sixteen years of age:—

STATE.	$.	cts.	STATE.	$.	cts.
Massachusetts	21	74	Vermont	7	55
Nevada	19	28	Indiana	7	37
California	14	92	Oregon	7	14
Nebraska	17	02	Maryland	6	55
Connecticut	12	89	Minnesota	6	62
Rhode Island	12	73	Wisconsin	7	06
Illinois	13	26	Maine	6	57
New Jersey	10	15	Delaware	5	80
Iowa	12	17	Mississippi	4	98
Kansas	11	31	West Virginia	3	70
Michigan	9	61	Missouri	3	62
New York	10	16	Louisiana	3	44
Ohio	9	24	Arkansas	3	13
Pennsylvania	9	23	Kentucky	2	48
New Hampshire	7	18	Virginia	2	80

See Commissioners' Report 1873, page 12.

For purposes of comparison with the home system I have also set out in the following table the amount raised by current taxation *per capita* of the whole population, men,

---

[1] St. Louis Report, 1872, p. 9.

women, and children, in the States named. The whole public school expenditure including endowments, is very considerably in excess of the amounts stated:—

State.	Revenue raised by Taxation, 1873.	Entire Population, from Census of 1870.	Amount raised by Current Taxation per Head of Population.
Massachusetts	\$3,889,053 £729,197 8 9	1,457,351	\$2.66c. 9s. 11½d.
New York	\$10,305,397 £1,932,261 18 9	4,382,759	\$2.35c. 8s. 9¾d.
Pennsylvania	\$7,548,149 £1,415,277 18 9	3,521,951	\$2.14c. 8s. 0¼d.
California	\$1,423,719 £266,947 6 3	560,247	\$2.54c. 9s. 6¼d.
Connecticut	\$1,203,842 £225,720 7 6	537,454	\$2.23c. 8s. 4¼d.
Illinois	\$6,675,097 £1,251,580 13 9	2,539,891	\$2.62c. 9s. 9¾d.
Indiana	\$1,482,279 £277,927 6 3	1,680,637	.88c. 3s. 3½d.
Iowa	\$3,898,702 £731,006 12 6	1,194,020	\$3.26c. 12s. 2½d.
Kansas	\$931,958 £174,742 2 6	364,399	\$2.55c. 9s. 6¾d.
Kentucky	\$838,000 £157,125 0 0	1,321,011	.63c. 2s. 4¼d.
Louisiana	\$493,845 £92,595 18 9	726,915	.67c. 2s. 6d.
Maine	\$849,775 £159,332 16 3	626,915	\$1.35c. 5s. 0¾d.
Maryland	\$1,093,721 £205,072 13 9	780,894	\$1.40c. 5s. 3d.
Michigan...............	\$2,561,133 £480,212 8 9	1,184,059	\$2.16c. 8s. 1d.
Minnesota	\$814,891 £152,792 1 3	439,706	\$1.85c. 6s. 11¼d.
Mississippi	\$1,089,685 £204,315 18 9	827,922	\$1.31c. 4s. 10¾d.
Missouri	\$1,145,384 £214,759 10 0	1,721,295	.66c. 2s. 5¾d.
Nebraska	\$111,018 £20,815 17 6	122,993	.90c. 3s. 4½d.
New Hampshire ...	\$434,150 £81,403 2 6	318,300	\$1.36c. 5s. 1d.
New Jersey...........	\$2,426,705 £455,007 3 9	906,096	\$2.67c. 10s. 0d.

Table continued from preceding page :—

STATE.	Revenue raised by Taxation, 1873.	Entire Population, from Census of 1870.	Amount raised by Current Taxation per Head of Population.
Ohio	$6,739,344 £1,263,627 0 0	2,665,260	$2.52c. 9s. 5¼d.
Rhode Island	$556,250 £104,296 17 6	217,353	$2.55c. 9s. 6¾d.
Vermont	$415,432 £77,893 10 0	330,551	$1.25c. 4s. 8¾d.
Virginia	$850,000 £159,375 0 0	1,225,163	.69c. 2s. 7d.
West Virginia	$693,059 £129,948 11 3	442,014	$1.56c. 5s. 10d.
Wisconsin	$1,810,096 £339,393 0 0	1,054,670	$1.71c. 6s. 4¾d.

For the year ending 31st August 1874, the expenditure from the Education Grant for public elementary education in England and Wales, was £1,268,773 8s. This included the grant for day and evening schools, the amount advanced towards furnishing and building school premises, the annual grant to training colleges, and the cost of administration and organisation of districts. During the same year, the income derived from School Board rates was £136,693 8s. 1d. The population of England and Wales in 1871, was 22,712,266. The amount raised for education by taxation last year was, therefore, 1s. 2¾d. per head of population. If we add the voluntary contributions (£616,326 1s. 8d. during the year), the whole expenditure out of taxation and voluntary contributions was 1s. 9¼d. per head of population.

IV. DONATIONS.

In estimating the sources of educational revenue in America, private benefactions cannot be left out of the account, although they are mostly devoted to secondary education by the establishment of colleges and universities. These institutions do not stand in a hostile relation to the public school system, since they are chiefly intended to take up the work of higher education at the point where the public school leaves it.

From the statistics of educational benefactions for 1872, contained in the Report of the Commissioner of Education, it appears that in that year 9,958,494 dollars was the sum total reported to the Bureau. Of this amount, 6,282,461 dollars were devoted to the establishment of colleges and universities, 1,155,856 dollars were for the benefit of theological institutions, 10,422 dollars for schools of law and medicine, and 482,000 dollars for agricultural and scientific schools. Other sums were left for the superior instruction of women, for libraries, and normal schools, and academies. "Beyond all these," says the Commissioner, "there are doubtless numerous, and, in some cases, large benefactions to education, individual and denominational, of which this office has no specific information." [1]

The Connecticut Report, 1871, says: "The last decade is unprecedented in the number and amount of gifts and legacies for learning. The amount is probably greater than that given for the same objects in any previous fifty years. The donations for colleges, seminaries, schools, academies, and libraries in Connecticut is nearly three millions of dollars." [2]

Special mention must be made of the magnificent gift of Mr. Peabody in aid of education in the South. Of this fund "the amount now available is, in round numbers, two million dollars, and yields an annual income of a little over one hundred and twenty thousand dollars. Besides this there are Mississippi and Florida Bonds, amounting to about fifteen

---

[1] Report of Commissioner of Education, 1872, p. lxi.
[2] Connecticut Report, 1871, p. 83.

hundred thousand dollars, from which nothing is at present realised. According to the donor's directions, the principal must remain intact for thirty years; the trustees are not authorised to expend any part of it, nor yet to add to it any part of the accruing interest. The manner of using the interest, as well as the final distribution of the principal, was left entirely to the discretion of a self-perpetuating body of trustees. Those first appointed had, however, the rare advantage of full consultation with the founder of the trust while he still lived, and their plans received his cordial and emphatic approbation." [1]

Donations are not made out of this fund to colleges, academies, or any private, sectarian, or charity schools. To free schools, continued about ten months in the year, the trustees pay sums varying from 300 dollars to 1,000 dollars, according to the average attendance. The people are required to pay for current expenses twice, and usually three times, as much as they receive from the fund, and to bear all expenses of erecting, and repairing, and furnishing school-houses. They are to grade their schools, and provide a teacher for every fifty scholars. The avowed object and purpose of the Board of Trustees is "to strengthen the State system of public schools by rendering them superior to private schools." [2] The design of Mr. Peabody was to inaugurate a movement by which the disasters of the South might be repaired from the abundance of the North. His example has been followed by others. The amount paid to any school is in no case large; but as a stimulus to public exertion, as well as to private munificence, the endowment has already produced most valuable results.

---

[1] Virginia Report, 1871, p. 33.   [2] Arkansas Report, 1873, p. 17.

(c) *Total Abolition of Rate-bills (School Fees)*.

When the Bishop of Manchester visited the States, now ten years ago, rate-bills were in use in New York State, Connecticut, New Jersey, Rhode Island, and Michigan. In his report, Bishop Fraser says they were chiefly met with in the rural districts of New York State. In the city of New York the schools were wholly free, and also, as is well known to the present writer, in many rural districts. At the time of the Bishop of Manchester's visit the agitation against rate-bills was at its height in New York, and within two years a free school law was passed. Rate-bills had been the subject of contention in New York State for over twenty years. About the same time they were abolished in Rhode Island. In Connecticut they had given rise to more disputes than all other parts of the system put together; [1] and in that State they were shortly afterwards disused. New Jersey and Michigan followed the example of New York, Rhode Island, and Connecticut, and in 1871 the rate-bill had entirely disappeared throughout the Union. It was time it was abolished, for it was everywhere described as the "odious" rate-bill.

I propose to show, from the reports of the States where the system of rate-bills was in use during recent years, what have been the results of making the schools wholly free.

The report of New York State, issued at the close of 1870, being the third year of the Free School Act, states that better results were produced during that year than ever before: "The attendance in the rural districts, in 1867—the last and most successful year of the rate-bill system—was for an average term of only thirty weeks and three days, while that of each of the three years following was for an average term

---

[1] Connecticut Report, 1867, p. 88.

of thirty-two weeks and four days. The average length of time each pupil attended school, in the rural districts, was more than 16 per cent. greater in 1870 than in 1867."

"The average number of pupils, for the whole State, in attendance each day of the entire term, in 1870, was 16,284 more than in 1869, and 64,748 more than that for the shorter term in 1867," ([1]) the last year of rate-bills.

The same report says that the rate-bill plan "repelled attendance by directly taxing it." ([2])

In the same year the County Commissioners for New York, almost without exception, report that the free school law had been received with universal satisfaction by the people.

The report for the next year (1871) shows that the average attendance in the rural districts was nearly 17 per cent. greater than in any year of the rate-bill system, while the increase in school population since 1867, when that system was abolished, was less than one and a half per cent., and the average length of school terms had advanced more than seven per cent. The average attendance in 1871 was greater by 73,691 than in 1867. ([3])

The report for 1873 says that "the statistics for the year are distinguished by the unprecedented aggregate and average attendance at the schools, which exceeds that of any previous year by several thousands. This is not a spasmodic increase, but is the product of an uninterrupted growth that has characterised the returns each year since the free school system was inaugurated." ([4])

"The free school system, inaugurated in 1867, has been so successfully vindicated by its results that it may be deemed secure. Under its operation the aggregate yearly attendance

---

[1] New York State Report, 1871, p. 10.   [2] Ibid, p. 62.   [3] New York State Report, 1872, p. 10.   [4] New York State Report, 1874, p. 7.

of pupils at the public schools has increased nearly eighty-two thousand, and the average daily attendance nearly eighty thousand." [1]

The Commissioner of Public Schools for Rhode Island reports results equally gratifying. He says of the city of Providence, where the schools were free, that "the effect has been in the highest degree satisfactory; and notwithstanding the indifference of some and the opposition of others to the free schools, the number of children in schools has largely increased, and the percentage of those who do not attend school largely diminished." [2]

In New Jersey the free school law has given a new impulse to education, and vigorous efforts are being made to overtake the necessities of the State. The Board of Education report in 1872: "There has been a large increase in the number of pupils attending the public schools, and we may safely infer, from the absence of all complaint, that our school machinery is working to the satisfaction of the entire community." [3] The State Superintendent reports: "The free school law of New Jersey went into operation the 1st of September, 1871. During the year for which this report is rendered, therefore, all the children of this State have had an opportunity of attending school free of charge. The results of the first year's experience under the working of this law are most gratifying. There has been a liberal increase in the salaries paid to teachers, and the time the schools have been kept open has been considerably increased." [4] "The law gives general satisfaction. It is popular in all parts of the State. The unanimity with which the bill passed the Legislature was most gratifying to its friends, but far more

---

[1] New York State Report, 1874, p. 57.   [2] Rhode Island Report, 1871, p. 22.
[3] New Jersey Report, 1872, p. 5.   [4] New Jersey Report, 1872, p. 9.

gratifying has been the hearty endorsement given it by the people." (¹)

The Michigan report, issued shortly after the abolition of the rate-bill, says: " In consequence of the schools being free, the length of time they have been held has been greatly increased. In some districts they are said to have nearly twice the length of school that they have previously had. The advantages of the free school system are so manifest that it was adopted in most of the cities and large towns several years since, the rate-bill being abolished by public vote. A larger number of children are found to attend the public schools, and there is far less irregularity of attendance." (²)

The Connecticut Board of Education, in their report for 1869, say: " The reports come to us from all parts of the State of a largely increased attendance of the children of those parents who were unable, or more frequently unwilling, to pay the charges for tuition; and while we have no sympathy with this last class of parents, we rejoice that their children need no longer suffer for this their parents' neglect." (³)

The Secretary of the Board, Mr. B. G. Northrop, says: " The law has received an emphatic ratification from the people. The rate-bill is buried beyond the hope of resurrection. If any 'mourners go about the streets,' the procession is a small one. There is little prospect of an 'about face' and another march towards the dark ages. No such retrograde movement ever occurred in this country. Wherever once repealed, the rate-bill has never been re-enacted. In many States, for long periods, and under varying circumstances, the rate-bill has been fully and fairly tried, and everywhere it has been 'found wanting.'" (⁴)

---

[1] New Jersey Report, 1872, p. 10.
[2] Report of Commissioner of Education, 1870. Title, Michigan, p. 185.
[3] Connecticut Report, 1869, p. 5.
[4] Ibid, p. 17.

In the following year Mr. Northrop was able to refer to the test of experience. He says: "The free school law has accomplished more than its friends promised. The unanimity of its adoption by the Legislature and its welcome by the people were favourable signs. But the test of experience is still more decisive. The actual results of the first year's trial demonstrate the necessity and wisdom of the law. They show that nearly six thousand children were kept from school by the rate-bill." [1]

The Report for 1871 shows results still more remarkable: "The increase in the whole number registered the first term of free schools, as reported last year, was 6,208, and for the corresponding term now reported 5,744, or an increase in two years of 11,952. How beneficent that legislation which has led nearly 12,000 children to school, and thus to a higher future." [2]

The increase in attendance in the year previous to the adoption of free schools was only 432. [3] With the large increase of attendance under the free school law, the duration of the schools has also made a considerable advance. [4] In his last report (1873) Mr. Northrop says: "Our people believe in free schools, and are determined to maintain them. The old rate-bill is abandoned 'for good' in Connecticut, and is now unknown in this country. It is a proud fact that the public schools of every State are free." [5]

The testimony of the State Superintendents and Secretaries in all these States is strengthened by the reports of the County Superintendents. A large volume might be filled with extracts from their reports, proving the universal delight with which free schools have been received.

---

[1] Connecticut Report, 1870, p. 29.   [2] Connecticut Report, 1871, p. 19.
[3] Connecticut Report, 1870, p. 5.   [4] Connecticut Report, 1871, p. 5.
[5] Connecticut Report, 1873, p. 30.

This testimony points to two conclusions—first, that the exaction of school fees is a serious bar to attendance; and, secondly, that free schools can be kept open for longer periods than schools not free. The people are willing to pay taxes for the support of free schools where they will not contribute towards the expense of education by means of school fees.

(d) *Free Schools, the People's System.*

If there is one question upon which the citizens of the United States are practically unanimous, it is in support of free schools. The gauge of public interest in the system is the burden of taxation which the people are willing to bear for its maintenance. It has been shown what this amounts to. The Superintendent for Pennsylvania says that in every district except one the schools are put in operation by the free suffrages of the people; it is the people's system. ([1]) The Superintendent for Iowa says that the opposition of wealth has long ceased to exist. Wealthy men are the most liberal in their views, and the most active friends of popular education. The taxes which are levied to support the schools are self-imposed. "However much our people may disagree on other subjects, they are practically united upon this." ([2])

It will be seen that upon other points of the system there is a division of sentiment, but as to the propriety of retaining the free character of the schools I can find but one opinion—at any rate, so far as the elementary schools are concerned. A small minority are opposed to free high schools. "Doubts, questionings, murmurs of discontent, mingled with

---

[1] Pennsylvania Report, 1873, p. xii. [2] Iowa Report, 1873, p. 17.

voices of direct opposition or appeals for reconstruction and improvement, are coming up from every quarter of the Union—from the old States as well as the new. This statement is not to be understood as affirming or implying that the public opinion of any State having a well-established system of common schools has become hostile to the system as such, or to the policy of free schools supported and controlled by the State. It is believed that no instance of that kind has occurred, or is likely to occur, but, contrariwise, that on the main question the sentiment of the States and of the nation as the aggregate of States is as sound and as firm as ever." (¹)

This feeling exists where we should hardly expect to find it. The Superintendents for Virginia say : " The favourable advance in public sentiment has continued, as is unequivocally shown by the testimonies of County Superintendents on pages 31-33. The evidences of this, however, are patent to every observing eye. The platforms of both political parties, and the political speeches made during the canvass, would have placed the fact beyond a doubt, if there had been no other evidence." (²) And again : " The struggle which the school system has heretofore been compelled to wage for its existence is over." (³)

The report from West Virginia is that " opposition is withdrawing, and, by its practical results, our system is daily recommending itself to the judgment and affections of the people." (⁴)

The Hon. Warren Johnson, State Superintendent for Maine, writes : " Free education for all is the instinctive demand and prime necessity for all republics." " Society must assume the responsibility of ordering the education of youth. This responsibility cannot be left with the in-

---

¹ Illinois Report, 1872, p. 47. ² Virginia Report, 1873, p. 2.
³ Virginia Report, 1873, p. 19. ⁴ West Virginia Report, 1872, p. 9.

dividual, with benevolent associations, fraternities, or religious bodies, or to charity. The old brotherhoods of France, the Established Church of England, the parochial, denominational schools everywhere, have failed to accomplish the purpose. Society, through its organic forms of municipalities, State or National governments, must issue the fiat, 'Free education for all.'" [1]

Mr. Thos. W. Harvey, State Commissioner for Ohio, says: "The people, in the past, have shown their ability and willingness to guard, foster, and protect the common school, the pride, the boast, the glory of our nation. They will continue to do this in the future." [2]

This is confirmed by the reports for Cleveland and Cincinnati, both in the same State. The former affirms that the schools are constantly growing in effectiveness and in the confidence of the people; [3] the latter, that the schools never stood higher in public confidence. [4]

The Washington Report (1872) says that no tax is so cheerfully paid as that for school purposes. [5]

The Superintendent for Louisiana refers to the hold which the system of free schools has taken on the affections of the people. [6]

The Superintendent for California says: "The people are so much in earnest in their support of the public schools, that in 1873 they voluntarily taxed themselves 10·48 per cent. more than they did in 1871." [7]

The State Board of Rhode Island report that "at no period in the history of the State has there been a more profound interest manifested in the prosperity of our common schools." [8]

---

[1] Maine Report, 1872, p. 100.
[2] Ohio Report, 1873, p. 56.
[3] Cleveland Report, 1872, p. 14.
[4] Cincinnati Report, 1869, p. 22.
[5] Washington Report, 1872, p. 3.
[6] Louisiana Report, 1873, p. 11.
[7] California Report, 1873, p. 42.
[8] Rhode Island Report, 1871, p. xi.

Between 1854 and 1871, a period of eighteen years, the city of New York contributed in taxes, over and above what she received, more than five and a half million dollars to aid other portions of the State for the support of public schools. The Board of Education ask: " Could a stronger statement than that contained in these figures be made, illustrating the high appreciation that the people of the metropolis entertain in relation to the necessity and importance of supporting and developing a sound system of public instruction ?" [1]

From Maryland it is reported that "the popular feeling in favour of public schools is more unanimous and more intense now than at any previous time." " Every effort on the part of School Boards to furnish better accommodation and better teachers has been responded to by the people, and has resulted in an increase of pupils and in a higher appreciation of the school system." [2]

The Superintendent for Indiana says that " the enemies of free schools have either been converted or have sunk away in sullen silence." [3]

The Superintendent for Kentucky refers to the " futility of opposition " to the free school system.

In Michigan, the healthy public sentiment in relation to the free schools is proved by the fact that the amount paid in salaries has increased from about half a million dollars in 1860 to over a million and a half in 1873. [4] In the sparsely settled districts of this State, and under all the disadvantages which attend new settlements, the most commendable and extraordinary efforts are being made to obtain good schools.

In proof of what the inhabitants of the State think of free schools, Massachusetts points to the increase of 100 per cent. in the amount of school taxation in seven years.

---

[1] New York (City) Report, 1871, p. 16.
[2] Maryland Report, 1873, p. 9.
[3] Indiana Report, 1872, p. 11.
[4] Michigan Report, 1873, p. 55.

We have seen already, in speaking of rate-bills, the opinion of those States where the schools have recently been made free.

There can be no doubt that the State Superintendents are in the best position to gather the suffrages of the people on this subject; but if we go deeper and examine the reports of the County Superintendents and of local School Committees we arrive at precisely similar results. Now and then a grumble is heard about heavy taxes, but the reports which record them are of the most exceptional character, and suffice only to prove the general rule. A more frequent complaint is that the incidence of taxation is unequal, especially in New York State and in Missouri. In twenty-one counties of Illinois the Superintendents report almost perfect unanimity of public feeling in favour of the system, while in two counties only is there any opposition. In Virginia, the Superintendents of ninety-three counties report a gain in public sentiment, while five only report unfavourably. In Missouri, nine counties report dissatisfaction on account of school taxes, whilst sixty-seven state that public opinion is strongly in favour of the system.

This description answers for the whole Union. Those who have known America best and longest will agree that, whether the attachment of Americans for free schools is founded on good and solid reasons or otherwise, there can not be the slightest doubt that it exists, and that it forms one of the most striking features in the national character.

It must be said, however, that in recent years there has been manifested a feeling, partial in extent and evanescent in character, that the State should provide for elementary instruction only. That this limitation of free education has not a large number of advocates may be gathered from the fact that the Superintendent of only one State, so far as I can ascertain, advocates it. The Superintendent for Maryland favours a small fee for attendance at the high schools. (¹) In Michigan, the legal right of a district to levy taxes for providing instruction beyond ordinary English branches has been formally challenged and decided. In the case of Stuart v. Kalamazoo School District, it was contended that the laws of the State could not be construed to authorise district schools to be supported free of tuition in other than primary English branches, nor to authorise a district high school to be established and maintained in any other way than by charges for tuition. The Court decided that the law authorised the establishment of high schools, and that a tax for their support was in accordance with the provision of the Constitution.

The Commissioner of Education, in his last report, refers with gratification to the fact that the opposition to free high schools has been checked, and that there has been no confinement of the State provision to the rudimentary and lower schools—no stopping at "the point where, to the poor man, the question of expense obliges him to arrest the further progress of his children." (²) Mr. Dawson observed this difference of opinion in Ohio: "There is difference of opinion as to how far education should go, and as to whether the higher education, which can be but the good fortune of the few, ought to be paid for by the many. That question will have to be discussed hereafter in England and in America. All agree that all ought to have enough to start them in life, and to make them intelligent citizens; all are not agreed that the Latin language or the higher mathematics shall be taught at the public expense." (³) The whole subject is debated at length in the reports of several States. From these I gather that there is a consensus of opinion amongst educational officials that the present basis of the free school should not be narrowed.

---

[1] Maryland Report, 1873, p. 15.   [2] Report of Commissioner, 1873, p. xxi.
[3] "In Ohio." *Gentleman's Magazine*, March, 1875.

The tendency is rather in the direction of an enlargement of the present privileges of free schools. Thus, in the matter of school books, I find there is a considerable demand that they should be provided at the public cost. One reason for this, no doubt, is the text-book difficulty, arising out of the number of different sets of books used in the same State, and sometimes in the same school district. But apart from this difficulty, which is, however, of no slight dimensions, there is a growing feeling that with free schools free books ought to be supplied. It is argued that books are part of the school apparatus and machinery, and ought to be provided by the same means. In some of the largest cities of the Union this has been the rule for many years. The Bishop of Manchester found it in operation in New York city. ([1]) School books are free in Philadelphia where no scholar is required to purchase a school book, except to replace one lost or injured. ([2]) The Boston Board of Education recommended the adoption of free books in 1869. ([3]) In Baltimore, the practice is for the Board to supply books and to make a charge for their use. In many districts of Iowa, books are purchased by School Boards for the use of pupils. ([4])

The opponents of free schools in England have endeavoured to show that the free system is being undermined by the increasing preference of the people—especially of the richer class—for private schools. I have sought diligently for evidence upon this subject, and the bulk of that which I have been able to collect is opposed to this view. It has been supported in this country chiefly by extracts and notes taken from the report of the Bishop of Manchester, and used without reference to their context. I do not for a moment impugn the fairness of Bishop

---

[1] Fraser's Report, p. 55. [2] Philadelphia Report, 1872, p. 276.
[3] Boston Report, 1869, p. 8. [4] Iowa Report, 1872, p. 32.

Fraser's report; nor do I class him with those "enemies" of the free school system, and of most other free institutions, who, to use his own words, " enumerate with ungenerous pleasure" those defects of the American school system and social organisation which are "patent to the eye of the most cursory observer." Mr. Collings has exposed, in the appendix to his pamphlet on American schools, the manner in which evidence is got up against the system. ([1]) This, however, has not prevented later writers from following the same method. Of these the most recent and, amongst several zealous competitors, the most flagrant offender is the Rev. Dr. Rigg. ([2])

Of the relative positions of public and private schools Bishop Fraser says: "By the theory of a common school system, scholars of every rank are supposed to come within the sphere of its operation. But actual—I don't know whether they can be called natural—distinctions cannot be disposed of by a theory, and, as a matter of fact, social distinctions do tell with a very marked effect upon American schools. Speaking generally, they are in possession of the great middle class, the artisans, storekeepers, farmers. The system works with a much nearer approach to its idea or theoretic perfection in the country, where ranks are more equalised, and there is no one rich and no one poor, than it does in the cities and towns. Yet even in country districts aristocratic feelings and prejudices, very foolishly and unhappily, it must be admitted, are beginning to prevail. And in all the cities, New York, Newhaven, Hartford, Providence, and even in Boston, the wealthier class, indeed all who can afford to do so, almost without exception, send their children to private schools. Of the persons whose acquaintance I made in the country, most of whom I should

---

[1] "Outline of American School System," by Jesse Collings, p. 51.
[2] See Appendix A.

rate at about the same level of social rank and social feeling as myself, I do not remember one who used, either for sons or daughters, the common schools. In all these cities there are finishing schools for young ladies, just as there would be in cities of the same character among ourselves; and there are private day or boarding schools for boys, at which they remain till they are fit for college." (¹)

"At Yale College, Newhaven—which, and Harvard University, near Boston, are the Oxford and Cambridge of America—I was informed that, though a large proportion of the students had been educated in the common schools, yet, as a general rule, they finished off with a year's preparation in a private school, with a view to a more exclusive reading in the classics."(²)

"There can hardly be said to be any competition between these different classes of schools—the common school on the one hand, and the academy or private school on the other. They exist side by side in an amicable way, because, apparently, there is a demand for both. In wealthy neighbourhoods the latter flourish and abound; where property is more equally distributed, it is to the interest of the inhabitants to support the former." (³)

Assuming that these extracts represent the case correctly at the time of Bishop Fraser's visit, it is worth while to enquire what has been the tendency since.

There were at that time fifty-nine academies and six hundred and eleven private schools in Massachusetts. In 1869, the private schools had decreased from six hundred and eleven to four hundred and eighty-one, (⁴) and in 1873 the number returned was four hundred and sixty-three. (⁵) In 1873, the Secretary of the State Board of Education wrote: "We have over fifty academies, many of which

---

[1] Fraser's Report, p. 99.   [2] Ibid, p. 100.   [3] Ibid, p. 101.
[4] Report of Commissioner of Education, 1873, p. 166.   [5] Ibid, p. 176.

have outlived the wants which called them into being, and are struggling for a precarious existence." (¹)

Mr. Philbrick, the Superintendent of the Boston schools, in his last report, says : " It appears that while the population of the city from 1856 to 1873 increased 55 per cent., and the pupils in the public schools increased 51 per cent., the number of the pupils in the private schools actually decreased." (²)

Of the private schools and academies in New York State, the report of the Superintendent, issued in 1870, says : " The State does not monopolise the work of school instruction, or attempt to exclude others from it. On the contrary, outside and independent of its own public system, it tolerates un-incorporated private schools, and, up to the present time, has chartered about forty literary colleges and four hundred and twenty academies. Twenty-two of the colleges, with some changes in names and plans, are still in operation. Of the academies, about two hundred are conducted under their original charter; about eighty have been absorbed in the organisation of Union free schools, and the others are either dormant or dead." (³) The School Commissioner for Cortland County (N. Y.) says : " Private schools, always exerting, to a greater or less extent, a deleterious influence on the public schools, do not flourish under the operation of the free school system. Most of the academies are unable to compete with free schools, and are rapidly giving place to Union schools." (⁴)

In four years, in Ohio (between 1870 and 1873), the number of pupils attending private schools decreased by nearly one half—viz., from 10,500 to 5,945. (⁵) The Report suggests, however, that this large decrease may be partly accounted for by errors in enumeration.

In Illinois there was a large decrease, between 1870 and

---

¹ Massachusetts Report, 1873, p. 190.   ² Boston Report, 1874, p. 414.
³ Report of Commissioner of Education, 1870, p. 227.
⁴ New York State Report, 1871, p. 210.   ⁵ Ohio Report, 1871, p. 31.

1872, in the attendance at private schools; (¹) but in 1873 it appears to have again risen. The report for Illinois, for the year 1867-8, says: "The number of private schools has decreased rapidly during the last four years until 1868, when there is an apparent increase of thirty-eight over the last year. This is only apparent, not actual, and is due to an imperfect enumeration in the city of Chicago. The large number of private schools in that city is partly caused by the inadequate accommodation afforded by the public schools. So extraordinary is the growth of the city, that although several large new school buildings are added every year, the increase in the number of seats does not keep pace with the increase in the population." (²)

The report for Maine, 1871, says of academies: "The total number of such institutions is sixty-seven. An examination of these returns discloses the fact that, while a few of the highest seminaries, fostered by denominational sympathy and aid, have developed to a vigorous and healthy existence, the great majority are in a feeble and precarious condition. Their resources are insufficient for the support of the schools, and their constant application to the State Legislature for aid is a confession that they are unable to stand alone." (³) The report for the same State for the following year says: "The academies, the former real high schools of the people, are gradually disappearing from the field, where at the proper time they did a noble and faithful educational work." (⁴)

The scholars attending private schools in Connecticut had decreased from 10,364 in 1869 (⁵) to 9,029 in 1872. (⁶)

On the other hand, in New Jersey, between 1871 and

---

[1] Illinois Report, 1872, p. 2. [2] Report of Commissioner of Education, 1870, p. 112. [3] Report of Commissioner of Education, 1872, p. 142. [4] Maine Report, 1872, p. 90. [5] Connecticut Report, 1869, p. 108. [6] Connecticut Report, 1873, p. 146.

1873, there was an increase of attendance at the private schools amounting to nearly 6,000. This is accounted for by the fact, already referred to, that the public school accommodation was deficient. ([1])

The Rhode Island report for 1873 says: "As the schools of the State have become more efficient than private institutions, we have found patronage withdrawn from the latter, and that attendance upon the former has improved. That improvement still goes on." ([2])

The Superintendent of the city of Williamsport (Penn.) says: "In our first report, made in 1868, soon after the office of Superintendent was created, the following language is found—'But very few, if any, of the children of those families which move in the most fashionable circles attend the public schools; a large number of select and private schools are well sustained in our midst from this circumstance. While some parents consider it a disgrace for their children to attend public schools, there are others who send to private schools from the fact that the higher branches of a liberal English education are not taught in our first grade public schools.' What a change has taken place . . . an entire change in public sentiment, from that of opposition to that of cordial support of the schools, and the consequent discontinuance of half a dozen private enterprises, the pupils of which are now enrolled on our public school register." ([3])

Iowa reports for 1872 a very considerable increase in pupils attending private schools. This is partly explained by the fact that schools are opened as private enterprises during the excessively long vacations of public schools. ([4])

In Virginia there has been a complete absorption of private schools since the inauguration of the free school system. ([5])

---

[1] New Jersey Report, 1872, 1873.　[2] Rhode Island Report, 1873, p. 8.
[3] Pennsylvania Report, 1872, pp. 249-51.　[4] Iowa Report, 1873, p. 13; ibid, 1871, p. 150.　[5] Virginia Reports, 1871, pp. 5-7; 1872, pp. xii. 3.

The Wisconsin report for 1871 states that "the fact noticed last year may be repeated with emphasis—namely, that there is a tendency to the extinction rather than increase of academies, arising from the fact that the high schools, normal schools, and the preparatory departments of the State University and the colleges absorb the larger share of academical students." [1]

The report for Washington (1872-3) says: "During the year twenty-eight new private schools have been established in Washington, and during the same period twenty-five were discontinued, in most instances for lack of support, many students preferring to avail themselves of the increased facilities afforded by the public schools." [2]

Going farther West, the reports from California, Nebraska, and Minnesota show that the attempts to conduct private schools in competition with public schools almost invariably end in failure; and the reports of the County Superintendents throughout the Union confirm this testimony.

There will be found, of course, in every community a certain number who will prefer to educate their children in private schools; but that neither in North nor South, East nor West, in large cities nor in rural districts, are the schools regarded as the schools of the poor, is a fact capable of easy demonstration.

In Boston, the examinations are now arranged to accommodate those parents who wish to take their children out of town before the beginning of the long vacation. [3] The Superintendent says, in a late report: "If there are Boston citizens who desire that the schools should be kept down to a pauper level, and that they should be attended only by the children of the poor, they never give public

---

[1] Report of Commissioner, 1872, p. 358.
[2] Washington Report, 1872-3, p. 92.   [3] Boston Report, 1869, p. 223.

expression to such sentiments. A high English educational official, while on the way with me to visit one of our grammar schools, enquired about the social grade of the children in the public schools; he wanted to know especially if professional gentlemen sent their sons to them. My answer was, 'At the school to which we are now going, you will find the son of the Chief Justice of the Commonwealth; at a school not far from it you might find the son of the Governor, and at another the son of the Mayor of the city." ([1])

The following is a list of the numbers and occupations of parents whose children attend the schools of Detroit:— Clergymen, 71; physicians, 90; lawyers, 57; teachers, 22; editors, 24; architects, 35; musicians, 37; civil officers, 110; military officers, 21; policemen, 62; firemen, 53; merchants, 910; grocers, 308; bankers, 25; insurance men, 62; persons of leisure, 135; shipowners, 57; jewellers, 36; book-keepers, 210; travelling agents, 153; clerks, 447; civil engineers, 45; agents, 266; conductors, 98; sailors, 234; engineers, 255; bakers, 99; tailors, 212; butchers, 186; brewers, 71; saloon-keepers, 141; teamsters, 186; expressmen, 47; telegraph men, 19; printers, 129; carpenters, 1,206; moulders, 195; machinists, 444; blacksmiths, 254; wagon-makers, 52; draymen, 97; hackmen, 14; barbers, 78; washerwomen, 124; day labourers, 1,168; boarding-house keepers, 88; masons, 238; plumbers, 68; shoemakers, 337; tinsmiths, 69; painters, 215; farmers, 129; cabinet-makers, 92; peddlers, 296; gardeners, 72; sailmakers, 24; photographers, 23; widows, 542; manufacturers, 508; unclassified, 945. ([2])

In St. Louis there are in the schools, 7,243 children of mechanics; 2,228 children of manufacturers; 3,336 children of merchants; and 1,071 children of professional men. Besides these, the parents are classified under the heads of

---

[1] Boston Report, 1874, p. 229.   [2] Michigan Report, 1873, p. 316.

agents, artists, boarding-house keepers, boatmen, butchers, clerks, confectioners, draymen and teamsters, farmers and gardeners, day labourers, laundresses, public officers, saloon-keepers, and seamstresses. (¹)

The Superintendent for Gallipolis (Ohio) says: "The public schools here have greatly advanced in public favour, and to-day they are cherished and patronised by nearly all, and certainly by the best citizens of the place." (²)

The Superintendent for Virginia put this question to the local authorities, "Have all classes of society been proportionately represented in the schools?" with this result: "We have reports on this subject from forty-nine counties. In forty-one counties the public schools were attended by all classes alike, high and low, rich and poor. In the other eight counties many of those who were able to give their children private schooling did so." (³)

One of the most remarkable features of the American free school is its almost infinite power of assimilation, and this is one of the greatest works which the school does. It draws children from all nations together, and marks them with the impress of nationality. Mr. Dawson says: "The school has more to do than to educate the children: it is the mill, so to speak, into which go children of English, Scotch, Irish, German, Russian, Italian, and Scandinavian parents, and come out Americans. Africa contributes its negroes, and now Asia is sending its Chinese. All must learn English, and the result will soon be that the population of the United States will be the most homogeneous of nations." (⁴) It is by means of the free common school that there is an American nation. Without it the nation would long ago have been split up into as many sections as Germany before the Empire. It is not too

---

[1] St. Louis Report, 1872, p. 19. [2] Ohio Report, 1873, p. 221.
[3] Virginia Report, 1871, p. 152.
[4] "In Ohio." *Gentleman's Magazine*, March, p. 341.

much to say that it was the teaching of the free school that saved the Union at the time of the civil war. Some of the good results of this school-fellowship of classes and of races are noticed by Mr. Dawson: " Far from the great cities there is little or no choice of schools; there is but one school in many places, and that is a good one, and all classes of children go to it. If anyone does not choose that his children should mix with all the children of his neighbours, he must have them taught at home or send them away to some boarding school. I was unable to see or to hear of any ill effects arising from this mingling of classes, and I attribute the superior good manners of (what would be called in England) the lower classes in the United States to this early meeting with those above them. Possibly, some vain ambition may be stirred up, or some undesirable finery may be worn; but these are small evils compared with the strong feeling of fellow-citizenship which is created." [1]

There is one thing, and one thing only, which appears to threaten the common school—that is, the Catholic question. Wherever large numbers of Roman Catholics congregate, parochial schools are opened, and the children of Catholics are withdrawn from the public schools. In the large cities where many private schools are found, the great proportion of them are of this character. There are a few other sectarian schools in the States, but at present the Catholics stand alone as a denomination in their hatred or fear of free schools. When other sects follow their example it will be an evil day for the American common school, and, as I think, for the nation.

---

[1] "In Ohio." *Gentleman's Magazine*, March, p. 341.

III.

ATTENDANCE.

(*a*) Annual Enrolment — (*b*) Average Attendance — (*c*) Period of Attendance—(*d*) Failure of Indirect Compulsion—(*e*) Trial of direct Compulsion—(*f*) Demand for Direct Compulsion.

(a) Annual Enrolment.

In the competition for improved methods and results in school affairs which, happily, now engages such general attention in many countries, it is becoming well understood that a large number of scholars on the register does not count for much. Unless the attendance of the whole school is for a certain period, and very regular, the devotion of teachers and the most scientific methods can accomplish comparatively little. Indeed, there is a kind of attendance—the hanging off and on of children—which, while it does them very little good, is a positive injury to the rest of the scholars. This is a lesson which we are learning in England; and as the League has done something to enforce it, I shall not be thought to over-rate the significance of the facts in stating the progress which has been made in the United States in the enrolment of scholars. A large attendance, even though it be at intervals and uncertain, indicates that the public mind is partially awake to the importance of education, but that the waste and obstruction which are caused by irregularity are not understood; and this feeling respecting the necessity of instruction is one of the first requisites in the work of national education.

It may safely be affirmed that there are very few native American children—at any rate, in the Northern and Western States—who do not attend school during a certain period of their lives. What is called "absenteeism," which means the total neglect of school advantages, is chiefly found amongst the foreign population. There is no large class born in these States to whom the inside of a school is an absolute mystery. That the attendance of a considerable proportion is much too short and too irregular is more than probable, as will be seen; but the first steps—the provision of accommodation and the registration of scholars—have long ago been taken.

In the following States the enrolment of children, without distinction of age, colour, or nativity, and including both public and private schools, exceeded, in 1873, the whole number between the ages of five and fifteen:— California, Connecticut, Illinois, Indiana, Iowa, Kansas, Massachusetts, Michigan, Minnesota, Nebraska, New Hampshire, New Jersey, New York, Ohio, Pennsylvania, Vermont, and Wisconsin.

In the remaining States the percentage of enrolment of the population between five and fifteen was as follows:— Alabama, 37·8; Delaware, 59·4; Florida, 41·6; Georgia, 30·7; Kentucky, 66·08; Louisiana, 41·8; Maine, 90·4; Maryland, 67·3; Mississippi, 70·17; Missouri, 88·2; North Carolina,

H

51·4; South Carolina, 45·7; Rhode Island, 91·0; (¹) Tennessee, 49·7; Texas, 56·6; Virginia, 51·2; West Virginia, 67·19.

These calculations are made from statistics contained in the Reports of the Commissioner of Education for 1872 (p. 946) and 1873 (p. 512). The numbers of children between five and fifteen are based upon the returns of the United States Census, 1870, an allowance having been made for an increase between 1870 and 1873. I am unable to give precisely similar figures for England—there is no international uniformity of statistics—but for the purposes of comparison it may be well to state the results as nearly as they can be ascertained. The last census gives the number of scholars (children in school) in England and Wales under fifteen as 3,563,888, while the total population of school age (between three and thirteen) was 5,374,301. This gives a percentage of enrolment upon the school population of 66·3. The number at school over fifteen is not included in this estimate, but this omission may safely be set off against the numbers in the States under five and six years of age omitted from American calculations, who, being under instruction at home and in private schools, are as much entitled to rank as "scholars" as large numbers of those included in our English census. From these figures it would seem that in 1871 England occupied a position, as to enrolment of pupils, between the border States and the old slave States—below Maryland and Missouri, and above Virginia, the Carolinas, and other Southern States. Allowing for a considerable increase in the enrolment between 1871 and 1873, we still should not at that time reach the standard in Mississippi and Missouri; but it is satisfactory to know that great and rapid improvement is now being made in this respect.

As regards the United States, the facts are under-stated

---

[1] Rhode Island Report, 1874, p. 49.

rather than otherwise, as a reference to the Reports will show. The enrolment throughout the Union (exclusive of territories) was, in 1873, about 60 per cent. of the whole population between five and twenty-one, according to the census of 1870.

The Superintendent for Pennsylvania says: "The school age with us is between six and twenty-one, and the probable number of persons between these ages is now about 1,200,000. Of these we had enrolled during the past year, in public schools, 834,020; in private schools, soldiers' orphans' schools, orphan homes and asylums, academies, colleges, &c., probably 50,000 more; making in all 884,020, or in round numbers 900,000. Of the 300,000 children of school age not in school, the great majority, without doubt, are between fifteen and twenty-one years of age, having obtained a greater or less degree of education, and are engaged in learning trades, &c.; but a careful observer cannot but be convinced that there are many thousands of our youth growing up to manhood almost wholly ignorant and uncared for." [1] The population of Pennsylvania (between five and fifteen) in 1870 was 854,340; [2] less by nearly 50,000 than the numbers in school.

In Iowa, in 1872, 71 per cent. of the population between five and twenty-one were enrolled in the public schools alone. [3]

The Report for New Jersey (1872) shows that 77 per cent. of the population between five and eighteen attended school (public or private) for some portion of the year. [4]

The Illinois Report for 1872 gives the enrolment in public schools for the year as 75 per cent. of the population between six and twenty-one. [5]

The Report for Connecticut (1873) shows that 94 per

---

[1] Pennsylvania Report, 1873, p. 14.
[2] Report of Commissioner of Education, 1872, p. 946. [3] Iowa Report, 1872, p. 10.
[4] New Jersey Report, 1872, p. 22. [5] Illinois Report, 1872, p. 7.

cent. of the children between four and sixteen attended schools of all kinds during the previous year. (¹)

The Report for Ohio (1871) states that over 78 per cent. of the population between five and seventeen were enrolled during the year. "It may safely be affirmed that, within the last school year, only about one fifth of the youth of Ohio, between the ages of five and seventeen years, were not enrolled in any school. To comprehend the full significance of this fact, we must bear in mind that many children, whose instruction and training have been quite up to the average standard of popular education in the State, leave the common school before they are seventeen years old, to engage in some other employment, or to enter academies or colleges, and that in many cities and towns children are forbidden by law, as in some localities they are forbidden by custom, to enter the schoolroom before they reach the age of six years." (²)

The Superintendent for New York State says: "Including the number reported in attendance upon private schools and academies, more than 80 per cent. of all children in the State, between five and twenty-one years of age, attended school some portion of the last year—a number larger than the entire population between the ages of six and seventeen years." (³)

In comparing the attendance at school in the State of New York with that in Prussia, he adds: "But our period of pupilage is eight years longer than that of Prussia, which includes only those between six and fourteen years of age, and our ratio of attendance is correspondingly less by reason of the greater number embraced in our enumeration. Making a just allowance for the number of those below six years of age who are not sent to school because of their infancy; and another

---

[1] Connecticut Report, 1873, p. 26.   [2] Ohio Report, 1871, p. 23.
[3] New York State Report, 1871, p. 10.

just allowance for those between fourteen and twenty-one, who have acquired a sufficient business education, and have betaken themselves to active pursuits; and still another just allowance for those who, although they do not attend school during any one particular year, have attended, or probably will attend, during several of the other fifteen years of the school period, and I believe it is a fair conclusion that the school attendance in our State is at least 90 per cent. upon a basis like that of Prussia." [1]

At a meeting of the National Educational Association, held at St. Louis in 1871, in the course of a discussion upon compulsory education, the Hon. E. E. White, of Ohio, said: "Recent statistics which I have seen show that 18 per cent. of the entire population of Prussia are in school in a given year. Ohio statistics for last year show that about 22 per cent. of our population were enrolled in the schools, and, making a liberal reduction for errors, the statistics will still show, I think, that the school attendance is as large a per cent. of the population in Ohio as in Prussia." [2]

In the Report of the Commissioner of Education for 1872, statistics are given of the school attendance in fifty of the principal cities throughout the Union, having populations ranging from 942,292—that of New York city—to 27,000 that of Nashville, Tennessee. From these statistics the Commissioner arrives at this conclusion: "If the enumeration of the school population for all the cities were confined to the population between six and sixteen years of age, and the number of pupils in parochial and private schools were fully reported, the total enrolment in the public and private schools would probably cover about 90 per cent. of the youths between these ages." [3]

---

[1] New York State Report, 1871, p. 64.
[2] Proceedings of National Educational Association, 1871, p. 223.
[3] Report of Commissioner of Education, 1873, p. xxix.

In the Northern and Western States, there can be no doubt that, although isolated places may be found where there are considerable deficiencies, yet upon the average they have arrived at what in England would be considered a very ample registration of scholars. In the States of the South, where free school systems have only been in operation for a short time, much remains to be done, but the progress has been rapid when we take into account the difficulties under which the work has been conducted.

(b) Average Attendance.

We are all agreed that one of the most important facts in regard to a school system is the degree of regularity with which scholars attend; yet this is a point about which it is not always easy to arrive at a correct conclusion. In the United States the methods of calculating average attendance are not always uniform, so that fair comparisons between states and cities do not at once appear on the face of the statistics obtainable. Still less is it a simple matter to draw a comparison which shall convey the exact relations of England and the various States, for then we have to compute the irregularities which are known to prevail in this country.

In America there is a keen competition between some of the larger cities to show a high average of attendance. It is considered a point of honour to stand well in this particular. In England, besides the spirit of rivalry, there is a much more powerful and direct incentive to exhibit good results, since the Government grant depends largely upon this return.

How this rivalry operates in some cities in the United States may be best illustrated by an extract from a speech made at a meeting of the National Educational Association, held at St. Louis, in 1871. In the discussions of the "Department of School Superintendence," Mr. W. R. Creery, of Maryland, said: "School statistics are valueless for purposes of comparison, because there is no uniformity in the language used, and no common understanding of the methods from which the various results are derived." "Again, the admirers of high percentage of attendance create wrong impressions, and give to the enemies of public schools an opportunity to make unfavourable contrasts upon unfair bases. School reports fall into the hands of a great many people, who, from a single item, draw a wholesale conclusion. It is a very pretty showing to have 95 or 96 per cent. of a school in attendance. The community in which this state of affairs is presented may be regarded as appreciating the whole subject of education to the value of 10 per cent. more than any other city, which can justly show but 85 per cent. of school attendance. The truth may be that the latter people love the cause as ardently as the former, but show it in a different way." [1]

Americans are not slow to borrow from other nations, and it has been suggested that they should adopt the English plan of dividing the State taxes upon the basis of average attendance.

I find that many of the school officials are pressing this reform upon State Legislatures. It may well be doubted, however, whether in England this mode of apportioning the grant has been productive of unmixed good. The reports of Her Majesty's Inspectors in recent years point to the conclusion that the system has operated not so much to secure increased attendance as to encourage irregular modes of keeping registers, which cannot be too strongly condemned. The

---

[1] Proceedings of National Educational Association, 1871, p. 226.

report of the Committee of Council for 1872–3 is especially instructive upon this subject. There is hardly an Inspector who does not refer to the irregularities which prevail. Mr. Stokes noticed in his district a method of keeping school registers which has, at least, the merit of simplicity. He says: "The worst of all methods is where the neglect of any entry at all—*i.e.*, a blank in the record—is assumed to mean presence; so that whenever the class rolls are not marked, all children are counted present." [1]

No doubt, the attention which has been called to this matter in recent years will lead to improvement, as it has already caused the issue of more stringent regulations by the Education Department; but it will still remain certain that very considerable deductions must be made from the averages given in our reports before they can be received as sufficiently accurate to be made the basis of reliable estimates.

The average attendance, as frequently stated in the reports of cities in the United States, is calculated, not in reference to the number enrolled, but to the "average number belonging." The latter number is based upon a standard sometimes arbitrarily selected by a School Board or a teacher, and differing in various cities. The rule as adopted in Chicago, Cincinnati, St. Louis, and some other cities, is as follows:—

"In all cases of absence of pupils from school, whether with intention of returning or not, and whether the absence be occasioned by sickness or other causes, including even the suspension of the pupil, and excepting only the case of transfer to some other school in the city, the pupil's name shall be kept on the roll as 'belonging' for three days, and dropped uniformly on the beginning of the fourth day, in case he does not return." [2]

---

[1] Report of Committee of Council, 1871-72, p. 73.
[2] St. Louis Report, 1872, p. 158.

The object of stating this item of "number belonging" is to show, " by comparison with the number in attendance, (*a*) the importance attached to regular attendance on school by the community ; (*b*) indirectly how much influence the teacher exerts on the pupils, and through them on the parents ; (*c*) local and temporary causes interfering with attendance—such, for example, as epidemics, local excitements," &c.

"The entire number enrolled, compared with average attendance, shows more general causes, such as are not dependent to so large a degree on the inclination of the parent or pupil, or the energy and ability of the teacher. For instance, the poverty of the people causes the withdrawal of pupils, to place them at work during certain seasons of the year. But the "number belonging," compared with the number attending, indicates causes dependent, to a large degree, on the tone of the community, the will or inclination of parent and pupil, and the influence of the teacher. Hence the latter item indicates a field wherein much can be done for the improvement of the schools, and, indirectly, of the tone of the community ; while very little, comparatively, can be done to influence the former item—the entire number enrolled." [1]

Another authority thus explains the advantages of keeping both methods of calculation : "(1) The total enrolment, compared with the actual average attendance, shows the irregularity of population, and the insufficiency of zeal or means on the part of the people at large to continue their children at school the whole scholastic year. (2) The average 'number belonging,' compared with the average daily attendance, shows the temporary irregularity, and indicates the strictness of discipline on the part of the teacher, the moral tone of the pupils, and, to a large extent, the prevailing tone of the community." [2]

---

[1] St. Louis Report, 1872, p. 159.
[2] Proceedings of National Educational Association, 1871, p. 227.

In the State Reports the item "number belonging" is very seldom given, and we have materials for examining the attendance at school in two lights only—(1) in comparison with the number enrolled, and (2) in comparison with the school population between certain ages. An investigation of the figures not only shows the comparative advancement of the different States, but leads to one important conclusion applicable to all—that under the most popular school system in the world it is impossible to dispense with laws for compulsory attendance.

The numbers enrolled and the average attendance in public schools in nearly all the States are set forth in the Report of the Commissioner of Education for 1873, p. 510. A calculation of the percentages, as shown in the following table, gives some most curious results:—

State.	Number Enrolled.	Average Attendance.	Per Cent.
Alabama	103,615	73,927	71· 3
California	107,593	69,461	64· 5
Connecticut	114,805	67,599	58· 8
Florida	18,000	14,400	80· 0
Georgia	76,157	32,240	42· 3
Illinois	655,508	329,799	50· 2
(¹) Indiana	465,154	298,851	64· 2
Iowa	347,572	204,204	58· 7
Kansas	121,690	71,062	58· 3
Louisiana	57,433	34,000	59·19
Maine	122,442	103,548	84· 5
Maryland	130,324	59,001	45· 2
(²) Massachusetts	276,602	205,252	74· 2
Michigan	324,615	170,000	52· 3
Minnesota	124,583	54,895	44·06

[1] Taken from State Report, 1874, p. 6.
[2] Taken from State Report, 1873, p. 150.

Table continued from preceding page:—

STATE.	Number Enrolled.	Average Attendance.	Per Cent.
Mississippi	148,780	125,000	84·01
(¹) Missouri	371,440	210,692	56· 7
Nevada	3,848	3,322	86· 3
New Hampshire	69,874	47,759	68· 3
(²) New Jersey	178,826	99,444	55· 6
New York	1,036,999	503,240	48· 5
North Carolina	146,737	97,830	66· 6
(³) Ohio	694,348	407,917	58· 7
Pennsylvania	834,020	511,418	61· 3
Rhode Island	28,245	22,435	79· 4
Texas	129,542	83,000	64·07
Virginia	160,859	91,175	56· 6
West Virginia	81,100	61,244	75· 5
Wisconsin	281,708	180,185	63· 9

In England, for the same year, there were on the registers of public elementary schools 2,218,598. The average attendance was 1,528,453; the percentage of attendance 68·8. (⁴) It must not be overlooked, however, that in all the Northern and Western States, the enrolment in America embraces a much larger school population than the enrolment in England.

In his report to the Schools Enquiry Commission, Bishop Fraser gives the percentage of "attendance" upon "enrolment" in five States. In Massachusetts it was 80; in Rhode Island, 78; in Connecticut, 72; in Pennsylvania, 64; and in Ohio, 57. (⁵)

In comparison with these results, Bishop Fraser states those arrived at in England under the Duke of Newcastle's

---
[1] Taken from State Report for 1873, p. 7. [2] Taken from State Report, 1872, p. 8.
[3] Deducting re-enrolments, the percentage is 59·18. State Report, 1873, p. 17.
[4] Report of Committee of Council, 1873-4, p. ix. [5] Fraser's Report, p. 94.

Commission. In ten "specimen districts" the average attendance upon enrolment was 76 per cent. Upon these statistics Bishop Fraser based the conclusion that the percentage of attendance in America " is no better than, indeed hardly so good as, the average condition of schools among ourselves." ([1]) This deduction has given great satisfaction to many people in England who were content with our system of education before the Act of 1870 ; but it seems to me that it was a very hasty, and, if improvement is to be our object, a perilous judgment to arrive at upon the materials at hand. That the figures represent the degree of regularity *within prescribed limits* is true, but they tell nothing whatever of the hold which a school system has upon the population. A very select enrolment will give a very high average attendance, as in the case of Florida, which, in the above table, stands much higher than New York. It is clear that as a school system reaches lower down and takes in the poorest class, embracing "the mass of apathy, thriftlessness, and ignorance," it must become proportionately more difficult to present a high average attendance, and, without a stringent system of compulsion, impossible to do so. The only way to show how far a system embraces the many is to compare the attendance with the school population.

The school population in England and Wales (between three and thirteen) was, at the last census, 5,374,301. The average attendance in 1873 was 1,528,453, giving 28·4 as the percentage of attendance.

In the following table the school population for all States is taken from the returns of the last United States Census (1870), and the numbers in average attendance from the Report of the Commissioner of Education, 1873, except for Indiana, Massachusetts, Missouri, and New Jersey. The average

---

[1] Fraser's Report, p. 93.

attendance in these States is derived from the State Reports:—

STATE.	Population between 5 and 15.	Population between 5 and 21.	Average Attendance.	Per Cent. of Attendance on Population.	
				Between 5 and 15.	Between 5 and 21.
Alabama	273,464	414,117	73,927	27·02	17· 8
Arkansas..............	128,836	201,302	32,863	25· 5	16· 3
California	110,480	152,610	69,461	62· 8	45· 5
Connecticut	107,974	170,425	67,599	62· 6	39· 6
Florida	51,637	77,633	14,400	27· 8	18· 5
Georgia	324,751	490,956	32,240	9· 9	6· 5
Illinois	661,614	977,508	329,799	49· 8	33· 7
Indiana	452,789	675,893	298,851	66· 0	44· 2
Iowa	320,404	467,547	204,204	63· 7	43· 6
Kansas	88,420	129,287	71,062	80· 3	54· 8
Louisiana	180,491	271,769	34,000	18· 8	12· 5
Maine	135,334	215,133	103,548	76· 5	48·13
Maryland	193,466	294,350	59,001	30· 5	20·05
Massachusetts (¹) ...	282,485	462,398	205,252	73· 0	44· 3
Michigan..............	285,341	429,175	170,000	59· 5	39· 6
Minnesota	118,167	166,223	54,895	46· 4	33·02
Mississippi	222,087	337,502	125,000	56· 2	37·03
Missouri	466,971	684,942	210,692	45· 1	30· 7
Nevada	4,399	6,457	3,322	75· 5	51· 4
New Hampshire......	60,070	98,453	47,759	79· 5	48· 5
New Jersey...........	209,585	316,942	99,444	47· 4	31· 3
New York	966,852	1,506,289	503,240	52·04	33. 4
North Carolina	285,144	435,085	97,830	34· 3	22· 5
Ohio	670,844	1,016,272	407,917	60· 8	40·13
Oregon	23,767	33,578	15,329	64· 5	45· 6
Pennsylvania	854,340	1,295,823	511,418	59· 8	39. 4
Rhode Island	42,837	69,639	22,435	52· 3	32· 2
Texas	228,618	339,344	83,000	36· 2	24· 4
Virginia	314,021	474,850	91,175	29·03	19· 2
West Virginia	120,689	178,393	61,244	50· 7	34· 3
Wisconsin	285,551	416,921	180,185	63· 1	43· 2

I have not been able to procure the average attendance in Delaware, Kentucky, Nebraska, South Carolina, Tennessee, and Vermont, so that these States are omitted.   ¹ Massachusetts Report, 1873, p. cv.

A comparison with this and the preceding table will show that while in England we have a more select enrolment, and consequently a more regular attendance, than in many of the States—some of them the principal Northern and Western States—yet that, so far as concerns our hold upon the great mass of the population, we stand only on a level with some of the most backward of the old slave States. This reflection is the more serious when we remember that in the foregoing calculations the whole of the school population, native and foreign, white and black, are included. I do not forget that our average attendance is estimated upon a longer school year than that in most of the States, but against this fact may be set the later school age in the United States; and when allowance is made for every difference which would tell in our favour, there can be but one conclusion—that in the work of getting the masses into school we are still far behind a country in which absenteeism and irregularity of attendance are admitted, on all hands, to be the most crying evils under which their system labours.

The percentage of average attendance upon "the number belonging," as given in some city reports, will hardly be of great interest in England, for the reason that the method of calculation, and any advantages which it affords, are very imperfectly understood. Yet, as the percentage of average attendance is founded upon a much more limited registration or enrolment under this method, it affords a more equal basis of comparison with our average attendance upon enrolment than when the total enrolment in the States is estimated. I will give a few examples of the results in different cities, but I do not claim for them any special value. Any estimate or comparison which leaves out of account a large proportion of the school population can only prove deceptive, and give warrant for a false security. The school officers in the United States do not blink the difficulty which the absence of compulsory laws entails upon them, but in a country where so much depends upon the true comprehension by the people of the work to be done, it is above all things desirable that the exact outcome of their system should be set before them. This is not done when high averages, based upon arbitrary methods of calculation, are set up for admiration. If it is necessary to retain " average number belonging " as a computation to enable the State Superintendent to direct his energies in the best manner, it appears to me that it should be kept for the use of school officials only.

The following table shows the results of this calculation for some principal cities : —

Year of Report.	City.	Total Enrolment.	Number Belonging.[1]	Average Attendance.	Per Cent. of Attendance on Enrolment	Per Cent. of Attendance on Number Belonging.
1874	Boston ...	50,000	44,942	41,613	83·2	92· 5
1873	Chicago ...	44,091	28,831	27,003	61·2	93· 6
1874	Cincinnati..	26,795	21,564	20,609	76·9	95· 5
1873	Cleveland...	15,085	10,362	9,676	64·1	93· 3
1874	New York[2]	215,545	—	117,239	54· 4	—
1874	Philadelphia	92,036	—	79,565	86· 4	—
1872	St. Louis ...	30,294	22,010	20,479	67·6	93·04
1873	Washington	8,935	6,890	6,417	71·8	93· 4

[1] In Washington called the Average Enrolment.

[2] The above figures for New York include evening schools, corporate schools, and coloured schools. In his last report the Superintendent says : "The average attendance and yearly enrolment as shown in the preceding exhibit, present a very great discrepancy, the former being only about 55 per cent. of the latter. As I have stated in previous reports, this is, to a certain extent fictitious. As many pupils are constantly passing from school to school, in consequence of a change of residence and from other causes, and as each school returns all the pupils who attended during any portion of the year, without regard to their attendance at any other school, the same pupils are consequently counted several times in the aggregate of the different returns. Were some means devised to correct this statistical inaccuracy, the number showing the general enrolment for the year would be considerably

It will be evident from a glance at these figures that the vital calculation is that of average attendance upon enrolment.

These cities do not all rank as high as the cities of Pennsylvania taken together, where I find that the average attendance in the cities and boroughs having 5,000 inhabitants or upwards, was 80 per cent. of the enrolment. The latest returns which I have been able to obtain from some of the largest towns in England show the following results:—Liverpool: "Number on the roll," February 1875, 57,698 ; average attendance, 38,449 ; per cent. of attendance, 66·6. Leeds: "Number on the roll for the month ending February 28, 1875," 44,498 ; average attendance, 27,531 ; per cent. of attendance, 61·8. Bristol: "Number on the rolls," 19th February, 1875, 25,182 ; average attendance for the four previous weeks, 17,807 ; per cent. of attendance, 70·7. Newcastle-on-Tyne: Number on books, January, 1875, 17,444; average attendance, 12,149; per cent. of attendance, 69·6. Birmingham: Number on the books, week ending 4th June, 1875, 51,334 ; average attendance, 34,718 ; per cent. of attendance, 67·6. Manchester: Number on the books week ending February 27th, 1875, 48,275 ; average attendance, 32,407 ; per cent. of attendance, 67·1. The general average is thus slightly in favour of the American towns. It will be seen that the number on the roll does not mean the total enrolment for the year, but the number on the books at a given period ; in reality, "number belonging," though not "average number belonging." In comparing the English and

---

reduced ; and I see no reason for continuing a practice which, in a serious manner, impairs the accuracy of our returns, and at the same time gives a false impression as to the actual number of children who attend the schools. I recommend, therefore, that the records of the schools and the methods of making the returns of attendance be so modified as to correct this error, which, besides what has already been stated, seems to indicate that the pupils are very irregular in their attendance ; whereas, in fact, they are quite remarkable for regularity as well as punctuality."

American towns, it must also be remembered that here compulsory bye-laws have been in operation for several years, while of the American cities above given, Boston and Washington are the only ones in which compulsion has been tried at present. The practical conclusion is that greater stringency is required in England in the application of compulsion, since in the chief American cities (New York, perhaps, excepted) they are doing as well without compulsion as we are with it. If the rural districts were taken into the calculation for the States a very considerable falling off would be found; especially in the new and thinly-populated States the average for a whole State is deceptive. The percentages in the towns are high; in the country necessarily low, because of the isolated situation of large numbers of the population. You do not find good roads, trim fences, and the common evidences of civilisation in every school district out West. Neither has the Constitution provided for every parish an "educated gentleman" by profession, for generations past. All this must be considered in forming an estimate of what the common school has done and is doing in the States.

The obstacles to regular attendance and the temptations to absenteeism and truancy throughout the Union are very great, and arise in no slight degree from the new character of the country and its social conditions. The constant influx of a foreign element acts as one of the chief hindrances, as the process of assimilation must necessarily be gradual. It is the policy of the nation to welcome all additions to the numbers of the people, and the impediments which arise from this cause are very seldom made the subject of complaint by the State Superintendents; but the State Reports nevertheless abound with evidence that this difficulty is not the least under which the work goes on. The County Superintendents very frequently refer to the fact.

The Report for Connecticut (1872) says: " A large proportion of these uneducated children are of alien parentage, and know only a foreign tongue. Living as they do in compact manufacturing villages, and associating mostly with those of their own race, they remain ignorant of the English language." (¹) "Most of the French Canadians, when they come to this State say they are to stay but a few years; when they have got a little money they shall return to Canada. But very many who come with that purpose remain here." (²)

The School Commissioner for Rhode Island says: "It will be noticed that there are very great differences in the several towns in the proportion of children who did not attend school, and that the greatest percentage of absentees is in those towns which have the largest foreign population by parentage." (³) And again: "It will be found in all cases that there is a direct relation between the number of absentees from school, and the number of children of foreign parentage."(⁴) "A greater proportion of the truancy and absenteeism from school is among the children of foreign parentage, and is greater in the country towns which have a large foreign population than in the city of Providence." "The greater portion of those in the State who cannot read and write is amongst the foreign population, and chiefly among those born in foreign countries." (⁵)

The other adverse influences which act chiefly in the rural districts are almost inseparable from the climate and the unsettled state of many parts of the country. In the winter bad roads—often impassable on account of snow—and the severity of the weather tell against the schools; and the heat of the summer is even more trying than the cold of winter; so much so that it is often impossible to keep the schools open. Sickness is a most formidable opponent, and I

---

[1] Connecticut Report, 1873, p. 7.   [2] Ibid, p. 22.
[3] Rhode Island Report, 1871, p. 21.   [4] Ibid, p. 22.   [5] Ibid, p. 24.

find that many schools are constantly broken up by small-pox panics. The demand for juvenile labour is also very great. Cotton-picking in the South, and corn and fruit gathering in the North and West, empty the fall schools; while in manufacturing and mining States, such as Connecticut, Massachusetts, Rhode Island, and Pennsylvania, the drain upon the schools arising from the demand for children's labour is constant and immense.

How to overcome these obstacles is the problem now uppermost in the minds of American educationists. No one pretends that attendance at school is sufficiently regular. In writing on this subject, the State Superintendent for New Jersey says: "We are making reasonable and satisfactory progress in all matters pertaining to the schools, excepting this one. Except in rare instances, all the money needed for the maintenance of the schools is freely voted; the school terms are being gradually lengthened; every year more care is exercised in the selection of teachers, and better salaries are paid them; the school buildings are all the while being improved, and increased vigilance is exercised by school officers in their work of supervision. In the matter of attendance, however, we seem to be making no advancement whatever. In our efforts to make our school system productive of the greatest good, irregular attendance must be regarded as the greatest obstacle we now have to contend with." ([1])

This is true not only of New Jersey, but of nearly every State in the Union. Compulsion is the greatest want under which the American system labours.

(c) *Period of Attendance.*

It is impossible to ascertain, even approximately, from

---

[1] New Jersey Report, 1872, p. 21.

the materials supplied by the reports, the length of time spent in school by children in the States.

The information which is to be had may be classed under two heads—(1) the school age ; (2) the school year.

(1.) THE SCHOOL AGE.

The legal school age in the several States is as follows :— From 4 to 21 in Florida, Maine, New Hampshire, and the city of Washington. From 5 to 21 in Alabama, Arkansas, Delaware, Iowa, Kansas, Minnesota, Mississippi, Missouri, Nebraska, New York, and Virginia. From 6 to 21 in Illinois, Indiana, Louisiana, North Carolina, Ohio, Pennsylvania, and West Virginia. From 4 to 20 in Wisconsin and Oregon. From 5 to 20 in Maryland, Michigan, and Vermont. From 6 to 20 in Kentucky. From 6 to 18 in Georgia, Nevada, Tennessee, and Texas. From 5 to 18 in New Jersey. From 4 to 16 in Connecticut. From 4 to 15 in Rhode Island. From 6 to 16 in South Carolina. From 5 to 15 in California and Massachusetts. ([1])

As very few of the State Reports distinguish the ages of scholars in their enumeration or enrolment, it does not appear how many years are spent in school upon the average in different States. Without doubt, the vast majority of children leave school before fifteen or sixteen. In the winter, however, when many kinds of labour are out of the question, there is often a large influx of scholars between fifteen and twenty-one. The average for a State, even if it could be obtained, would hardly be a reliable basis of opinion, since the extremes between cities on the one hand, and isolated villages on the other, are so far apart. Thus I find in one town of Ohio, Gallipolis, that 38 per cent. of the pupils are over sixteen years of age.

---

[1] Commissioner's Report, 1873, p. 510.

The following table practically illustrates the ages of scholars in particular towns :— ([1])

State.	Town.	Whole No. Enrolled.	No. over 16 years of age.	Per Cent.
New York	Fulton	1,239	390	31· 4
"	Geneva	1,427	500	35·03
"	Bath	725	75	10· 3
"	Greenwich	270	50	18· 5
"	Watertown	2,004	430	21· 4
"	Whitehall	870	120	13· 7
Massachusetts	Amherst	849	120	14· 1
"	Canton	717	100	13· 9
"	Rockport	806	200	24· 7
"	Sandwich	793	117	14· 7
"	Ware	657	116	17· 6
New Hampshire	Nashua	2,211	702	31· 7
Minnesota	Mankato	1,125	175	15· 5
"	Minneapolis	2,298	290	12· 6
"	Rochester	945	150	15· 8
Maine	Gardiner	860	160	18· 6
"	Farmington	528	80	15· 1
"	Eastport	600	140	23· 3
"	Ellsworth	1,700	400	23· 5
"	Bath	1,716	290	16· 8
Michigan	Ann Arbor	1,788	295	16· 4
"	Battle Creek	1,383	215	15· 5
"	Manistee	809	100	12· 3
"	Owasso	727	110	15· 1
Iowa	Muscatine	1,400	300	21· 4
"	Oskaloosa	1,010	260	25· 7
"	Winterset	445	50	11· 2
Indiana	Anderson	650	150	23·07
"	Goshen	699	113	16· 1
"	South Bend	1,500	392	26· 1
"	Vincennes	1,123	200	17· 8

[1] Commissioner's Report, 1873. See table, p. 514.

Similar instances will be found scattered all over the Union, but these percentages are very high, and must not be taken as representing an average. In those towns which have no high schools, the proportion of children in school over sixteen must be very small. Even if the numbers above this age attending the public schools were given, we should still be unable to arrive at a just estimate of the numbers under instruction, since it is at about this age that the "academy" often comes in to supplement the work of the common school.

In Maine, the average school period ranges from the age of six years to sixteen—ten years. ([1])

In Rhode Island, on an average, the children leave school before fourteen. ([2])

The School Commissioner for Ohio has collected statistics which he says "indicate that the average length of time spent by each youth in the *public* schools is from five to six years. Of course, a large number attend school a much longer time, and a few perhaps, never avail themselves of common school advantages." ([3])

The average age of pupils in the public schools of West Virginia, in 1872, was eleven and a half years, ([4]) the school age beginning at six.

In Massachusetts, in 1872, over 8 per cent. of the pupils in attendance were between fifteen and twenty-one years of age. ([5])

In Ohio, in 1873, the pupils between sixteen and twenty-one constituted over 12·6 per cent. of the average enrolment. ([6])

In England and Wales the percentage of children over fourteen in schools receiving grants, in 1874, was ·99 ; ([7]) but

---

[1] Maine Report, 1872, p. 8.   [2] Rhode Island Report, 1871, p. 41.
[3] Ohio Report, 1871, p. 9.   [4] West Virginia Report, 1872, p. 6.
[5] Massachusetts Report, 1873, p. 150.   [6] Ohio Report, 1873, p. 15.
[7] Report of Committee of Council, 1874-5, p. 3.

this must not be put in comparison with the American figures. Private schools in England do the work which in the States is frequently done by public high schools, and, consequently, the numbers over fourteen under instruction do not appear in the enrolment of our public elementary schools.

There can be no doubt, however, that, as a general rule, children remain at school much later in America than in England. While their higher age gives them a great educational advantage over English scholars, it is, on the other hand, unfavourable to average attendance.

(2.) THE SCHOOL YEAR.

The legal school year varies in different States, and the actual school year—the period for which the schools are taught—differs again in many States from the term required by law.

The Report of the Commissioner of Education (1872) states the average period during which the schools were taught in the principal States as follows: California, 6 months 10 days; Connecticut, 8 months $12\frac{1}{2}$ days; Illinois, 6 months 27 days; Indiana, 5 months 16 days; Iowa, 6 months 14 days; Maine, $106\frac{1}{2}$ actual working days; Massachusetts, 8 months 28 days; Michigan, $7\frac{1}{2}$ months; Minnesota, 6 months 18 days; Mississippi, 5 months 10 days; Missouri, $4\frac{1}{2}$ months; Nevada, 8 months 10 days; New Hampshire, 4 months $4\frac{1}{2}$ days; New Jersey, 8 months 18 days; New York, 35 weeks 1 day; Ohio, 152 days; Pennsylvania, 6 months; Rhode Island, 34 weeks 2 days; Vermont, 6 months; Virginia, 5 months 15 days; Wisconsin, 7 months. ([1])

In most of these States the period during which the schools were open was in excess of that required by law.

---

[1] Commissioner's Report, 1872, p. 609.

The school terms throughout the Union are being gradually lengthened, but it will be a long time before the American schools reach the English scale. The average duration of schools in England and Wales is not given in the Government returns, but the number of school meetings (400) required to secure a grant cannot be held under forty weeks, and it is probable that the average is considerably in excess of that period. From the school registers of one of the best schools in Birmingham, which I have before me, it appears that the school was open for forty-six weeks in 1874. With the opportunities afforded by the length of the school year in this country, it is humiliating to reflect that so few attendances are actually made. Out of the whole number of scholars on the register last year, only about half made 250 attendances. These attendances would be made in twenty-five weeks.

From a return issued by the Education Department it appears that in the four counties of Dorset, Nottingham, Suffolk, and Warwick, about 18 per cent. of the scholars attending public elementary schools made less than 50 attendances, over 30 per cent. less than 100, over 40 per cent. less than 150, and over 50 per cent. less than 200. At a meeting of the Manchester School Board, held on the 26th of last April, Mr. Bremner presented a statistical report of 8 elementary day schools in that city (4 Church schools, 3 British, 1 Roman Catholic), containing a total of 5,110 children. Of this number 3,105 had attended during the year only 100 single times, and under. Of these 3,105 children, an analysis showed that 955 had attended twenty times only during the year, 312 thirty times, 312 forty times, and 252 fifty times, 281 sixty times only—in all over 2,000 had attended sixty times, and under. ([1])

---

[1] *School Board Chronicle*, May 8th, 1875.

In the State of New York, in 1872, the average time each pupil in the rural districts attended school was sixteen and nine-tenths weeks; in the cities, nineteen and three-tenths weeks. ([1]) When the large enrolment is taken into account this is a very good average.

The Cincinnati Report for 1874 gives the attendance in the district schools of the city as follows: Less than 8 months, 34·6 per cent.; 8 and less than 10 months, 26·9 per cent; total less than 10 months, 61·5 per cent.; continued through the year, 38·5 per cent. The attendance in the intermediate and high schools was even better than this. ([2])

In Cleveland, for 1873, the period of attendance of the scholars is reported as follows: Less than 6 months, 35·7 per cent.; less than 8 months, 47·8 per cent.; 8 and less than 10 months, 24·6 per cent.; total less than 10 months, 72·4 per cent.; 10 months or the entire year, 27·6 per cent. ([3])

The average length of school attendance in Iowa is less than four months. ([4])

The percentages of the number enrolled attending school in New Jersey, in 1872, were: Between 8 and 10 months, 15 per cent.; between 6 and 8 months, 17 per cent.; between 4 and 6 months, 19 per cent.; less than 4 months, 40 per cent. ([5])

These are very inadequate materials upon which to found any general conclusion as to the length of time spent in school in each year, but they are the only ones which the reports afford. There is a very general agreement in the States—first, that the school terms must be lengthened; and, secondly, that attendance must be made compulsory.

---

[1] New York State Report, 1873, p. 10. [2] Cincinnati Report, 1874, p. 104.
[3] Cleveland Report, 1873, p. 39. [4] Iowa Report, 1872, p. 38.
[5] New Jersey Report, 1873, p. 17.

(d) *Failure of Indirect Compulsion.*

Laws for regulating the employment of children in various departments of labour, based on the same principle as the Factory Acts and the Agricultural Children's Act in England, have been tried in several States. As in England, so in America, they have had a very partial success, and in the great majority of cases have failed to fill the schools, or to protect the children against the cupidity of parents or the temptations of the labour markets. Even in States where the law has been worked with the fullest co-operation of employers, the results have not been encouraging, since children have been removed into neighbouring States where no restriction is placed upon their employment; and in those States where the law has been ignored by the parents and employers alike, it has been practically a dead letter.

The history of the Factory Laws in Pennsylvania is a most disheartening story of failure to protect children in the enjoyment of school rights. The law forbids altogether the employment of children under thirteen years of age. Children between thirteen and sixteen can be legally employed only nine months in the year, and for no period unless they have attended school for three consecutive months in the preceding year. The practice is very different.

Mr. W. W. Woodruff, who was appointed to visit the mills, factories, and mines in Eastern Pennsylvania, in 1873, states the result of his inspection. "It was found that no attention whatever is paid to the laws prohibiting the employment of children under thirteen years of age; nor to the one forbidding the employment of children between the ages of thirteen and sixteen more than nine months in any one year, and not at all unless they shall have attended school at least three consecutive months within the same year. Many manufacturers were entirely ignorant of the existence of such a law; others seemed to have some vague ideas that at some indefinite past time some laws—they did not know what—touching this matter had been passed. One manufacturer said that when the law of 1849 was enacted there was an attempt made in his factory to obey it, but it was found that no other manufacturers in the vicinity were even attempting to obey the law; and the result was that his hands began to leave him and go to neighbouring factories where their children would be employed. So the effort to obey the law was abandoned."

"There was very little variation in the results obtained at different factories of the same kind. In the cotton factories it was found that from one fourth to one third of the persons employed are under thirteen years of age. In the woollen factories more skill is required, and but few under thirteen years of age are employed."

"In rolling mills, boys have not sufficient strength for the labour required until they are fourteen or fifteen years of age. So in these mills the law is seldom violated."

"The views and opinions of those engaged in manufacturing were solicited upon the general subject of the educational needs and opportunities of the children in their employ, and in regard to the best practicable way of meeting the exigencies of the case. In some of the factories it was thought by the officers that all the children could read and write. In some others, nothing was known by the officers in regard to it. They made no enquiries into such matters; if the children employed did their work properly, the employers were content, and did not interest themselves further. The general testimony was that it is a rare thing for parents to take their children from the factories to send them to school. It is easier for the average parent to understand the value of three dollars in hand every Saturday than it is to comprehend what an education may do for the future of his child." (¹)

Mr. Woodruff refers to some noble examples of care manifested by employers in the welfare of children. Mr. Samuel P. Crozier, of Upland, Delaware, has opened a reading-room, night school, and lyceum, and erected a bathing-house in connection with his factories; and such instances of the recognition of responsibility by masters are, happily, not rare in the States. But in the keen rivalry of commerce, the child more often goes to the wall. In the cotton manufactories there are many kinds of labour which children can perform better than adults, while it costs only one third as much. Again, if the factories of one State are not allowed to employ children, while those of the adjoining State are under no restriction, the result is disastrous to the former. These reasons have not only operated against the Factory Laws, but also against the adoption of direct compulsion.

The law of Connecticut, passed many years ago, provided that no child under fifteen should be employed in any manufactory or business unless he should have attended school at least three months in the preceding year. The penalty for breach of this law was formerly 25 dollars, but it was, nevertheless, very commonly disregarded. In 1869 the law was amended: the age under which a child might not be employed was reduced to fourteen, and a higher penalty of 100 dollars was substituted in case of its violation. The Amendment Act also provided that an agent should be appointed to secure the due enforcement of the law. The State Board of Education appointed Mr. Henry M. Cleveland agent for this purpose, and he made his first report in 1870. If this law has failed in Connecticut, it cannot be because there was no one whose duty it was to enforce it. Four different classes of officers—

---

[1] Penn. Report, 1873, p. xxxvii.

school visitors, state attorneys, grand jurors, and the agent of the Board of Education—were instructed to co-operate in carrying out the law. Mr. Cleveland visited nearly all the manufacturers in the State, and submitted to them a plan for carrying the law into effect, under which they were invited to divide the children in the mills into two or three classes, and to send out to school one class the first succeeding term, another class the second term, and the third class the third term, so that each child might get three months' schooling during the year succeeding the date of the arrangement. Nearly all the manufacturers gave their cordial assent to this plan, and pledged themselves to its execution by signing a voluntary agreement as follows:—

"We hereby agree that from and after the beginning of the next term of our public school, we will employ no children under fourteen years of age, except those who are provided with a certificate from the local school officers of actual attendance at school the full term required by law."

While the manufacturers were ready to do their duty, the parents were not, in all cases, and the agent says: "I found some parents unwilling to take their children out of the mills, and positively refusing to send them to school after they were discharged." [1] Some of the children, when they were discharged, were carried into the neighbouring states of Massachusetts and Rhode Island. Mr. Cleveland says of a similar law passed in Massachusetts in 1867: "It is conceded that the law has not answered the expectations of its friends." [2] The statistics of the Massachusetts Bureau of Education confirm this view.

That the Connecticut law has not wholly remedied the evils against which it was directed is evident from the report for the following year, 1871. Mr. Cleveland, after a year's

---

[1] Conn. Report, 1870, p. 21. [2] Ibid, p. 20.

experience under the Act, says: " Facts conclusively show that very many children have been sent out of the mills who have not entered the public school, and in many cases where ample room and a full supply of teachers had been provided. Realising the necessity, in a republic, of universal education, I cannot hesitate to say that we ought to incorporate the principle of compulsory attendance into our school system in this and in every State in the Union." ([1])

In the following year the Legislature of Connecticut passed an Act for compulsory attendance.

The law of Rhode Island prohibits the employment in the factories of children under twelve years of age, and also between twelve and fifteen years, unless they have had at least three months' schooling in the previous year. The law also provides that no child under fifteen years of age shall be employed in the factories more than nine months in any calendar year. But the law is inoperative. The reports of the manufacturing districts supply constant examples of its violation. The Board of Education, reporting in 1872, say: " In the former report the notice of your honourable body was directed to the employment, in manufacturing and other establishments, of children who are thus deprived of the privilege of school instruction. The evil referred to is a very serious one. The law regulating the matter has long been inoperative." ([2])

It would be impossible that the law should have been tried under more favourable conditions than existed both in Connecticut and Rhode Island, where the employers were, almost without exception, strongly in its favour. The parents, irritated by the exclusion of their children from the factories, either removed them to other States or left them to run about the streets. This is precisely the class of parents for whom compulsion is needed, and who are amenable to no other

---

[1] Conn. Report, 1871, p. 12. [2] Rhode Island Report, 1872, p. 13.

influence. Why they should be regarded with so much tenderness does not clearly appear. But notwithstanding the cumulative proof of the failure of these indirect compulsory laws, it may be assumed that the "patch and repair party," both in the United States and England, will continue to advocate them.

(e) *Trial of Compulsion.*

When compulsion was first advocated for England it was said to be unsuited to the "genius" of the people. The same thing has been said across the Atlantic. "The wedge of despotism;" "the first step towards centralisation;" "opposed to the genius of American institutions"—these are phrases which have often been heard in the past, and will, no doubt, be heard again; but the Americans, while always jealous of the safety of their institutions, are the last people in the world to be frightened by phrases, and so the idea of compulsion has been steadily growing for many years. Its universal adoption throughout the States is now, as in England, only a question of time.

Compulsion has hardly been enforced a sufficient length of time in any State to test its operation thoroughly by experience, except, perhaps, in Massachusetts. In all the other States where it has been adopted it is a very recent importation. It will be of use, however, from such materials as can be obtained, to ascertain how the law has been received.

The States in which compulsory laws, of more or less stringency, are in operation are Massachusetts, Maryland, Connecticut, Michigan, New Hampshire, Nevada, New York, Texas, and District of Columbia.

Truant laws will be found on the Statute Books of Maine, Rhode Island, Wisconsin, and other States, but they are permissive, and are not generally obeyed.

The law of Massachusetts is somewhat similar to our present law in England. There is compulsion in theory for the whole State; there may be compulsion actually or not, as the inhabitants of a district choose.

By the General Statutes, parents and guardians are required to send to school, at least twenty weeks during the year, all children between the ages of eight and fourteen years, under a penalty of 20 dollars for each offence against the law. Moreover, no child under ten years of age can be legally employed in any manufacturing or mechanical establishment. No child between the ages of ten and fifteen shall be so employed who has not attended some day-school three months, or sixty school-days, within the year next preceding such employment, under a penalty of 50 dollars against employer and parent. ([1])

Towns are required to appoint truant officers, and make other provisions for carrying the law into effect. As there is no penalty annexed for a breach of the law on the part of corporate authorities, the Acts, so far as they require municipal action, are virtually permissive, and, like most permissive legislation, they fail to secure the object aimed at. Out of 342 towns only 127, in 1873, had made the provisions concerning truants required by law. The Board of Education, in their annual report, recommend the adoption of "a more stringent system of compulsion, with the necessary agencies for its efficient administration. For want of such agencies the existing compulsory provisions are not generally carried into effect. Towns are required to appoint truant officers, but as there is no penalty annexed, the requirement is largely ignored." ([2])

---

[1] General School Statutes, pp. 59, 62. Massachusetts Report, 1873, p. 17.
[2] Ibid, p. 19.

The law fails for the same reason that the Agricultural Children's Act has failed in England—it is not sufficiently stringent, and there is no one whose special business and duty it is to see that it is enforced. Amateurs do not readily come forward to undertake offices of this kind. Where the law is put in force, there it succeeds. Take for instance the case of Boston. Mr. John D. Philbrick, the late superintendent of schools for the city, in his report for 1872 said: "It appears that the whole number of pupils of all ages belonging to the public and private schools is considerably in excess of the number of persons in the city between five and fifteen years of age; that the number between these ages belonging to the public and private schools is 92 per cent. of the whole number in the city; that of the 7 per cent. not attending school, six sevenths are pretty well accounted for; making 99 per cent. in school or accounted for, while 1 per cent. remains unaccounted for. This statement of the case respecting the school attendance in this city seems to afford evidence for the belief that the number of children who are growing up without acquiring at least the rudiments of education is quite small. During the past ten years I do not remember to have met with the case of a child who had resided in the city until the age of fourteen without learning to read and write."

"Our truant officers are expected to look after all children not attending school, who are found in the streets without any lawful occupation. From their reports, and from information derived from other sources, I had good reason for believing that they are faithful and efficient in the performance of their duty. But as I occasionally hear it said in educational speeches, or read in some newspaper communication, that there are several thousand—from ten to fifteen thousand, I think, is the number named—vagrant urchins in the streets, growing up in ignorance, idleness, and vice, I thought

I would try to find where they were. Accordingly, a week or two ago, on a bright and sunny morning, taking care not to select a holiday, I set out on a voyage of discovery. I went to all the railroad stations, I drove round the marginal streets, scanning the wharves and alley-ways, keeping a sharp look-out for boys and girls of school age. The result of this perambulatory expedition, which occupied two or three hours, was quite extraordinary in respect to the smallness of the number of children of school age that were found at all. Every one found was stopped, and his case enquired into. The whole number found was hardly more than could be counted on one's fingers, and among them there was only one who had not a good reason for being out of school. This was a truant who had slipped through the fingers of his teacher and escaped the vigilance of the truant officer. The next day being fine, I continued the survey, going through nearly all the streets of a densely-populated section of the city. The result was about the same as that of the preceding day. The few children found, with one exception, gave good reasons for their absence from school. He was a licensed newsboy, and was generally found in school. A similar district in another part of the city was inspected on the third day. It was the same thing over again. I propose to repeat this survey of the streets when the spring opens." ([1])

"As I have already intimated, the truant law, which has been in operation for twenty years, has proved a powerful auxiliary in the warfare against ignorance. Indirectly, the truant officers have performed a very valuable service, which perhaps was not anticipated when the truant law was enacted. They have, to a very great extent, been the means of making those classes of persons who do not appreciate the value of education at least feel the disgrace of voluntary ignorance."([2])

---

[1] Mass. Report, 1873, p. 196.   [2] Ibid, p. 197.

The New Hampshire law, passed in 1871, provides that every parent or guardian having the control of a child between eight and fourteen shall cause such child to attend school at least twelve weeks in each year, unless excused by the School Committee of the town. The penalties incurred for violation of the law are 10 dollars for the first offence, and 20 dollars for a subsequent offence. It is the duty of School Boards to sue for penalties thus incurred, upon written notice served by a taxpayer, stating by whom, when, and how any such penalty was incurred. [1]

The weak place in this law is that it makes any taxpayer an informer, and there are very few taxpayers who will accept the office. Consequently, in some districts the law is inoperative. The Superintendent of Public Instruction sends me the following statement respecting the working of the law:—

"The compulsory law of New Hampshire is working better than its most sanguine friends anticipated. The State Superintendents, since its enactment, have been earnest to secure its efficient enforcement, with the following encouraging result:

	1872.	1873.	1874.
Children between 4 and 14 not attending school....	4,602	3,680	2,593
Decrease..	—	922	1,087
Percentage of non-attendants to number registered	·063	·052	·037

In other words, the non-attendance has been diminished 44 per cent.

The law is pretty well enforced in most of the larger places. A great difficulty now is, that in the outskirts of most of the country towns there still remain a few families from whom the centralisation of population has withdrawn the schools. To compel the children of such to go three or

---

[1] Report of Commissioner of Education, 1873, p. 250.

four miles to school seems hard, while to sustain a good school for only two or three pupils seems almost an equal burden. Yet nearly every country town presents from one to a dozen just such cases—children who seldom or never enter a school-room, or are entered on the returns to the State—children growing up in ignorance, to be the scourge of the next generation. The problem of their education is one of the most important now before our people. The same question is coming up in the mountainous districts of other States."

By the Connecticut law, passed in 1872, all children between eight and fourteen are required to receive not less than three months' schooling. It is too soon almost to speak of the results of the law. The State Board of Education, immediately upon its passing, appointed an agent to supervise its enforcement. Some extracts from his first report show the early effect of the statute. "I know from observation that boys cannot be found in the streets of New Haven in school hours; even the lads who were accustomed to wait at the depot to 'shine your boots' are missing. They have gone to school. Possibly, children who have not attended school as the law requires are employed in factories, stores, or shops in New Haven; but in the largest manufacturing establishment which we visited in the city, no boys under fourteen years of age were found who had not certificates that they had attended school three months during the year." "In Hartford the truant law is faithfully enforced by two officers detailed for that purpose." "In New London, the police, under direction of the school visitors, take charge of all boys at play or loitering in the streets in school hours, and in that city the laws relating to attendance at school are well enforced. The school visitors of the town of Windsor Locks have appointed one of their number to attend to the enforcing of these laws, and I was informed that this duty is faithfully discharged, and with good effect. Other places where the requirements of the law are systematically obeyed or enforced might be named, but these are sufficient to show that no part of the law need be considered a dead letter." [1]

The compulsory law for Michigan, passed in 1871, is the same, almost word for word, as the New Hampshire law. Parents are required to send children to school for twelve weeks in each year, of which six weeks are to be consecutive, unless excused by the School Board. Directors of School Districts and Presidents of School Boards are required to publish notices of the law. The directors or presidents are required to take action against parents to recover penalties on receiving written notice from any taxpayer of a violation of the law.

This statute is in great danger of becoming a dead letter. It contains that which in England, and in almost every other country, would be fatal to its success—it depends for its results upon the action of amateur detectives. A very short time has elapsed since the law was passed, and already there is evidence of its partial failure, notwithstanding that when enacted it was accepted with almost universal satisfaction. The Hon. Oramel Hosford, in writing to Mr. Northrop, of Connecticut, said: "I do not remember that any law bearing upon the school interests of the State was ever received with such universal favour as this one. The press, without distinction of party, very generally commend it, and very few of the people were heard to speak against it."

The State Superintendent, in his report for 1872 (p. 18), said: "The moral effect of the law was very manifest. Many children found their way to the school-room, not waiting to

---

[1] Connecticut Report, 1873, p. 19.

be compelled to attend by the force of law. The final results can only be determined by the faithfulness with which the law is executed. The law is sufficiently exacting to meet all cases, and if there is any failure it must be in its vigorous execution."

The report for 1873 gives the number of children between five and twenty in the State as 421,322. Of these 324,615 attended school during the year. The average attendance for the school year (over seven months) was about half of the latter number—say 162,000. The number of children between eight and fourteen years of age subject to the compulsory law was 181,604. Under this exhibit it would therefore be possible for all the children between eight and fourteen to have attended school during three months of the year. This assumption, however, is negatived by the reports of the County Superintendents. A circular letter issued by the State Superintendent to the County Superintendents requested that, in their official reports for the year, they would state to what extent the compulsory law had increased the attendance upon the schools. I have gone through the replies of the County Superintendents, with the following results: Out of fifty-three County Superintendents whose reports are printed, twenty-nine state that the law has been almost wholly disregarded, and that no attempts have been made to enforce it. Seventeen report that the silent influence or moral effect of the law has had a valuable influence in securing attendance. Three report attempted prosecutions, failing on technical grounds, and four others make no allusion to the law. A few extracts from the reports will show where the difficulty lies. The Superintendent for Macomb County says: "The compulsory law exists in this county only in name. Known violations of the law occur in nearly every district without notice. The inhabitants of districts, when offences are committed, seem to regard *a prosecution* in the light of *personal difficulties,* and refrain from any litigation in the matter." (¹)

The Superintendent for Sanilac County says: "The principle and intention of the law may be right, but the larger proportion of the individuals who violate this law cannot be reached by it. You cannot interest men to such an extent in the intellectual welfare of their friends' children that they will excite a feeling of hatred in the neighbourhood by prosecuting those who do not send their children to school. (²)

The Superintendent for Calhoun County writes: "The compulsory law has increased the attendance by its silent influence on the public mind." (³)

The Superintendent for Charlevoix County reports: "The compulsory school law has had a decidedly good effect in lessening the amount of school vagrancy. This law, in connection with free schools, has reduced the number of cases of unnecessary absence from school almost to a minimum." (⁴)

The Superintendent for Grand Traverse County says: "In some localities, and with a certain class of people, its influence is apparent in an increased attendance of a very backward set of children, who appear to have been much neglected." (⁵)

But it is apparent that unless the law is enforced when violated, the moral force which at first attended it will very soon evaporate. The Superintendent for Shiawassee County reports: "The Compulsory Act, having never been enforced in our county, is losing its effect". (⁶)

The compulsory law for Nevada was only passed in 1873, and that for New York in 1874. It is therefore too soon to

---

[1] Mich. Report, 1873, p. 155.   [2] Ibid, p. 181.   [3] Ibid, p. 115.
[4] Ibid, p. 120.   [5] Ibid, p. 126.   [6] Ibid, p. 182.

obtain any information respecting the working of compulsion in those States.

What is wanted in America to make compulsory laws thoroughly successful is a strong administrative department at the head of the system in each State. The principle of local self-government must be supplemented by State control. The absence of this feature is painfully evident in the working of the Michigan law ; and before compulsion can accomplish its best results, some State machinery will have to be called in.

In all the States where compulsion is now legal it has been felt desirable to move cautiously, and not to bring the principle into odium by making its application too stringent. For the same reason, in most States the law at first required only three months' school during the year. This has been generally enlarged to six months, and in some States to nine months. So the measures for effecting compulsion which have already been passed are only regarded by American educationists as tentative, and they look forward to the time when attendance at school for much longer periods can be secured.

(f) Demand for Direct Compulsion.

Notwithstanding the assertion here and there that America is not Prussia, and that compulsion is not compatible with free institutions, there is no reform so urgently and so generally demanded as one which shall remedy the present irregularity in attendance at school. I know of but one State Superintendent who, within the last four or five years, has offered strenuous opposition to a compulsory law. The Hon.

Abram B. Weaver, Superintendent for New York State, in his report for 1871, argued at length that compulsion was unnecessary, or at any rate that better teaching was a more pressing reform. But public opinion was too strong for Mr. Weaver, and last year the Legislature passed a compulsory law—not a very stringent law certainly, but one which will be sufficient to test the operation of the principle.

Within the last two or three years the State Legislatures of Indiana, Ohio, Illinois, Maine, Iowa, Wisconsin, and California have had compulsory bills under their consideration, but they have not hitherto escaped the perils which everywhere seem to beset desirable legislation. During the present year the Pennsylvania Legislature has had under discussion a bill for compulsion. The constant effort to secure the passage of these laws sufficiently indicates the direction which public feeling is taking, but there are more positive proofs of the strong support which compulsion has in America.

A few short extracts from the reports of the State Superintendents will show how urgently a compulsory law is desired by educationists.

The Superintendent for Pennsylvania, in his report for 1872, says, referring to irregularity of attendance: "I have, in previous reports, pointed out this great evil and the dangers it threatens, and, as wisely as I might, suggested remedies for it. I can do no more. The case needs prompt legislative action." [1]

In the report for the following year he recurs to the subject, and urges the passing of a "general law making it the duty of all parents, guardians, and employers to see that all children under their control attend school, for a certain number of months in the year, up to a certain age." [2]

The Superintendent for Illinois refers to compulsion as

---

[1] Penn. Report, 1872, p. xxii. [2] Penn. Report, 1873, p. xxiv.

the " most important school question of modern times." He says : " Given all other elements, as lands, buildings, equipments, funds, and teachers of the best quality, and in costliest profusion, there yet remains another essential condition— pupils. If these are wanting, or to the extent that these are wanting, there is no education. To that extent treasure is wasted, time is lost, and the system is a failure." [1] After a most careful examination of the arguments for and against compulsion, Mr. Bateman concludes his able paper by maintaining that it has been proved that the intervention of the Legislature, by means of compulsion, is necessary to perfect the American school system—that such intervention is not unconstitutional or tyrannical; "that it puts the right of the child to be educated above the right of the parent to keep it in ignorance; that it protects the many who do educate their children against the counteracting influence of the few who will not; that it shields the innocent from cruel wrong, since starving the mind is worse than abusing the body; that it is grounded upon the belief that to bring up children in ignorance, wilfully and without cause, is a crime, and should be treated as such ; that such conduct on the part of those having the control of children, being a fruitful source of criminality, should be under the ban of legal condemnation, and the restraint of legal punishment; that the allegations as to the incompatibility of such laws with the nature and spirit of our political system are unfounded, as also are the apprehensions concerning the assumed harshness and severity of their enforcement; that the operation of such laws in many of the most enlightened States of Europe is a vindication of their wisdom and beneficence, affording an example that may be safely followed; that there is no proof that the masses of our people are opposed to such legislation, but, on the con-

---

[1] Illinois Report, 1872, p. 187.

trary, that there is good reason to believe that general enlightenment on the subject would result in a general approval of the measure; that the exclusively voluntary policy has been, and is, but partially successful, while the accelerated influx of foreigners renders the adoption of new measures of education without delay a grave political necessity; that the proposed legislative intervention is but an affirmation of the irrefutable truth, that if it is right to tax all for the education of all, then it is equally right to see that all are educated; that it is in the line of a general human right, and of a fundamental right of children, and is compulsory only as that right must be protected against any and all infringements; that it is required to fully utilise the vast resources already devoted to public education, and to prevent enormous and increasing waste of money, property, and effort ; and, finally, that it is demanded by the clearest principles of justice, both to children and taxpayers—by the franchises conferred and implied in the Bill of Rights embodied in the Constitution—by consideration of the highest political wisdom, and by the facts and exigencies that now exist in this State and in every other State of the Union." ([1])

How great is the waste caused by irregularity is shown by the Superintendent for Iowa. He says: "The average length of time the schools have been taught is six months and ten days, while the average length of school attendance is less than four months. We thus provide and pay for two and one half months of school more than would be actually required to instruct the number registered if they attended regularly. The cost of maintaining these two and one half months of unnecessary school, exclusive of school-house building, is 1,171,300 dollars, or 5-13ths of the whole cost for the year." ([2])

---

[1] Illinois Report, 1872, p. 225.   [2] Iowa Report, 1873, p. 38.

The Superintendent for Maine, in discussing the statistics of illiteracy and the remedy, says : " To the thoughtful citizen no other remedy can be apparent than that the State shall insist upon some acceptable measure to secure the education of all its youth. Every taxpayer should insist upon coercive education, for it is only thus he will obtain compensation for his own time, labour, and business vigilance, represented in his contribution to the public treasury ; only thus that he will obtain fulfilment from the State of the compact she makes with him to return an intelligent community for the tax thus imposed upon him." " The State needs it as a safeguard against the pressing demands of capital for cheap labour, raw muscle, mere human working machines, and against the incoming tide of immigration and ignorance, to supply this demand."[1]

The Superintendent for Ohio says : " Truancy and absenteeism are evils for the cure or prevention of which no laws have been enacted; attendance at school is entirely optional. Children unable to read or write may be employed on the farm, or in mine, workshop, or factory. The State does not interpose to protect them against the avarice of thoughtless parents or the rapacity of employers. There is, however, a growing sentiment in favour of stringent laws against truancy and the employment of illiterate youth in industries of any kind, when such employment is a virtual denial of school privileges. Our people desire to see the results of compulsory laws, although it is questionable whether they are ready to sanction their enactment." [2]

In Indiana, compulsory education has been advocated for a long time past. The Superintendent, speaking of the reception of compulsion in Michigan, says : " I doubt not that a judicious law, compelling attendance upon the schools, would meet with similar favour in Indiana. It rises above

---

[1] Maine Report, 1872, p. 92.   [2] Ohio Report, 1872, p. 37.

all partisan considerations. Such a law would be the best friend of the orphan and neglected. It would open to thousands a door of hope, that is now probably closed for ever. The public is ready for this measure. It can be enforced. It will break up old and bad habits, and form new and better ones. Its adoption will mark a new and better era in educational matters, and erase from the census reports the figures that tell the disgraceful story of our illiteracy." ([1])

The Superintendent for Missouri, who, though not strongly in favour of compulsion, says that "universal education must at all hazards be secured," reports as follows: " Within twelve months past public sentiment within this State has experienced a remarkable change in respect to enforced attendance. This fact is indicated with emphasis by the complexion of educational meetings in which an opinion has been expressed by vote. Meetings of teachers and citizens in Jackson, Cooper, Jefferson, and Butler Counties took strong ground in favour of the proposition. In the published minutes of the Teachers' Institute, held at Lee's Summit in December last, I find the following minute : ' Resolution on compulsory education for all pupils between the ages of six and fifteen adopted ; 53 in favour, 18 negative. The citizens were then invited to vote, and stood 5 to 1 in favour of the resolution.'" ([2])

The Superintendent for Nebraska says : " Our system should secure a good education to every child. Call it ' compulsory' if you please, but no child should be allowed to reach the age of sixteen years without enjoying the advantages of school a sufficient length of time to enable him to learn to read and write." ([3]) " The fact that the great majority of educated minds in all States now endorse the movement, is itself no feeble argument in its favour." ([4])

---

[1] Indiana Report, 1872, p. 117.   [2] Missouri Report, 1873, p. 77.
[3] Nebraska Report, 1873, p. 40.   [4] Ibid, p. 50.

The Superintendent for California advocates compulsion in a long and able paper, and says the people are prepared for it. "The only time the people have had an opportunity to express their will, they have declared themselves overwhelmingly in favour of compulsory education." ([1])

The school organisation in the Southern States is probably not sufficiently complete to allow the early application of a compulsory law, but even in these States compulsion has its friends. The Superintendent for Louisiana says: "Where the parent fails to do his duty to his child, is it not the duty of the State to provide for the wants of that child? If we desire to reduce our large percentage of illiteracy, we must establish such State laws as will compel our youth to avail themselves of educational privileges. City ordinances must be passed prohibiting truancy, and, as in other cities, providing the means for the same. To this matter, and in recommendation of such legislation as may be necessary to effect the desired object, I especially call the attention of the State Board of Education." ([2])

At the meeting of the National Teachers' Association held in St. Louis in 1871 the question was discussed. This meeting was attended by the best known educationists from twelve States, and the following resolution was passed unanimously:—"That to secure universal education in this country, our present system of voluntary school attendance should be supplemented by truant laws, reformatory schools, and such other compulsory measures as may be necessary to reach that class of youths now growing up in ignorance." ([3])

The reports of the State Superintendents are but the reflex of the opinions expressed by school officers throughout the States. The more minute the examination of this subject

---

[1] California Report, 1873, p. 23. [2] Louisiana Report, 1873, p. 286.
[3] Iowa Report, 1871, p. 60.

the more apparent it becomes that American educationists will spare no pains and omit no means, however stringent, to place their system upon the highest possible level, and to secure the utmost efficiency. When Bishop Fraser visited the States he found that " from many sections of the community, and especially from those who would be called the educationists, the cry was rising, both loud and vehement, that greater stringency was required in the law, and that compulsory attendance was the proper correlative of free schools." ([1]) From that time until the present the advocates of compulsion have been constantly increasing in numbers, and the demand for this reform has daily grown more emphatic. Every year will now probably add to the number of States adopting the law, until it covers the whole Union.

---

[1] Fraser's Report, p. 39.

IV.

RELIGION AND MORALS.

(*a*) LAW AS TO RELIGIOUS INSTRUCTION — (*b*) BIBLE READING; MORAL TEACHING — (*c*) THE RELIGIOUS DIFFICULTY.

(*a*) *Law as to Religious Instruction.*

If anyone were able to lay down, precisely and authoritatively, the law of each State upon the subject of religious teaching in school, it is probable that there would be a great future saving of work for American lawyers and jurists. Up to a certain point, and covering a large practical field of operations, judicial opinions are very much in harmony; beyond it, and still embracing a wide range of controversy, very opposite views prevail. In the absence of a federal law upon the subject a conflict of opinion would appear to be inevitable.

In the case of "Minor *et als. v.* Cincinnati Board of Education," the Superior Court of Cincinnati was called upon to decide whether the Bible might be lawfully excluded from the common schools under the law of Ohio. The arguments in this case have been published, and occupy a closely-printed octavo volume of some five hundred pages. A very large share of attention is devoted to the legal question, respecting which, in the end, there was a difference of opinion amongst the judges. I cannot attempt to lead English readers through the maze of statutes, judgments, and authorities, bearing both on matters of law and of fact, which were adduced in this case. It will be quite sufficient to indicate the general policy of legislation, showing how far there is concurrence of opinion, and where the points of difference arise.

In a work regarded as of much weight in the United States—" Cooley's Constitutional Limitations "—the author includes as one of "those things which are not lawful under any of the American Constitutions," the "compulsory support, by taxation or otherwise, of religious instruction." If by "religious instruction" is meant the teaching of the distinctive theology of any particular sect, then this view of the law harmonises with the public sentiment and practice in most of the States. If, on the other hand, under the term "religious instruction" is included general Christian culture —the reading of the Bible, the repetition of the Lord's Prayer, and the singing of religious hymns—then the law, if this be law, is habitually violated, not by any means in every school district, but certainly in every State of the Union. From the context, however, it appears to be clear that Judge Cooley intends the words "religious instruction" in their most comprehensive sense. "Not only is no one denomination to be favoured at the expense of the rest, but all support of religious instruction must be entirely voluntary." Again: "Whatever establishes a distinction against one class or sect is, to the extent to which the distinction operates unfavourably, a persecution; and if based on religious grounds is religious persecution."

But the view apparently held by Judge Cooley, that under

L

the State Constitutions secular instruction only can be legally given in the common schools, although it is maintained by more than one eminent lawyer, is not the one generally accepted. The ideal set up by American legislators was absolute religious equality; but that ideal is not practically reached. By almost universal assent, distinctive denominational teaching is prohibited in the public schools. This arrangement no sect, the Roman Catholic excepted, wishes to disturb. It is also illegal to endow or subsidise out of public funds schools under the control of any sect; and this law is almost universally recognised and obeyed, the only exception that I know of being in the State of New York, where from time to time small grants have been made to Roman Catholic schools.

To the extent above indicated, the principle of religious equality is secured by the State Constitutions, and sometimes by additional provisions in the school laws of particular States, although quite as often the latter are altogether silent on the subject. But here the doctrines of perfect religious equality and freedom of conscience meet, in practice, their limit. The authors of the typical State Constitution and the founders of the common school system appear to have held that these doctrines could be consistently maintained in conjunction with a large amount of Christian and Protestant instruction in the schools—instruction which in England is often depreciated as "colourless," but which, nevertheless, is very full of colour in the eyes of a large section of the religious world. And the conviction that this kind of teaching is not out of harmony with absolute religious equality exists very generally throughout the States, although, as will be seen, it is at intervals somewhat rudely shaken.

Formerly, in the New England States, where the common school system was originated at a time when there was little divergence of religious belief amongst the inhabitants, religious instruction occupied a much more prominent position in the school than at present. And it is in these States still that religious exercises in the schools, such as prayer, the reading of the Bible, and the singing of hymns, are mostgeneral.

The chief difference in the statutory provisions of different States, where any such provision is made, appears to be in the amount of discretion which is vested in the teacher or school officers. A few illustrations will enable English readers to form their own conclusions.

In Massachusetts, Bible reading appears to be compulsory, it being the duty of the School Committee " to require the daily reading of some portion of the Bible in the common English version." (¹)

By the law of New Jersey, it is not lawful to introduce " in any school receiving its proportion of the public money, any religious service, ceremony, or forms whatsoever, except reading the Bible and repeating the Lord's Prayer." (²) By a later statute it is provided that no portion of the school fund " shall be apportioned to, or be used for, the support of sectarian schools." (³)

In Connecticut the Bible is generally read, but it does not appear to be compulsory—the discretion being vested in the Board of Visitors. (⁴)

In New York State, the law provides that "no school shall be entitled to, or receive, any portion of the school moneys, in which the religious doctrines or tenets of any particular Christian or other religious sect shall be taught, inculcated, or practised, or in which any book or books containing compositions favourable or prejudicial to the particular doctrines or tenets of any particular Christian or

---

[1] Fraser's Report, p. 24. On reference to the General Statutes (p. 27), I find that there is a Conscience Clause for the protection of children whose parents object to Bible reading.   [2] New Jersey School Law, Article ix, sec. 65.
[3] Act of 1871, section 4.   [4] Connecticut Report, 1871, p. 180.

other religious sect, or which shall teach the doctrines or tenets of any religious sect. But nothing herein contained shall authorise the Board of Education to exclude the Holy Scriptures, without note or comment, or any selections therefrom, from any of the schools provided for in this Act; but it shall not be competent for the said Board of Education to decide what version, if any, of the Holy Scriptures, without note or comment, shall be used in any of the schools. Provided, that nothing herein contained shall be so construed as to violate the rights of conscience as secured by the Constitution of this State and of the United States." [1]

The law of Rhode Island appears to leave the question to the discretion of School Boards, the practice varying in different towns.

The school laws of Ohio contain no provision respecting religious teaching, but the Bill of Rights embodied in the Constitution of 1851 declares that, "religion, morality, and knowledge, being essential to good government, it shall be the duty of the General Assembly to pass suitable laws to protect every religious denomination in the peaceable enjoyment of its own mode of public worship, and to encourage schools and the means of instruction." Under this provision it was held, upon appeal to the Supreme Court of the State, in the case of Minor *et als. v.* Cincinnati Board of Education, that the School Board might legally prohibit the use of the Bible.

The school law of Iowa "forbids the exclusion of the Bible from the public schools, and, at the same time, provides that the pupil shall not be required to read it contrary to the wishes of his parents or guardian." [2]

The law of Indiana says: "The Bible shall not be ex-

---

[1] Randall's History, p. 138.   [2] Iowa Report, 1871, p. 38.

cluded from the public schools of the State." (¹) A note to this section of the Act, by the Superintendent of Public Instruction, thus interprets it: "No school authorities have the right to prevent the teacher from using the Bible in his school, and none have the right to compel him to use it. The privilege of introducing the Bible into the free schools of the State is fully secured by this section. Most Christian teachers will be disposed to read the Scriptures daily in their schools." (²)

The law of Illinois permits, but does not compel, the use of the Bible in the public schools. It authorises Boards "to grant the temporary use of school-houses for religious meetings and Sunday schools." (³) But School Boards "are strictly forbidden to use, or to allow or cause to be used, any school funds or property of any description, under any circumstances whatever, for any sectarian purpose, or to support or help to support any school or other institution of learning of any kind or grade whatsoever that is under the control of any church or sectarian denomination." (⁴)

In Missouri "there is no statutory law either prohibiting or requiring the introduction of religious teaching into any school." (⁵) The State Constitution, Article 10, prohibits any appropriation, payment, or grant from any public fund whatever, in aid of any creed, church, or sectarian purpose, or to help, support, or sustain any sectarian denomination or school. (⁶)

The law of Kentucky provides that "no books, tracts, papers, catechisms, or other publications of a sectarian, infidel, or denominational character shall be used or distributed in any common school, nor shall any sectarian or infidel doctrine be taught therein." (⁷)

---

[1] Indiana School Law, 1865, sec. 167. [2] Indiana School Law, p. 59.
[3] Illinois Report, 1872, p. 19. [4] Illinois Report, 1872, p. 129.
[5] Missouri Report, 1873, p. 62. [6] Missouri Report, 1873, p. 62.
[7] Kentucky School Law, Article 10, section 8.

The school law of West Virginia embodies a provision somewhat similar to that which the League has recommended for adoption in England. The trustee of the schools may allow the houses "to be used for the purpose of holding religious meetings and Sunday schools, equally by the various religious denominations that may apply for the same, under such regulations as to the care of the same as he may prescribe." ([1])

The school laws of other States which I have examined, such as California and Wisconsin, make no mention of Bible reading, but prohibit the use of sectarian books in the schools. In other States, such as Mississippi and Nebraska, I find no provision whatever on the subject in the statutes, though possibly the State Constitutions may contain some.

(b) Bible Reading; Moral Teaching.

The "Statement of the Theory of Education in the United States," published by the National Bureau, contains the following general explanation: "Sectarian instruction is not given in the public schools. Religious, particularly sectarian, training is accomplished mainly in families, and by the several denominations in their Sunday schools, or in special classes that recite their catechisms at stated intervals during the week. It is quite a common practice to open or close the public schools with Bible reading and prayer. Singing of religious hymns by the entire school is still more common." ([2])

An examination of the State reports shows Bible reading to be the rule, but subject to important exceptions. The

---

[1] West Virginia School Law, chap. 123, section 15.
[2] Statement of Bureau, p. 18.

Bishop of Manchester said in his report: "It is true that everywhere—at least, I believe everywhere—under the system, provision is made for reading the Bible." ([1]) If he had said that everywhere Bible reading was allowed, the statement would have been more accurate. Bible reading was not universal in the States at the time of Bishop Fraser's visit. It is still less universal now. Perhaps in all the schools of the New England States the Bible is read; I know of no exception. In New York State, although the law does not permit *School Boards* to exclude the Bible, yet, as a matter of fact, it is often excluded, both in the schools of New York city and other parts of the State. ([2])

In 1872 the Bible was read in only 10,856 out of the 15,999 schools of Pennsylvania. ([3])

In some of the largest cities of the West the Bible is not read. The Superintendent of the St. Louis schools says: "I cannot find that our schools have, ever since their foundation in 1838, permitted so much as the reading of the Bible in them. I believe that this perfect secularity has done much to bring about the perfect intermingling of all denominations in our schools which has existed for so long." ([4])

Since the decision of the Supreme Court in "Minors *v.* the Cincinnati Board of Education," the Bible has been excluded from the schools of Cincinnati.

A census of the schools under this head would probably show that there is a considerable minority of schools in every State save, perhaps, in New England, which are purely secular. No such census has been taken except in Pennsylvania.

Probably in Iowa or Indiana, where the statutes say that the Bible shall not be excluded, it is read in nearly all the

---

[1] Fraser's Report, p. 160.
[2] Randall's History, p. 203.
[3] Pennsylvania Report, 1872, p. xiii.
[4] St. Louis Report, 1872, p. 17.

schools. In Missouri, Illinois, Michigan, Ohio, and some other Western States, there is good reason to believe that this is not the case. Recent State reports contain very little information on the subject, but such as they do contain more than suggests a doubt as to the universal use of the Bible.

The Superintendent for Antrim County, Michigan, says: "In some of our schools the reading of Scripture was practised as an opening exercise, and in most cases where it had not been practised, I succeeded in prevailing on the teachers to introduce it." [1]

The Superintendent for Huron County (Michigan) writes: "Many of the teachers asked me the question, 'Shall we read the Bible in school?' I answered that I was no partisan in religion or politics, that I encouraged a moral, scientific, and practicable education, and that they could use their own discretion about the matter of reading the Bible." [2]

The Superintendent for Washtenaw County (Michigan) says: "During the summer term, in the rural districts, sixty-eight teachers, or 46 per cent. of the whole number, used singing in the opening exercises; eighty-four, or 57 per cent. of the whole, read the Bible; thirty-three, or 22 per cent. of the whole number, opened school with prayer. During the winter term, forty-nine practised singing, seventy-two read the Bible, and thirty-five opened school with prayer." [3]

The school officers of Illinois who refer to the subject do not speak of the reading of the Bible as a matter of course. The Superintendent for Hardin County says: "I am glad to say that the Bible is in general use in all the schools in our county." [4] The Superintendent for Mercer County

---

[1] Michigan Report, 1873, p. 102.
[2] Michigan Report, 1873, p. 134.
[3] Ibid, p. 195.
[4] Illinois Report, 1872, p. 262.

says: "Most of our teachers make use of the Bible in their schools by reading some portion every morning, and, so far as I know, none object to its use." (¹)

In other States the practice, though general, appears to vary as to extent and manner.

In Camden County (New Jersey) the Bible is read for ten minutes before the roll-call, (²) thus introducing a time-table conscience clause.

The rules of the Washington public schools require the reading of the Bible, without note or comment, as an opening exercise, the use of the Lord's Prayer being left to the discretion of the teacher. (³)

The Bible is in general use in the Rhode Island schools, though the regulations under which it is read vary in different towns. In North Providence the rule is as follows: "All the public schools may be opened in the morning by reading a portion of the Scriptures, which may be done by the teacher alone or in connection with the older pupils, the whole school being required at the same time to suspend all other subjects, and to give proper and respectful attention; and this exercise may be followed by prayer or not, at the discretion of the teacher." (⁴)

In East Providence the rule is that teachers "shall open the morning session of each school with reading from the Bible as a devotional exercise."(⁵)

In the evening schools of Providence, in the literature class, the Bible is read in comparison with early English productions, to afford an insight into the etymology of the language. (⁶)

In Philadelphia at least ten verses of the Bible must be

---

¹ Illinois Report, p. 281. ² New Jersey Report, 1872, p. 31.
³ Washington Report, 1873, p. 202. ⁴ Rhode Island Report, 1871, p. 53.
⁵ Rhode Island Report, 1872, p. 64.
⁶ Rhode Island Report, 1873, p. 15.

read, without note or comment, at the opening of the schools. A suitable hymn may also be sung. (¹)

The correct conclusion appears to be that a very wide discretion as to the use of the Bible is reposed in the School Boards and in the teachers, but when it is read it is nearly always without note or comment. The custom in regard to requiring the attendance of pupils during the reading also varies, but the instances in which pupils are withdrawn appear to be few, the conscience clause, such as it is, and where it is in use, being of very small practical use.

Besides the reading of the Bible, provision is made in nearly every State, either by express legislative enactment, or by the regulations of School Boards, for giving moral instruction.

The statutes of Maine require the teacher to "impress on the minds of the youth committed to his care and instruction the principles of morality and justice, and a sacred regard for truth, love of country, humanity, and a universal benevolence; sobriety, industry, and frugality; chastity, moderation, and temperance, and all other virtues which are the ornaments of society; and to lead those under his care, as their ages and capacities admit, into a particular understanding of the tendency of such virtues to preserve and perfect a Republican Constitution, and secure the blessings of liberty, and promote their future happiness; and the tendency of the opposite vices to slavery, degradation, and ruin." (²)

In Boston, the school regulations require that "instruction in good morals shall be daily given in each of the schools, and the principles of truth and virtue faithfully inculcated upon all suitable occasions." Mr. Philbrick, in his last report, says: "In the programme of the primary schools moral

---

¹ Philadelphia Report, 1871, p. 273.   ² Maine Report, 1872, p. 162.

instruction is not set down as a separate subject for instruction, except in requiring the 'repetition of verses and maxims,' meaning verses of poetry and moral maxims. In the programme of the grammar schools the specific requirement under this head is: morals and manners, by anecdotes, examples and precepts, and by amplifying and applying the hints and suggestions relating to those topics contained in the reading lessons. In the high schools moral philosophy is a distinct branch of instruction." [1]

The Superintendent of the St. Louis schools says: "Moral education is a training of the will, and not of the intellect; consequently, it relates to the formation of habits. The duties of (1) punctuality, (2) regularity, (3) silence, (4) truth, (5) industry, (6) respect for the rights of others, are enforced continually in and about the school, as indispensable to the management of it." [2]

The regulations throughout the Union respecting the teaching of morality are much the same in substance. The practice, no doubt, varies widely—the instruction being more general in some cases, more definite in others, and depending always in an important degree upon the character and opinions of the teacher.

It is sometimes asserted in this country that many children are sent to private schools because the moral discipline is better in them than in the common schools. The allegation is twofold—first, that the children attending common schools are often of immoral character, and, secondly, that the tone of the schools is wanting in morality, or is "irreligious." In answer to the first charge, it may be said that it would be strange if, under a system which embraces all classes, some children were not found whose moral training had been neglected, but, that as a class, the pupils of the

---

[1] Boston Report, 1874, p. 348.   [2] St. Louis Report, 1872, p. 16.

public schools are less moral than others has never been substantiated. Isolated instances are to be found. I find a charge of the kind admitted by the Superintendent of the St. Joseph schools, Michigan. At the risk of having it taken out of its setting, and widely circulated to the disadvantage of the common school system, I quote the passage: "So far as I have observed, there is but one valid objection urged against the public when compared with the private schools, and that is the charge of immorality. Such of our religious friends as are interested in sectarian or denominational schools, together with that portion of our community who look upon the public school system as plebeian in character, seize this thumbscrew and turn it with a vengeance. There is some truth in this charge." ([1])

In the course of a long and extensive reading of authorities on American education, this is the only instance in which I have found the accusation admitted, that the public schools are less moral than the private schools; although I have met with occasional complaints that insufficient attention is given to moral instruction. The balance of testimony is quite the other way. Mr. Edward Shippen, formerly President of the School Board of Philadelphia, wrote a letter to Mr. Follett Osler, which was read at the first annual meeting of the National Education League, in which he said, "I candidly tell you that in placing my children at school, I would infinitely prefer placing them in public schools than private schools, and, in doing so, I would thus consult the better their moral, spiritual, and scholastic welfare." ([2])

The Secretary of the Connecticut Board of Education says: "It is the testimony of one of the most eminent educators of our State, that 'public schools are better, as well

---

[1] Michigan Report, 1873, p. 361.
[2] Report National Education League, 1869, p. 185.

as far cheaper, than private schools. I believe the morals of children are better guarded in public than in private schools. From wide observation as to the influence of the two systems on the morals of pupils, I advocate the training of the children of all classes together in the public school.' A successful experience of thirty years as professor in Yale College gives weight to this opinion." (¹)

In reply to the kindred accusation, that the tendency of the common schools is irreligious, the Superintendent for Virginia says: "The infidel tendencies charged upon public schools do not exist. Modern heresy and scepticism are indeed found closely allied with intelligence, but it is not with the simple intelligence of the popular mind, which is everywhere true to the faith. The sources of infidelity are to be found in the temples, not in the synagogues, of learning."(²)

At the meeting of the National Teachers' Association, in 1870, the Hon. F. A. Sawyer, United States Senator said: " I have yet to learn that the pupils of private schools in which special moral and religious instruction is given are, on the whole, possessed of purer morals than those who rely upon the free common schools for their only instruction. I speak of this subject because I know that there are many Americans who decry our public school system, because they say it confines the pupil's development to his intellect, and leaves uncultivated that more important part of his nature upon which his value as a citizen and as a man depends, even more than it does upon his intellectual qualities. They say ours is a godless system; that it increases the power to do evil by stimulating and invigorating one set of faculties while it fails to give tone and vigour to another set, whose action and power become even more necessary to the educated than the uneducated man. I deny the existence of the fact. I claim

---

[1] Connecticut Report, 1869, p. 20.   [2] Virginia Report, 1871, p. 61.

that in general our public schools are not second, as agencies of moral influence, to any other in use outside of the family and the church; and I aver that the exceptions go not to prove the defects of the system, but the want of faithfulness on the part of those who have the appointment of teachers and the general supervision of the schools." [1]

The Bishop of Manchester wrote: " The intellectual tone of the schools is high; the moral tone, though, perhaps, a little too self-conscious, is not unhealthy; but another tone, which can only be vaguely described in words, but of which one feels one's self in the presence when it is really there, and which, for want of a better name, I must call the 'religious' tone, one misses, and misses with regret." [2]

Some readers will be tempted to ask where this latter tone is to be found, and how it is to be supplied. Is it found in the public elementary schools of England, or has it been produced by the religious instruction given in our schools for sixty years? Who that has heard the school-class gabble of Bible and Catechism in a National school can pretend that this is so? If anyone seeks convincing information on this subject, let him read the reports of her Majesty's inspectors previous to 1870, when they were at liberty to examine and report on religious instruction. The record that will be found, with only a partial exception, is one of carelessness, indifference, irreverence, and superficiality. Let Bishop Fraser himself be the witness as to the result of the English plan. " I do not think that it can be maintained that the religious teaching of our schools has produced religious intelligence or religious stability in our people; at any rate, not in that class of our people who, in their school days, had most of such teaching." [3]

---

[1] Proceedings of the National Teachers' Association, 1870, p. 208.
[2] Fraser's Report, p. 179. [3] Ibid, p. 323.

If we have nothing to learn from Americans on this subject, we have at least some valuable experience to place at their disposal, but it is not of a kind flattering to the methods we have hitherto pursued.

(c) *The Religious Difficulty.*

If a poll could be taken on the question, it would probably be found that a large majority of American citizens are perfectly satisfied with the general custom of Bible reading without note or comment. Yet the hostility to the prevailing practice cannot be described as insignificant. It has grown amazingly during the last twenty years, and appears to be still growing. There are two sections of educationists who are incessantly at work against the present system. There are the denominationalists, who desire that the public money should be handed over to their charge, *pro ratâ*, and the work of education left in their hands; and there are the educationists proper, the advocates of State secular education, who desire to exclude the Bible from the public schools. Here, then, are two camps, utterly repugnant to and irreconcilable with each other, who are for the present united in opposition to the custom of Bible reading, but with wholly different ulterior aims. It is almost needless to explain that the secular party draws material strength from the action of the sectarian party. It would be unjust to those who are opposed to Bible reading to say that they are exclusively animated by a spirit of antagonism to the denominationalists. No doubt, as a body they advocate the exclusion of the Bible on the ground of justice to all sects; but it is clear that every fresh effort made by the priest party to secure a division of the public funds largely recruits the ranks of those who see in purely secular schools the only sure and unassailable basis of a national system. The prevailing tone of the schools at present is Christian and Protestant. This, it is held, is unjust to the Jew and Roman Catholic. Whether the Roman Catholics, who constitute the main force of the sectarian malcontents, would be reconciled by a secular system, is a point in dispute. It is, however, clear that the ground of their objection, as understood by the community at large, would be greatly cut away from them if the schools were wholly secularised. To say that the teaching of reading, writing, and arithmetic, *plus* the reading of the Protestant Bible, is a Protestant, and therefore a sectarian, proceeding, is an intelligible position. That the teaching of reading, writing, and arithmetic alone, without any religious instruction whatever, is an irreligious or infidel, and therefore sectarian action, is a conviction which ordinary minds have hitherto been unable to comprehend or assimilate. Therefore, a considerable portion of the community say, "Let us have schools in no sense Protestant or sectarian. If, after putting our system upon this broad and just basis, Roman Catholics still refuse to come in, and insist upon having their own parochial schools—as all admit they have a perfect right to do—that is their own look-out. We are not concerned to meet an objection, even though it is said to be based upon conscience, if we are wholly unable to comprehend its nature. There is a religious equality and a religious freedom which all can understand, and which may be interpreted by the application of the golden rule. There are also 'the blind hysterics of the Celt.' The former we are willing to embody in our system; the latter we ought not to be asked to recognise. A Roman Catholic ought not to be compelled to support a system the prevailing tone of which is opposed to his religion; but he might as conscientiously refuse to contribute to the support of our Government because it is not conducted under ecclesiastical auspices, as to refuse to support schools in which no religious teaching is given."

This indicates accurately, I believe, the nature of the controversy as far as it has gone. There is a very small party in the country who, without making any change in the administration of the schools, desires to increase the amount of definite religious instruction in them; but it is not of sufficient strength to form a considerable element in the discussion. In fact, if it were not for the Roman Catholics, a chapter on the religious difficulty in the States might be as brief as the famous chapter on snakes in Iceland. It is mainly due to the presence of a considerable Irish population that it cannot be written, "There is no religious difficulty in the United States." Not that the difficulty is wholly Irish or Roman Catholic; but it would be a long time before any overt manifestation of it appeared were it not for the numbers and the energy of the Irish faction. Wherever Roman Catholics congregate in large numbers, there is an agitation of the public mind upon this question, and the waters are disturbed, too often without any healing results. Not that the discussion of the question is to be deprecated. So long as the tone of the schools is sectarian, and antagonistic to their faith, large numbers will sympathise with the hostility which is displayed by Roman Catholics towards the system. How it can be maintained that in such a city as New York the reading of the Protestant Bible in the schools can be just to the Roman Catholic parents and ratepayers, I for one do not understand. The question is not now whether their opposition to secular schools would be more or less strenuous, or whether, as many believe, the priests by whom they are led, object not so much to the Bible as to a liberal education. Those are questions which may fairly be discussed by

Protestants when they have washed their hands of every particle of injustice towards Roman Catholics, and purged their schools of all teaching which is hostile to Roman Catholicism. If the Roman Catholic faith and teaching are a standing menace to civil and religious liberty everywhere, the present practice of Bible reading in the public schools of America is not less a badge of Protestant supremacy. I think it is clear that Protestants should remove the latter before they are entitled to be heard about the former. If it be true, as it probably is, that the Roman Catholic hierarchy—and I think an important distinction should be made between the hierarchy and the community—would not be content with anything short of the division of the school fund, the last thing they would rejoice to see would be the expulsion of the Bible from the schools. It would deprive them of their present undoubted grievance. The *locus standi* from which they demand a division of the school fund would be gone immediately the Protestant custom of Bible reading were surrendered. They might still talk about their conscientious rights, and might still endeavour to keep up their parochial schools, but the answer to them then would be clear—" Enjoy your distinction and pay for it. Keep on your separate schools if you think fit; no one interferes with you."

In New York city, and in parts of the State, there has for many years been an intermittent conflict on this question. Previous to 1842, the school funds in the city of New York were raised by the Common Council, and by them paid to the Public School Society, a professedly secular organisation, having control of the public schools. In these schools the Bible was read, and the parochial schools were excluded from all participation in the funds. The agitation against this system, conducted by the Roman Catholics, was very vigorous; but it owed its partial success more to a really weak point in the system than to the power of the Roman

Catholic organisation. The Public School Society was not a representative association, and was practically irresponsible, as the management of a large proportion of the elementary schools is in England to-day. Against this feeble place in the system the artillery of the Roman Catholics was directed, and in 1842 an Act was passed for the election of the Board of Education in the city. By this and subsequent enactments the religious question was partially settled. I have already explained the law, which does not permit the Board of Education to exclude the Bible, nor does it allow them "to decide what version, if any, of the Holy Scriptures" shall be used in the schools. The matter appears to be left very much to the discretion of the teachers. As a matter of fact, the Protestant version is read in most schools, though I believe that the Douay version is read in some schools where there are large numbers of Roman Catholic children, and in others the Bible is excluded altogether. But the Catholics are not satisfied with the system. To the extent of making the public schools wholly secular, a large party are willing to accede to their demands; and this is the case not only in New York, but in the cities of the West, which are now manifesting a determination to strike out their own lines in educational matters.

It is a very significant fact that the report for the city of Chicago, in 1869, expressed an opinion against the advisability of reading the Bible in public schools, on the ground that as the people represent every shade of religious belief, and as all contribute to the support of the schools, they should be unsectarian in all respects. "Those of us who are Protestants would resent any attempt on the part of the authorities to require our children to listen to a daily lesson from the Douay Scriptures. Why, then, should we compel our Romanist neighbour to listen to the version of King James, or insist that the followers of Moses join in the reading of the New Testament?" (¹)

In discussing the question, the Superintendent for Iowa refers to the "wide and unfriendly diversity of public sentiment." "If the Bible used is a Protestant Bible, the Catholic children in attendance, even if excused from the exercise, are committed to the attitude of a false and hostile system of faith and worship; and precisely the same thing must befal the Protestant children if the version accepted by the Catholics is used in these opening exercises. If the New Testament is read, the Jew is offended; if it is omitted altogether, in accommodation to the Jew, the Christian comes in with a most decided protest. There would seem, therefore, to be no impartial course left but to banish the Bible altogether from the public schools . . . . . . Precisely to this conclusion have some of the most eminent divines and educators in this country arrived, and from it many, even after prolonged discussion of the topic, show no disposition to recede." (²)

The Superintendent for Missouri advocates the entire separation of religious and secular instruction, on the plan recommended by the National Education League and adopted by the Nonconformist Conference, and which has now been in use in the Birmingham Board Schools for over a year. Mr. Monteith thus states the principle of the Constitution: "By consulting the great charters, we find that under our Government the matter of religion is left entirely to voluntary thought and effort. Church and State are organically separate; and while it is not ignored but protected, religion is not affirmed by the State under any of its forms. While our civil principles distinctly affirm the doctrine of majority

---

[1] Report of the Commissioner of Education, 1870, p. 117.
[2] Iowa Report, 1871, p. 37.

rule, they do not sanction the application of this doctrine to matters of religious opinion. On the other hand, the genius of our institutions sacredly protects the smallest minority in the freest exercise of religious sentiment." (¹) As the following passage bears so directly upon the controversy in England, it will be read with more than ordinary interest in this country: "Complaint is made by some of the representatives of a great and powerful sect, that since their religious convictions will not permit them to send their children to schools where religious instruction is not practised, it is unjust to tax them to support the education that returns them no benefit. The same objection may lie with equal force against many of the public works and institutions that spring from public necessity. The City Government lays a system of water-pipes or gas-pipes, well supplied with their respective fluids, for public use, and says to its taxpayers, 'These improvements are necessary to the life and safety of the city. You must pay for their support, but you are not obliged to tap these pipes; you are at liberty to dig your own wells, build your own cisterns, and feed your own lights if you choose.' Is this a hardship? The State erects gaols, penitentiaries, poorhouses, and insane asylums, and says to us, 'You must pay for them, even though you furnish them no inmates.' Is this unjust?"

"Each year brings a new iteration of the criticism that the public schools are godless schools; that they turn loose upon the country a swarm of infidels, atheists, and criminals. Thus far this criticism stands in mere assertion; no facts or statistics are adduced to prove what is alleged. They do not tell us whether the Tweeds, Connollys, and their ilk attended public or sectarian schools. Until the facts and statistics are brought forward, the friends of public schools may rest easy, for the burden of proof is with the objectors. Observation

---

[1] Missouri Report, 1873, p. 58.

produces in me impressions quite opposite to the unsupported criticism referred to."

* * * * * *

"All that statistics have thus far asserted is, that ignorance and crime are everywhere closely wedded, and of all the means of prevention which the State has yet invented or established, the public school system is foremost and most effective." (¹)

But it is not only in the Western States that a more liberal feeling on the subject of Bible reading is being manifested. Mr. Northrop, of Connecticut, says: "Our school system should be unsectarian. Its primary purpose is intellectual training. In its practical workings it has always been essentially secular, while its moral influence has been great and good. The Bible is generally read without objection in our schools. Much as I value its influence and desire its continued use, I oppose coercion, and advocate full religious freedom and equality. Wherever there is opposition to this time-honoured usage, I would permit the largest liberty of dissent, and cheerfully allow parents to decide whether children shall read or not read it, or be present or absent when the Bible is read. Roman Catholic children may read from the Douay version, and the Jews from the Old Testament; or, still better, the teacher may read a brief selection; or, if it be preferred, let the Bible reading occur at the close of the session, after the objectors have retired. Compulsory reading will defeat its own aim, and induce resistance and reaction." (²)

The city of Cincinnati, however, has been the seat of the most important discussion on this subject. In November, 1869, an honest attempt was made by the Board of Education to bring the children attending Roman Catholic schools into the public schools, by passing the following resolutions:—

---

[1] Missouri Report, 1873, p. 63.   [2] Connecticut Report, 1870, p. 112.

"*Resolved*—That religious instruction, and the reading of religious books, including the Holy Bible, are prohibited in the common schools of Cincinnati, it being the true object and intention of this rule to allow the children of the parents of all sects and opinions in matters of faith and worship to enjoy alike the benefit of the Common School Fund."

"*Resolved*—That so much of the regulations on the course of study and text-books in the intermediate and district schools as reads as follows : ' The opening exercises in every department shall commence by reading a portion of the Bible by or under the direction of the teacher, and appropriate singing by the pupils,' be repealed."

Very decisive action against these resolutions was taken by some citizens of the city, for on the day after they were passed a petition was filed in the suit of " Minor *et al., v.* Cincinnati Board of Education," in the Superior Court of Cincinnati, to restrain the defendants from enforcing the resolutions. The petition alleged that the entire rule cited in the second of the foregoing resolutions was as follows :—
" The opening exercises in every department shall commence by reading a portion of the Bible by or under the direction of the teachers, and appropriate singing by the pupils. The pupils of the common schools may read such version of the sacred Scriptures as their parents or guardians may prefer, provided that such preference of any version, except the one now in use, be communicated by the parents and guardians to the principal teachers, and that no notes or marginal readings be allowed in the schools, or comments made by the teachers on the text of any version that is or may be introduced." This rule was adopted by the Board in 1852. The version of the Bible generally used was that known as King James's version. It was further alleged that the reading of the Bible without note or comment had been practised in the schools since their first

establishment, and that instruction in the "elemental truths and principles of religion" had always been given, "but no sectarian teaching, nor any interference with the rights of conscience, had at any time been permitted." Further, that in 1842 the School Board provided that no pupil should be required to read the Testament or Bible if his parent or guardian desired that he should be excused from the exercise. Moreover, it was alleged that a majority of the pupils received no religious instruction except that given in the schools, and that the enforcement of the resolutions would leave those children without any religious instruction whatever. The petition also asserted that the resolutions were contrary to law, and against public policy and morality, and that their enforcement would have the effect of making the schools deistical and infidel both in their purpose and tendency.

The answer of the Board asserted that the rules said to have been adopted in 1842 had long since ceased to be acted upon or to be recognised as of binding force, the same not being found amongst the rules published by the Board during the previous twenty-five years; and that the sole version of the Bible which had been read in the common schools at any time was King James's version. It was admitted by the defendants that numbers educated in the common schools received no religious instruction except that communicated in the schools; and while they acknowledged the necessity for such instruction, they denied that it ought to be imparted by the State.

Upon the pleadings of which I have stated the substance, the cause was argued, and every authority and argument on the subject was exhaustively discussed. The decision of the Court was that the resolutions were in violation of the law of Ohio, two of the judges being of that opinion and one dissenting. Judge Hagans said: "Our common schools cannot be secularised under the Constitution of Ohio. It is a serious question whether, as a matter of policy merely, it would not be better that they were, rather than offend conscience. With this, however, we have now nothing to do." (¹)

The decision of the first Court was reversed on appeal to the Supreme Court of the State, since when the schools have been wholly secular.

In this case the important question was raised whether the secularisation of the schools would bring in the Roman Catholics. It was admitted that their ulterior object was to secure a division of the school fund. On these resolutions of the Cincinnati Board, the *Tablet* said : " The School Board of Cincinnati have voted, we see from the papers, to exclude the Bible and all religious instruction from the public schools of the city. If this has been done with a view to reconciling Catholics to the common school system, its purpose will not be realised. It does not meet, or in any degree lessen, our objection to the public school system, and only proves the impracticability of that system in a mixed community of Catholics and Protestants ; for it proves that the schools must, to be sustained, become thoroughly godless. But to us godless schools are still less acceptable than sectarian schools, and we object less to the reading of King James's Bible, even in the schools, than we do to the exclusion of all religious instruction. American Protestantism of the orthodox stamp is far less evil than German infidelity."

This is doubtless in accordance with the instructions of the hierarchy, but it is satisfactory to reflect that its potency to secure obedience to its commands has not increased of late years. Recent discussions in England demonstrate that there is an appeal from the Romish priesthood to the members of the communion, and that even amongst the clergy of that

---

[1] Report of Trial, p. 370.

church, there are Catholics and Catholics. As a matter of fact, the public schools in America, even with Bible reading, are denounced as godless and irreligious; yet there are always large numbers of Catholics in them. Catholic parents, like other parents, are very much attracted by good schools. "The best method of counteracting sectarian efforts is to make our free schools better than any others; parents will not long consent to deprive their children of superior advantages to gratify denominational pride or bigotry." [1]

The Secretary of the Connecticut Board says: "The Irish and Germans evince commendable interest in our schools. Said a parent to me, 'I attended Church schools without learning enough to tell O from a cart wheel. I mean to give my children an education, for I have sadly felt the need of it.' At a late anniversary of one of the best high schools in Connecticut, the valedictorian was a Catholic Irish pupil. This honour was awarded her on the ground of scholarship, and for the last year the higher position of assistant-teacher in the same high school has been worthily filled by her." [2]

From a previous Connecticut report I extract the following:—"Strong testimony as to the good effects of free schools is given in an interesting letter, recently published, from the Rev. Sylvester Malone, a Catholic priest, of Williamsburg, New York, who visited schools in several Southern States, and whose letter evinces fairness and culture. After strongly commending schools for coloured children, supported by Northern benevolence, he speaks of a large free school in Charleston, which is in the hands of the city authorities, and is supported by them. 'There is a good staff of teachers, and, what is a very hopeful sign, they are all from the State of South Carolina. Over 800 children are instructed in the various branches—reading, writing, arithmetic, &c. The

---

[1] New Jersey Report, 1872, p. 43. [2] Connecticut Report, 1870, p. 113.

teachers assured us they were pleased with the progress, attendance, and obedience of the children of this school.'" (¹)

The following remarks, published in the *New York Independent*, are made by the Hon. A. M. Keily, Mayor of Richmond, Virginia, himself a Catholic:—"I assure my Protestant fellow-citizens that in what I have to say I express the convictions of hundreds of thousands of my fellow-Catholics, who gratefully remember the public schools as the source of whatever education they or their children possess, and who know that among the most distinguished laymen, and the most pious and learned and useful priests of the Catholic Church in America, are those whose only early secular training was in the public school. I formulate their opinion and my own when I say that the imparting of sound, useful, and exclusively secular knowledge, by teachers of suitable acquirements, skill, and character, chosen mediately by the people, and paid for out of the public treasury, is, under the conditions prevailing in the United States, a wise, beneficent, and just system, and impugns no rights of conscience." (²)

We know that Bishop Fraser found purely secular schools in New York under the control of Catholics. He says: "There appears to be no difficulty experienced in assembling children of all denominations in the same school-room; though here again, as before noticed in regard to social status, a sort of attraction by affinity seems to prevail, and you find in one school quite a cluster of Jews, another almost possessed by Roman Catholics. This is particularly observable in New York, where some quarters of the city are almost exclusively occupied by an Irish population. The effect in some schools has been rather curious. Under the influence of Roman Catholic trustees, there has not been any intro-

---

[1] Connecticut Report, 1869, p. 22.   [2] Missouri Report, 1873, p. 64.

duction of Roman Catholic teaching, but there has been an exclusion of the Bible." (¹)

The commands of the "Sovereign Pontiff," no doubt, have great weight with Catholics; but it will relieve many of them from a difficulty to learn, on high authority, that his utterances respecting mixed education are not made in the exercise of his infallibility. "And again, his infallibility, in consequence, is not called into exercise, unless he speaks to the whole world; for if his precepts, in order to be dogmatic, must enjoin what is necessary to salvation, they must be necessary for all men. Accordingly, orders which issue from him for the observance of particular countries, or political or religious classes, have no claim to be the utterances of his infallibility. If he enjoins upon the hierarchy of Ireland to withstand mixed education, this is no exercise of his infallibility." (²)

To conclude, the question resolves itself into this: As long as the public schools retain their distinctively Protestant tone and spirit, the Roman Catholic population will have a just ground of complaint, and will be shut out in large numbers from the benefits of the system. That ground of objection once removed—an objection which just men of all religious opinions can comprehend and appreciate—can the obstructive policy of the Romish Church withstand the all-absorbing power of the common school system over American citizens? This is a question which the future can alone answer; but it is clear that large numbers of Americans are anxious that the schools shall be made purely secular, both on the ground of justice to all sects, and also to relieve the system from a peril which now besets it.

"Whenever a contest is made which involves the principle underlying this matter, those who insist upon religious

---

¹ Fraser's Report, p. 165.
² Dr. Newman's Reply to Mr. Gladstone, p. 120.

instruction or religious ceremonies in the schools must give way, or the destruction of the free school system is simply a question of time. Insist upon such instruction or ceremonies, and one sect after another will strive for the control of the schools, and, failing in securing it, will demand, in tones that will be heard and obeyed, a division of the funds constituted by the State. The result will be several systems of schools instead of one, and no one of them will be efficient for the purpose which our school system now so well accomplishes in those States where it has had a fair development. Finally, the free common schools will disappear, and each religious sect will have its own schools in their place. This is the result sure, sooner or later, to come about, if the just demand that all religious education shall be excluded from the schools be refused, or if the public funds raised to support free common schools be divided and placed under the control of different sects. The schools will no longer, in fact, be free or common. The American school system will have been wrecked on the same breakers which have been fatal to so many good institutions in times past." [1]

The apprehension that the common school system will some day give place to the parochial system, which has failed in every country on the earth, may not be altogether groundless, but the contingency is a remote one. Not until the Conservative reaction, which its admirers claim is going on all over the world, becomes much more vigorous—not until the social forces which now operate in the Union are changed in their very nature—not until Western civilisation loses its power of assimilation—not until life and progress give place to decay and stagnation—not until America is reduced to wear the fetters which Italy has thrown off, will the parochial

---

[1] Speech of the Hon. F. A. Sawyer. Proceedings of National Teachers' Association, 1870, p. 209.

system become the school system of the United States. But an increasing number of Americans gravitate towards the conviction that, in order to place the common school system beyond all danger from ecclesiastical factions, and also as an act of justice which ought not to be delayed, it will be necessary to confine public instruction to secular elements only, leaving to the churches, the Sunday schools, and other religious agencies, which are not dormant in the States, the work of religious education.

V.

TEACHERS.

(*a*) Training—(*b*) Examination; Qualifications—
(*c*) Salaries and Social Status.

(*a*) *Training.*

There is no part of the American school problem more beset by difficulties than that which relates to the supply of competent and trained teachers. It is out of the question to strike a balance between the extremes which exist, and to give a fair description of the average American teacher. If anyone wished to find the best teacher in the world he might reasonably prosecute his search in the United States, and while upon the spot it might be very possible to discover the worst. In the process of settlement which goes on in the Union, all phases and conditions of life find a representation —from the highest cultivation and refinement, to the rudest and roughest struggle for existence. The nation is but a hundred years old, and even in some of the oldest States the wilderness is not wholly conquered; so that within a comparatively circumscribed area there are great diversities of social condition. In one place all the comforts and luxuries of an apparently old civilisation may be found, and not far off all the shifts and expedients of the backwoodsman's life are resorted to. The teacher penetrates everywhere, and his profession is marked by the varying shades which colour other features of American life. The cities and large towns possess a class of teachers not to be surpassed in the world. In the rural districts the teachers are often improvised, rough and ready, without experience, without training, and with little to recommend them except an unlimited fund of good intentions. The best teachers flock to the best markets—the cities and large towns—leaving the incompetent and inexperienced to be absorbed by the requirements of the sparsely-settled districts, where teachers who are unfitted for the work are often licensed of necessity —no others being available.

There are several conditions of the American system as it exists at present, and apparently almost inseparable from it, which have combined to prevent the profession from attaining the highest degree of usefulness. One of these conditions, which operates in a very injurious manner, is the shortness of the school term. Even in those States where the terms now extend to eight and ten months, they were originally much shorter, and the profession of the teacher was shaped under the influences of the former system, which commonly left him half a year without occupation and without salary. This state of affairs still continues in a large part of the Union. Moreover, it is an evil for which no summary remedy can be found. It is customary in this country to ascribe the brief school term to the fact that the schools are free, the theory being that only a certain sum is available for school purposes, and that when it is exhausted the school must be closed. There is no foundation for this belief. The length of the school term is not a question of money;

if it were it could be easily rearranged. No other people respond so readily as Americans to pecuniary demands for education. The school term is regulated by climate, by the labour market, and by the development and needs of particular States. The tendency throughout the States is to lengthen the terms, but this necessarily is a work of time.

How directly the length of the school term bears upon the occupation of teaching will be seen. During the vacations the temptation to seek other employment is threefold. In the first place, the teacher is generally poor, and can ill afford to take a long holiday. Again, if good for much, either for teaching or anything else, work will be one of his first necessities. Add to this that the avenue to a more remunerative career is always open, and it is clearly seen that the better the teacher the stronger are the inducements to change his profession. As a matter of fact, the frequent change of teachers is the most serious drawback attending the common school system.

Another drag upon teachers, as a class, has been the very inadequate payment they have received. The demand for teachers has been very great, but instead of operating to secure fair salaries, it has produced a class of make-shift teachers, who use the profession as a stepping-stone to something else. The office of schoolmaster standing socially high, offers excellent opportunities for introduction to desirable employment. This may be good for enterprising young men, but it is bad for education, and it largely explains the want of permanency and stability which has attached to the schoolmaster's profession in the States.

The large preponderance of female teachers in the States will always render the occupation of teacher more or less a temporary one. As a matter quite of course, women do not look to teaching as a lifelong career. In England scarcely one in twenty of the female teachers reaches her tenth year of service. Of the female teachers trained at Bishop's Stortford, it has been ascertained that their average school life was under five years. The proportion of female teachers in America is ten times greater than in England. Female teachers may have other advantages over males, and in the United States are generally conceded to have, but the length of their school life is not one of them.

To all these adverse influences it must be added that only of late years has teaching been recognised as a profession for which preliminary training is necessary, either in England or America. While from time out of mind all mechanical employments have required apprenticeship previous to practice, the highest and most responsible of all occupations has been left to the ignorance, the conceit, the dullness, or the inexperience of the chance comer and amateur—the man who is waiting for a wind. This is as true of England as of the United States. It is only during the past generation that normal training has been regarded as necessary. Dr. Hodgson, in his report to the Duke of Newcastle's Commission, said: "In the appendix will be found notes sufficient, I think, to justify the assertion that none are too old, too poor, too ignorant, too feeble, too sickly, too unqualified in any or every way, to regard themselves, and to be regarded by others, as unfit for school-keeping. Nay, there are few, if any, occupations regarded as incompatible with school-keeping, if not as simultaneous, at least as preparatory employments. Domestic servants out of place, discharged barmaids, vendors of toys or lollipops; keepers of small eating-houses, of mangles, or of small lodging-houses; needlewomen, who take in plain or slop work; milliners; consumptive patients in an advanced stage; cripples almost bedridden; persons of at least doubtful temperance; outdoor paupers; men and women of seventy and even eighty years of age; persons who spell badly (mostly women, I grieve to say), who can scarcely write, and who cannot cipher at all—such are some of the teachers, not in remote rural districts, but in the heart of London, the capital of the world, as it is said to be, whose schools go to make up two thirds of English schools, and whose pupils swell the muster-roll that some statistical philanthropists rejoice to contemplate, and to inscribe with the cheering figures 1 in 8." ([1])

If the minutes of the London School Board could show no other record of useful work, the Board would still deserve public gratitude for the clean sweep it is making of such teachers as these. But this extract shows the state of public sentiment on the subject only ten years ago.

The first normal school was established in England about 1812—the first normal school in America was established in Massachusetts, in 1839. In England we should probably have been without normal schools to this day, had not the Church seen a sectarian advantage in founding them. It is a lamentable confession that the country is still content to rely upon institutions which, although they receive public money, give no sufficient guarantee that they are performing public work efficiently.

It has taken something like thirty years to obtain a recognition of the necessity of training. It is only now that people are beginning to see that the training of a teacher requires as much public vigilance and wise legislation as the training of a soldier or sailor or important civil officer. Dr. Channing said that it required more wisdom to educate a child perfectly than to govern a state. Normal colleges are as necessary as medical colleges. The injury to the mind of a child caused by the stupidity of an ignorant teacher may not be as apparent, but is just as real, as the maiming of the body by the unskilful use of a surgical instrument; and the

---

[1] Report of Duke of Newcastle's Commission, vol. iii, p. 483.

want of skill in the first instance is of far more serious consequence than in the other, because large numbers are subject to it. The medical tyro does not get his chance every day; the incompetent teacher may work for months before he is discovered, and when known he is often tolerated.

It has been a favourite saying that the teacher, like the poet or the orator, is born and not made. At the most this must be taken to mean that some persons are better endowed by nature than others with the qualities requisite for teaching and governing a school. Granting that it is so, it is necessary that some process should be used to discover and select the natural teachers, and to weed out the incapables. It is only by the test of experience that the true teacher can be found. The use of a normal school, then, is evident; it is the touchstone which will declare the gifted teachers and detect the pretenders, instead of leaving the latter to prove their incompetency at the cost of the children's intellectual welfare.

The truth, probably, is that the vast proportion of those who undertake the work have the requisite natural capacity in a greater or less degree. This natural capacity, be it much or little, it is the office of the normal school to train, develop, strengthen, and stimulate.

In the true normal school, theory and practice are supposed to go hand in hand. The drill pursued affords students an opportunity of obtaining in a short time an amount of information and practical skill which even the best of them could only acquire by an experience of years in the duties of teaching.

The conversion to these views in the States, slow at first, is now practically complete, and the question is—How can the want be supplied? It is not a problem of ordinary magnitude. Indeed, there are numbers who assert that only dreamers can contemplate the ultimate establishment of a sufficient number of normal schools to supply the common schools with teachers. Let us see what has to be done.

The number of teachers required to instruct the children between six and sixteen is estimated by the Commissioner for Education to be 260,000. ([1]) In 1873 there were 113 normal schools in the States, having an enrolment of 16,620 students. The full course of a normal school is generally three years; therefore, assuming that the students attended the full course, the present normal schools would turn out about 5,500 annually. Very few, however, do attend the full course. Taking the school life of a teacher under a thoroughly organised system at twenty years, the annual waste in a supply of 260,000 teachers would be about 13,000. As only a small proportion of the students go through the whole course, it may be taken that 120 normal colleges would be able to turn out annually at least 7,000 teachers. Therefore, given an average school career of twenty years—which, however, I do not think is practically realised anywhere—the number of normal colleges in America would only have to be doubled in order to make up the required number of teachers annually. At the present rate of progress, it seems that this may be actually done in about five years. But the great difficulty lies in the length of the school teacher's career in America. At present it is estimated that teachers in the States do not continue in service on the average more than three years. ([2]) It is clear that the State Legislatures would never undertake to supply facilities for normal training on the basis of a three years' professional career for the students; neither would students be found for the normal schools, if they were truly training schools, and not merely a superior kind of academies,

---

[1] Commissioner's Report, 1873, p. xxxiii.
[2] Report of Commissioner of Education, 1872, p. xxix.

on such an assumption. If State normal schools of the same standard and character as those which now exist are to be multiplied sufficiently to train the whole staff of teachers required in the future, one of the first conditions must be that the professional career of the teacher is put upon a much more permanent footing. But it cannot be expected that, for many years to come, the occupation of the teacher in the United States will be of the same duration as in England. A large proportion of the teachers are women, with whom, in the opinion of Mr. Philbrick, late superintendent of the Boston schools, teaching must always remain substantially a temporary occupation.[1] An average school life of five years would be high for American teachers. This would require an annual supply of 52,000 teachers, to meet which about 1,000 normal training colleges would be necessary. At the rate of progress in America, even such a supply as this does not seem improbable; but in the meantime population is increasing, with population the number of scholars, and with them the number of teachers required. The normal school provision is not abreast of the organisation in other particulars, and while it is making up lost ground the whole system is at the same time making rapid headway. It therefore seems impossible to estimate a time within which normal schools, on the scale of those now existing, can be multiplied sufficiently to overtake the wants of the country. There are no sects in the States who are willing to come forward and undertake to train teachers in the interests of proselytism, and if there were, the nation would be unwilling to abdicate its functions in their behalf. At a meeting of the American Normal School Association, in 1870, the question of the supply of normal schools was discussed. Professor White, principal of the Normal School, Peoria,

---

[1] Proceedings of National Educational Association, 1871, p. 219.

Illinois, said: "Allowing that after States have become settled and their communities established, not more than 30 per cent. of the teachers change to other employments annually, the State of Illinois would need 24 such schools; Michigan, 12; Pennsylvania, 20; Massachusetts, 10. The annual expense of these schools would be, to Illinois, not less than 360,000 dollars; to Michigan, 180,000 dollars; to Pennsylvania, 300,000 dollars; to Massachusetts, 150,000 dollars. However profitable such an investment might be to these States, it would be impossible now, or at any time in the near future, to persuade the people to make so large appropriations for this purpose." [1]

In this view of the situation, the most eminent educators of the States appear to coincide. At the meeting of the Education Association held in 1871, the Hon. J. D. Philbrick, of Boston, speaking of the question as it concerned Massachusetts, said that it was not practicable to increase the number of schools of the existing pattern sufficiently to meet the requirements of the public schools unsupplied with trained teachers. The expenditure of time and money to complete the prescribed course in the existing normal institutions, is too great to be undertaken by teachers looking for remuneration to employment in the schools of the rural districts, with their present short terms and low salaries. Again, it would be impracticable in view of the large expenditure from the public treasury which it would require. [2]

The solution of the difficulty for the present, in the opinion of those best qualified to judge, lies in the establishment of a system of graded normal schools in each State. This was the suggestion made by Professor S. H. White, of

---

[1] Proceedings of National Educational Association, 1870, p. 29.
[2] Proceedings of National Educational Association, 1871, p. 216.

Illinois, in his paper, read at the Normal School Association in 1870. It was enforced by Mr. Philbrick, at the meeting of the same Association in 1871; and the committee appointed to consider the question reported in its favour in 1872. The specific recommendations of the committee were:—

"That in every State there should be established, according to its population and resources, one or more normal schools or colleges of a high order, for the special training of teachers for high schools, for the elementary normal schools hereinafter named, and for the preparation of superintendents of schools for counties and cities."

"That these higher normal schools should be supplemented in each county, where practicable, by an elementary normal school supported by the county, with State aid if such can be secured, for the training of those teachers who are to be employed in the primary and intermediate grades of instruction, and in the mixed schools of the rural districts." [1]

The State of Illinois has already authorised the establishment of county normal schools.

Some plan of this kind seems to be the only present mode of dealing with the difficulty. That the needs of the common schools are too urgent to be postponed is admitted on all hands, and it is not believed that the expense, however large, will be permitted to stand in the way. That would be, as the Superintendent for Virginia expresses it, "to work with dull tools in order to save the cost of a grindstone." General Eaton, the Commissioner for Education, advocates free tuition in normal schools: "Few, not intending to teach, would seek this kind of training, and diplomas or certificates should not be given, except on condition that the recipient bind himself or herself to render appropriate service in the schools of the commonwealth." [2]

---

[1] Proceedings of National Educational Association, 1872, p. 37.
[2] Report of Commissioner of Education, 1873, p. xxxiii.

The number of normal schools reported as in operation in the principal States in 1873 was as follows:—Pennsylvania, 10 ; Ohio, 10 ; ([1]) New York, 9; Illinois, 8; Missouri, 8; Massachusetts, 6 ; West Virginia, 5 ; Wisconsin, 4; Iowa, Louisiana, Maine, Minnesota, Tennessee, and Vermont, 3 each ; Alabama, California, Delaware, Georgia, Indiana, Kansas, Maryland, Mississippi, New Jersey, Virginia, and District of Columbia, 2 each; Arkansas, Connecticut, Michigan, New Hampshire, North Carolina, Oregon, Rhode Island, and South Carolina, 1 each. ([2])

Of the work which is at present done in these schools it is impossible, in my limited space, to give any account. The State Boards of Education and Superintendents who are best informed speak of the results in terms of the highest praise. These institutions chiefly supply teachers for the graded and high schools. The instruction in some of them is almost purely technical ; in others it is of a more academic character. Sixty-eight of the 119 reported have model or practice schools attached ; 90 provide instruction in drawing ; 39 have models, charts, &c., for freehand drawing; vocal music is taught in 96, instrumental music in 60 ; 68 possess chemical laboratories and apparatus ; 81 possess cabinets and apparatus for illustrating the laws of physics ; and 45 have cabinets of natural history.

American normal schools are generally of an unsectarian character, having voluntary religious classes in connection with them. Their efforts are concentrated upon the production of good teachers, instead of being wasted in acquiring the art of proselytism. In this respect, amongst others, they have an advantage over the ecclesiastical nurseries upon which England still relies for her teachers, and in which public money is

---

[1] Seven of these appear to be private.
[2] Report of Commissioner of Education, 1873, p. xxxi.

devoted to securing a thorough knowledge of the Book of Common Prayer, the thirty-nine Articles, and the Catechism.

The work of the normal schools in the United States is supplemented by several other agencies. While it is admitted that no other means yet discovered can compete with a well-organised normal school in the training of teachers, yet the other appliances in use in America form, in the aggregate, a powerful auxiliary in the work of preparation.

Large numbers of the private colleges have normal departments attached to them. There are between thirty and forty such colleges in the State of Ohio. Of these, the State Commissioner says that a commendable feature in them is the attention given to normal instruction. They are chiefly, no doubt, of an academic character. " Still, a limited amount of really valuable professional training is provided for, not only in these schools, but in a large number of seminaries and academies, especially in such as are dependent for their support upon the patronage of those who intend to teach a portion of each year, while preparing for college or pursuing a course of academic studies." ([1])

The Superintendent for Indiana says of the higher institutions for learning, not under the control of the State, that they have greatly aided in the free school work by furnishing many excellent teachers for the schools. ([2])

In the State of New York the work of the training schools is supplemented by normal instruction in academies and Union schools. The law provides that the sum of ten dollars shall be paid to each pupil, not exceeding twenty to an academy, instructed under a course prescribed by the Regents of the University, during at least one third of the academic year, in the science of common school teaching. The number of classes in which teachers' academies were

---

[1] Ohio Report, 1873, p. 26.   [2] Indiana Report, 1872, p. 147.

maintained in 1873 was ninety, and the number of pupils instructed was 1,589. (¹)

Many of the high schools throughout the States also have training classes, the object of which is to fit teachers for work in the common schools.

The State Board of Massachusetts employs special agents to visit schools and give teaching exercises.

But the most important auxiliary in the work of training are the Teachers' Institutes, which have become a prominent and universal feature of the American school system. These are meetings of teachers for the purpose of discussing methods and taking part in training exercises. They are, in fact, ambulatory normal schools, and are held in most counties once and sometimes twice a year. In some of the States they are compulsory, in others they are authorised by the Legislature, and appropriations are made for the expenses attending them. So far as I know, the Teachers' Institute is exclusively an American institution, but if the high value placed upon it by American educators is well grounded it ought not to remain so.

General Eaton, in his report for 1870, says: "Teachers' Institutes furnish a powerful and efficient means for instructing and inspiring teachers. They may be considered as normal schools of the lowest grade, affording the only means by which the great mass of teachers can, at present, be reached, and some better ideas of school instruction and school management can be imparted. If these are well conducted—if the plan is devised beforehand—if the work is done by skilled teachers who have given special attention to it, and in such a way as to elicit active thought and work from the institute, it is doubtful whether an equal amount of expense and labour to the same end will accomplish so valuable results." (²)

---

[1] New York State Report, 1873, p. 56.   [2] Commissioner's Report, 1870, p. 398.

The Superintendent for Iowa says : " The value of these institutes can hardly be overstated. Year by year they are becoming more valuable as their legitimate work is better understood, and as the number of teachers qualified to give thorough and practical instruction in them increases. The best educational talent of the State is now everywhere brought into requisition in these institutes." ([1])

The Commissioner for Ohio reports : " Institutes have long been regarded by teachers as very important educational helps. They are most largely attended, and their advantages best improved by the most intelligent teachers . . . . The acknowledged fact that schools are best taught and school affairs best administered in those counties where teachers take the most interest in institutes, is a sure test of their value and efficiency." ([2])

The Commissioner for Rhode Island writes : " The association of teachers in institutes and conventions has been found to be a very important auxiliary in the work of public education. Even in those States where good normal schools exist, the institute has been established and successfully maintained to supplement the work of the training school, and to refresh and stimulate the minds of teachers by the new methods of instruction and discipline which are so frequently adopted." ([3])

The Superintendent for Michigan says : " The uniformly good effects of these institutes in the past, have made them a prominent and interesting feature of our school system. They are a great auxiliary. No more powerful agency can be had to awaken an interest in the public mind, to assist in elevating the profession of the teacher, and to increase the efficiency and worth of our schools." ([4])

---

[1] Iowa Report, 1873, p. 64. [2] Ohio Report, 1871, p. 41.
[3] Rhode Island Report, 1871, p. 25. [4] Michigan Report, 1873, p. 10.

In contradistinction to Teachers' Institutes, what are called Normal Institutes are held in some States. These assemble for longer periods, and the instruction given in them is more exclusively technical. ([1])

It is admitted, however, on all hands, that whatever value the institutes may have as aids, they cannot adequately supply the place of regularly organised normal schools. At best the instruction given in them must be very brief, and on that account imperfect. That normal schools will be established in sufficient numbers to meet the wants of the country appears to be certain. The present aims of those who have at heart the improvement of the public school system are chiefly directed towards this end. It is a question of time.

The appreciation of training by teachers as a class, and the extraordinary efforts and sacrifices made by large numbers of them to obtain its advantages, merit a word of recognition. The reports of the normal school directors and the other officials cite constant instances of teachers who teach school for one term in order that they may obtain the means for passing another term at a normal school. By thousands of American teachers the work of qualification for their profession is carried on under sacrifices and discouragements of no ordinary kind, and subject to the primal necessity of earning their own living at the same time.

It is noteworthy that the English pupil teacher system has no advocates amongst the school officials of the States. The tendency is to raise rather than lower the age at which the work of teaching may begin. Already it is admitted many American teachers are too young for their work. The idea that anyone can teach the youngest children is rapidly going out of fashion. The Prussian method of placing the most mature and experienced instructors over the primary

---

[1] Iowa Report, 1873, p. 68.

classes is being adopted. "It is a regulation of the School Board of St. Louis, in assigning teachers, to place the very best ones in the lowest room of the school, and to pay them better than those teaching the next higher grades. The child is initiated at the start into the best department, and habits of diligence and attention." ([1]) "We need the best trained and most practically experienced teachers in our most elementary schools." ([2]) "The Germans are wise in putting the work of primary instruction into the hands of those who have been liberally educated as well as specially trained for their work." ([3]) These extracts show the spirit which animates the discussions upon this question. To subject the plastic mind of childhood to the barbarous experiments of boys and girls, is to create a wholesale destruction of material in the effort to produce good tools. Americans are in the advantageous position of not having to unlearn so injurious a practice.

(b) *Examination; Qualifications.*

Every teacher is required to undergo an examination, and to produce testimonials as to moral character. No one may teach without a license or certificate.

The practice respecting certificates varies in different States. In New York, teachers must be licensed by the State Superintendent or local officers appointed for that purpose, or must hold a normal college diploma. In Iowa, no person is authorised to teach without a certificate signed by the County Superintendent. In New Jersey, the State Board of Educa-

---

[1] Proceedings of National Educational Association, 1871, p. 114.
[2] Ibid, 1872, p. 134.   [3] Ibid, page 167.

tion and the County Boards of Examiners issue licenses. In Connecticut, teachers are licensed by Township School Boards; in Ohio, by County Examiners; in Rhode Island, by District Trustees; in Indiana, by County Examiners; in Missouri, by County Superintendents.

In most States diplomas are issued by State Boards of Education or State Superintendents. Normal school certificates also qualify for teaching.

There are several grades of certificates, available for different periods. The certificate in most general use authorises the teacher to follow his calling for a year only. This is the case in Iowa. In New Jersey, certificates are issued for three years, two years, and one year. In Ohio they are limited to two years. In Indiana the licenses are for two years, eighteen months, twelve months, and six months. In Missouri the time varies in different counties. In several States life diplomas are issued by Boards of Education.

The methods and standards of examination in the different States are multiform. In some States the Board of Education or the State Superintendents draw up the questions and determine the scale; in others, each body of examiners adopt their own standard. The former method prevails in New Jersey, Indiana, and other States; the latter is in use in Ohio, Missouri, and elsewhere. The regulations respecting the examinations of teachers appear to be responsible, to some extent, for the frequent changes which occur, and which form a special blot upon the American system. When a teacher is only engaged for a year, and at the expiration of that time has to undergo another examination, he must lack the sense of security which is partly necessary for successful work. To one who intends to follow the profession of teaching for life, an annual examination must be insufferable. That teachers do find these frequent examinations both expensive and embarrassing is clear from the reports. More than one Superintendent urges that justice to teachers requires that longer certificates should be granted.

The fact that the examiners are not in all cases teachers causes a good deal of friction at times. In Ohio, out of 264 County Examiners, only 136 are teachers, 45 being attorneys, 23 ministers, 20 farmers, 8 physicians, and the remainder of various employments. Although as a class they have the reputation of being " competent, just, prudent, and fearless," yet teachers reluctantly submit to their decisions, and are even too apt to believe that the leading object of the examination is to give the examiners a chance of showing off their own attainments.[1]

The want of uniformity must work prejudicially. Teachers who are rejected by one set of examiners are passed by another. In Knox County, Ohio, 97 per cent. of those examined passed and received certificates; in Muskingum, 55 per cent. of the candidates were rejected. This instance alone is sufficient to prove the necessity for some definite standard of qualification and uniform method of examination. Still it must be remembered that the examiners have frequently a very limited choice, and must either close the schools for lack of teachers, or accept the services of those who are, at the best, poorly qualified. The Superintendent for Missouri says that no uniform standard is at present possible in that State.

There is a general disposition on the part of officials to make the examinations more rigorous. In New Jersey, the Superintendent reports that about one fifth of the applicants fail. Every year more care is exercised in the selection of teachers. The object is to make the examinations more and more rigid every year, and thus continually to raise the standard of the teacher's profession in the State. The returns

---

[1] Proceedings of National Educational Association, 1872, p. 80.

bear evidence that the examinations are conducted with this view.

In Ohio, too, the County Boards of Examiners are raising the standard: "The indolent and incompetent have been compelled to prepare themselves by study for the business of teaching, or to seek some other employment." ([1]) In New York the standards have also been considerably raised within recent years.

Boston is the only large city of the Union where the provisions for examining teachers appear to be inadequate. Mr. Philbrick, the late Superintendent, constantly urged reform in this matter. In his last report he returns to the subject: "Where we ought to have examinations they are dispensed with; and where we ought not to have them they are sometimes insisted on, and probably it would not be far from the fact to say that as a rule they are not of the right sort." ([2])

The most important alterations respecting examination at which American educators are now aiming, are:

1. A comprehensive system of State, City, County, and Town Boards of Examination.
2. These Boards to be comprised of School Superintendents and professional teachers.
3. A graded series of certificates from life diplomas down to annual certificates to be granted upon actual examination.
4. Legal recognition by each State of professional certificates and normal school diplomas issued in other States. ([3])

Leaving their youth out of the account, the general testimony as to the worth of American teachers is very high.

---

[1] Ohio Report, 1873, p. 29. [2] Boston Report, 1874, p. 345.
[3] Proceedings of National Educational Association, 1872, p. 80.

O

Energy and enthusiasm are their predominant characteristics; what they lack in training and in scholastic attainments, they endeavour to make up by zeal and devotion to their work. No higher praise can be given to them than that of the Bishop of Manchester: "All sorts of plans are adopted in the different States to improve the quality and increase the quantity of the teaching power, but hitherto, it must be confessed, with very limited success; and more complete appliances for training teachers is still one of the things wanting to the perfection of the American system of public schools. At the same time, I must allow that the deficiency is very much less striking to the outward eye of a casual observer, than would be the case under similar circumstances in England, on account of the much greater natural aptitude for the work of a teacher possessed, as it appeared to me to be, by Americans generally, and particularly by American women. They certainly have the gift of turning what they do know to the best account; they are self-possessed, energetic, fearless; they are admirable disciplinarians, firm without severity, patient without weakness; their manner of teaching is lively and fertile in illustration; classes are not likely to fall asleep in their hands. They are proud of their position, and fired with a laudable ambition to maintain the credit of their school; a little too anxious, perhaps, to parade its best side, and screen its defects; a little too sensitive of blame, a little too greedy of praise; but still, as I judged them from the samples which I saw, and in spite of numerous instances to the contrary which I read of but did not see, a very fine and capable body of workers in a noble cause. . . . . Apart from the question of adequate training, I know not the country in which the natural material out of which to shape the very best of teachers is produced in such abundance as in the United States. That, with the shaping process so very imperfectly performed, the results are what they are is sufficient proof of the quality of the material." (¹)

(c) Salaries and Social Status.

If, however, America has some reason to be proud of her teachers, she has cause to be ashamed of the salaries paid to them. The stipends of male teachers are generally not much better than those of English curates, and frequently they are worse. Of Maine, where the salaries of women are lower than in any other State, the Superintendent says: "The female teacher in Maine cannot earn her living by teaching." (²)

The State Board of Maryland refer to counties "where teachers' salaries are so low that somebody must inevitably be cheated—the teacher if he is competent, and the public if he is not." (³)

The following table shows the salaries of teachers per month in the most important States:— (⁴)

STATES.	No. of Months School.	Males. $ c.	Females. $ c.
Massachusetts	9	93.65	34.14
District of Columbia	10	91.66	62.50
California	6⅓	84.28	63.37
Rhode Island	8½	75.72	41.97
Connecticut	8½	67.01	34.09
New Jersey	8½	65.92	36.61
Illinois	7	52.92	40.51
Michigan	7½	51.94	27.13

---

¹ Fraser's Report, p. 73. ² Maine Report, 1872, p. 33.
³ Maryland Report, 1873, p. 10.
⁴ See Commissioner's Report, 1872, p. 609. Ibid, 1873, p. 511.

STATES.	No. of Months School.	Males. $ c.	Females. $ c.
Mississippi	5⅓	51.32	51.32
New York	8½	49.53	49.53
Wisconsin	7	43.66	27.34
Pennsylvania	6	42.69	34.92
Missouri	4½	42.43	31.43
Ohio	7	41.00	29.00
New Hampshire	4	40.78	23.84
Iowa	6½	36.28	27.68
Maine	5	34.28	15.16
West Virginia	4	34.00	28.89
Virginia	5½	32.00	32.00

These figures will enable the reader to make his own calculations.

In Massachusetts, the average annual salary of masters is about 850 dollars; of mistresses, about 290 dollars. District of Columbia, masters, 916 dollars; mistresses, 625 dollars. California, masters, 530 dollars; mistresses, 400 dollars. New York, both sexes, 430 dollars. As the old custom of boarding around is now almost out of use, these figures represent the actual compensation which teachers receive. No one will be surprised that, under such a scale of remuneration, teachers are driven into other employments. In the great State of New York the average pay of teachers, male and female, is not more than £80 per annum.

It is encouraging to find, however, that salaries are going up. Many of the Superintendents of the best States refer to this fact with gratification. In Connecticut teachers' wages doubled between 1863 and 1870. The statement issued by the National Bureau says: "For some years there has been a steady increase in salaries." [1]

---

[1] Statement of Bureau, p. 19.

But if the teachers of the United States receive a very inadequate recompense for their services, they have some consolations which are denied to the masters of public elementary schools in England. They do not stand on the social level of the servants' hall. They are not expected to join with the occupation of teaching, that of beadle, parish clerk, verger, or sexton. If they are often compelled to resort to hard and sometimes menial work to eke out their scanty means of subsistence, the fact does not entail upon them the social ostracism which attends the schoolmaster's calling in this country. The Bishop of Manchester says : " As to the character and repute of the teacher's profession in America, it certainly stands very high. I do not suppose that there are any teachers of common schools or of high schools in America who mix as freely in the highest class of society as do the masters of the great public schools among ourselves ; but that is chiefly owing to the slenderness of their income not enabling them to afford to do so ; and, on the other hand, the teacher of the humblest district school occupies a far higher social position than the teacher of an elementary school in England." Again : " All hangs upon the teacher's personal character and qualifications ; as far as his profession is concerned he is on a level with anybody. I was occasionally invited to visit teachers at their homes. They appeared to me to live in a sort of cheerful and refined frugality ; able to exercise a hearty but inexpensive hospitality ; often relieving the monotony of daily toil by the cultivation of some recreative, but not uncongenial, study or accomplishment—a social position not altogether dissimilar to that so happily enjoyed by many an Englishmen clergyman." ([1])

In America the schoolmaster is a civil officer, and his profession is attended by the highest honour and respect. In

---

[1] Fraser's Report, p. 84.

England he has long been a Church official of the lower grade. As the parochial system never aimed at raising the children very high, it was the reverse of necessary that the schoolmaster should be a man of cultivation and refinement, and he has not been encouraged to seek superfluous learning or to aim at social distinction. The teachers of America and England have one bond of fellowship—they have been equally badly paid.

VI.

GRADES — RESULTS.

(*a*) GRADING — (*b*) COURSE OF STUDY — (*c*) PRACTICAL OUTCOME.

(*a*) *Grading.*

Grading, as understood in America, is the arrangement of children of about the same age, and of as nearly as may be similar attainments, in separate schools or departments, under separate teachers, so that the kind of instruction and discipline suited to individual scholars may be adapted to the whole class or grade. The advantages of such a division are that time is saved, distraction is avoided, and, by the introduction of a greater degree of method, efficiency is secured. The extent to which the system of grading can be carried with advantage depends upon circumstances—very much upon the size of the school, and much also upon the adaptability of school-houses.

Some of the benefits which the application of the principle secures are obvious. Under a system which aims to give something beyond the merest elements of instruction there are certain broad and natural lines where grading may be advantageously adopted. Studies adapted to the capacity of more advanced pupils cannot be successfully pursued where primary classes are under instruction. There are different methods of discipline and teaching suited to children of different ages and developments. The quietness and attention necessary to the progress of an advanced school, if enforced amongst primary scholars, would be injurious to them, mentally and physically; and, conversely, the change of attitude and the noise attendant upon primary instruction cannot be permitted in more advanced classes without an amount of distraction, and a relaxation of discipline detrimental to progress.

In most States the instruction of the youngest children is principally oral. The objective method is in very general use, and the mode of teaching is entertaining and varied. The restraints of discipline are gradually applied and frequently relaxed. The learning of letters and of numbers is relieved by alternate singing, marching, and playing. "The proper teaching of little children is a busy and rather a noisy affair, because little children are busy, noisy creatures; and when a class is under appropriate instruction, there can be no studying in that room by other children. It is out and in, up and down, saying and singing." [1] The necessity for the separation of these scholars is at once apparent, and experience has shown that the further the principle is carried and the more perfect the classification of scholars on the basis of age and attainments, the more appropriate may be the instruction given, and the more thorough and efficient will be the success of the system. The wide recognition of this fact has resulted, in the United States, in the adoption of the graded system wherever practicable.

---

[1] Virginia Report, 1872, p. 51.

The economy of the graded plan is also another strong recommendation, enabling, as it does, a specified number of teachers to superintend a larger number of schools. This is most evident in large cities, where, in proportion to the numbers educated, the cost is diminished. To give one illustration : " In Richmond (Virginia) it costs $43.29 cents. on an average to send a child to an ordinary school for nine months. The cost in the public schools, which are all graded, is $13.41 cents. for the same length of time. To educate the 4,600 which were taught last year in this city would have cost, at private rates, 199,134 dollars. The actual cost was 61,686 dollars, an annual saving to the city of 137,448 dollars. The sum thus saved is sufficient to educate all the children of the city on the public graded system." [1]

But the economy of time is even more apparent. On the graded system, not only can one teacher do the work of two, but the pupils of similar studies and acquirements can be gathered into classes of such numbers that a much longer time can be spent in drilling and explanation at each recitation. The teacher's labour is simplified, the classes are diminished, and there is much greater regularity and thoroughness of labour, and freedom from confusion and friction. Time is again saved in organising classes and adjusting studies and recitations, and the number of separate schools is reduced, while their worth and efficiency are increased.

A very healthy effect of distinct grading is that the emulation of the pupils is excited, and effort is created. The higher grades draw up the lower ones. The scholars are stimulated to greater diligence, which only requires to be wisely directed to produce most valuable results. When, however, it is not judiciously controlled, it culminates in

---

[1] Virginia Report, 1872, p. 57.

what is known as "high pressure" or over-study—an evil of which we seldom hear in the elementary schools of England.

The system of grading is also advantageous to the teacher. In a badly classified school is found every abuse; teachers hurried and fretted beyond measure; some pupils shuffling from one thing to another with such haste and irregularity as to occasion bewilderment; others, having excess of time to prepare for lessons, inclining them to listlessness or mischief.[1] Each teacher's work being laid out for the year, the comparative merits of teachers come out more decidedly under the graded system.

On the other hand, too strict grading has its drawbacks. The class is everything; the individual scholar is merged. Herein lies a danger of diminished individual development. When pupils are advanced by classes from one grade to another in regular order, there is a lack of flexibility or adaptation to individual requirements. Some pupils are likely to be advanced too fast, others to be kept back too long, and some to be cramped and hindered by the course of study. This is especially the case where promotions are made only at stated intervals—in some cities once, in others twice a year. Scholars who do not pass are kept back, sometimes too long, and there is loss of time as well as discouragement. This is guarded against in many cities by having frequent examinations for promotion. To promote the advancement of all, to force none beyond their capacity, to encourage the best scholars, to meet the case of irregular attendants, grades should be near together, and promotions frequent. While no pupil should be permitted to enter on higher work until the lower grade is completed, none ought to be compelled to wait for others. It is maintained that graded systems,

---

[1] Virginia Report, 1872, p. 44.

properly arranged, are capable of sufficient flexibility to meet all cases.

The larger the school the more perfectly can the system be carried out. It follows that the principle of grading is best adapted to large towns. The rural schools in the United States commonly consist of less than fifty pupils. A high degree of organisation under such circumstances is not possible. Yet, by means of "union" schools, the graded system is being gradually introduced in towns formerly under the district system, and having numerous small district schools. Large buildings, capable of holding all the children of the township, are now erected. The plans of American school architects are commonly adapted for a high school and schools of a lower grade in the same building. These "union school-houses" are now amongst the most familiar objects of the country.

It is, however, in the large cities that the practice of grading is most perfectly developed. "Six hundred elementary pupils of both sexes in one building, divided into ten grades, with a teacher and a room for each grade, now constitute the preferred type of a public school." [1]

Bishop Fraser says: "The 'grades' correspond somewhat to our 'standards' of examination under the revised code—promotion from one grade to another taking place at fixed periods, seldom oftener than twice a year, and always as the result of examination." [2]

The plan of teaching classes or grades in separate school-rooms has been adopted in some of the Birmingham Board schools, and also in London, I believe, and has given great satisfaction.

In New York city the elementary course is divided into primary and grammar departments. The primary schools

---

[1] Virginia Report, 1872, p. 60.   [2] Fraser's Report, p. 87.

are subdivided into six distinct grades, the grammar schools into eight grades. In the male grammar schools there are on the average thirty-five pupils, in the primary schools forty-eight pupils to a teacher.

The schools of Philadelphia are divided into four grades or departments—viz., primary, secondary, grammar, and high. "Each one of these grades is valuable both in itself and as an essential part of the system. Each one of the lower grades educates a large number of children who, from various causes, never advance beyond it. Each higher one carries to a more advanced stage the education of those who are sent up to it from the schools below." ([1]) The course of study in the high school is divided into eight classes, or grades lettered from A to H. The grammar, secondary, and primary schools are separated into sub-grades or divisions by a committee appointed by the Board. The number of these divisions appears to vary in different sections of the city. The course of study for each department (grammar, secondary, and primary) is laid down by the Board, and the studies are then apportioned among the several divisions in such manner as the principals of the schools think best. ([2]) Six months must be devoted to the instruction of each division in the studies allotted to it. Each division of grammar and secondary schools contains an average of forty pupils to each teacher; the average attendance in the primary schools is not less than forty-five to each teacher. Promotions from primary to secondary, and secondary into grammar schools are made half-yearly. Promotions from one division of a school to a higher division are made whenever the principal thinks the pupils require it.

In Boston the departments of the schools are (1) high, (2) grammar, (3) primary. Pupils are admitted to the

---

[1] Philadelphia Report, 1871, p. 7.   [2] Ibid, p. 82.

primary grade at five years of age. This course is arranged for six classes (or grades) and three years. The grammar schools are designed to receive pupils from the primary schools at eight years and upwards, and carry them on through a thorough course of practical elementary instruction. This course is arranged for six classes and "is intended to comprise about six years." (¹) The Superintendent, in his last report says: "The primary schools, from the time of their establishment in 1818 down to 1856, had been conducted on what we call the 'ungraded plan;' that is, the school taught by each teacher was a separate and independent organisation. The course of instruction was divided into six steps or classes, but each teacher had all the six classes in her room at the same time. She was fitting a class for the grammar school, teaching a class of a-b-c-darians, and carrying on the intermediate stages of the course simultaneously. This arrangement necessitated a great waste of teaching power. It was gradually changed by the substitution of what is known as the 'graded plan,' which assigns to each teacher, so far as circumstances will permit, only one class or grade of pupils. This arrangement requires the promotion of pupils every six months, from one primary teacher to another." (²)

The primary schools are now built, as a rule, to contain six school-rooms. A building of this description accommodates six schools, forming what is described as a group. About forty-five scholars are assigned to each teacher. (³)

The Cleveland public schools are classed as high, grammar, and primary. Each of these departments is subdivided into four grades; those of the high school being

---

¹ Boston Report, 1874, p. 383.   ² Ibid, p. 296.   ³ Ibid, p. 321.

numbered one to four, and those of the grammar and primary one to eight. ([1]) The average number of scholars to a teacher is forty-six. When the course first went into effect it was arranged that promotions from class to class should be made annually. There were several practical objections to this method, and the more liberal plan has been adopted of advancing the lower classes as soon as they are prepared. Whenever pupils give promise of ability to do the work of the higher class, they are permitted to go forward for trial. ([2])

In Cincinnati the schools are known as high, intermediate, and district. There are eight grades in the intermediate and district schools, lettered from A to H. The average number of pupils to a teacher is forty-one. The annual examination for transfer is held at the end of the school year, but classes may be transferred specially, if necessary. ([3])

There are three grades of day-schools in St. Louis—high, normal, and district. The latter include grammar, intermediate, and primary departments in the same building. ([4]) They are also sub-divided into seven grades. The schools are generally held in school-houses containing twelve rooms, having between fifty and sixty pupils in a room, and assigned to one teacher. The system of grading in operation at St. Louis is one of the most flexible in the States. Great care is taken that pupils may be advanced from grade to grade as they are prepared.

In Chicago, the first division of the schools is into high, grammar, and primary departments. The two latter departments or grades are sub-divided into ten other grades. Each teacher in the highest five grades is responsible for the instruction and discipline of forty-eight pupils; in the lowest

---

[1] Cleveland Report, 1873, p. 38.   [2] Cleveland Report, 1872, p. 44.
[3] Cincinnati Report, 1874, pp. 47, 220.   [4] St. Louis Report, 1872, p. 161.

five grades, of sixty pupils. Classes are examined for promotion whenever they are ready. (¹)

It will be seen that in the Eastern cities the classes are generally examined and promoted at stated intervals. In the West, the hard and fast line, which is one of the dangers of the graded system, is broken through, and individual promotion is more frequent.

Upon one or other of the models described, the systems of other large towns are based. In the smaller towns, wherever practicable, grading has been adopted. In 1872 there were three hundred and ninety-two cities in the United States having populations varying from one thousand upwards. In over three hundred of these "cities," the schools were graded. (²) The value attached to grading is shown by the fact that aid from the Peabody Fund is given only to graded schools.

(b) *Course of Study.*

Although, for the sake of convenience, the American schools are arranged under three heads—high, grammar, and primary—there are in reality but two courses of instruction, the higher course pursued in the high schools, and the elementary course carried on in the grammar and primary schools. It must not be supposed that the grammar grade answers to the grammar schools in England. On the contrary, the grammar grades are merely the higher elementary grades, and although the studies pursued in them range much higher than the standards of the English code, they still

---

[1] Chicago Report, 1873, pp. 105, 107.
[2] Report of Commissioner of Education, 1872, Table III.

comprise only the amount of instruction which, according to American views, should be given in an elementary school.

It is important to bear this distinction in mind. The primary schools and the grammar schools are but one course, and all children are expected to pass from the primary schools into the grammar schools. That the expectation is not always realised is too true, though in the vast majority of cases it is. The Superintendent for Boston thus explains the working of the elementary course in that city: " Our system of public schools nominally comprises three grades of instruction, but in reality only two—the elementary grade, including both the primary and grammar schools, and the higher or secondary grade, embracing all the different high schools. The line of demarcation between the primary and grammar schools is an arbitrary one, which was adopted merely for the sake of convenience in the organisation and management of the schools. It is not known to the law, and has no important significance in respect to the age, instruction, or destination of pupils. All the pupils of the primary schools are expected to pass into the grammar schools, and this expectation is practically realised." (¹)

The same description of the course is almost as true of New York. The Superintendent for that city says: "The distinction between primary and grammar school pupils is to a certain extent arbitrary. There is, in fact, but one course of instruction, extending from the lowest or alphabet grade to the highest in the grammar schools." (²)

In Cincinnati, Chicago, St. Louis, and Cleveland the elementary course, comprising primary and grammar schools, or " district" and " intermediate" schools, is divided into ten, eight, or seven grades. A child enters the primary school at the age of five or six, and continues in it for three or four

---

[1] Massachusetts Report, 1873, p. 183.   [2] New York City Report, 1874, p. 9.

years, at the end of that time passing into the grammar school, the grades of which extend over another four, five or sometimes, as in Boston, six years.

The course of study in the several departments and grades varies in the different cities, according to the views of the educational authorities. It is very difficult to institute any comparison between the grades in American schools and the standards of our English code. While the primary grades are often below our standards (especially in arithmetic), the grammar grades generally go far beyond our highest standards. An English child is introduced to the first standard at the age of seven, having had, it is presumed, some preliminary instruction in the infant school. Six years are assigned to the six standards, each standard being supposed to embrace a year's work. The American pupil enters school at five or six years of age, without any preliminary teaching. He commences, therefore, at the very bottom of the ladder. The first grade of the primary school is occupied in learning letters and numbers. The primary course generally comprises six grades as in New York and Boston ; or five grades, as in Cincinnati and Chicago. In point of time, it is supposed to occupy sometimes three years, as in Boston; sometimes four, as in New York ; sometimes five, as in Cincinnati. The aim in Boston is to pass all children into the grammar schools at eight years of age. In age, therefore, the lowest grade of the Boston grammar schools would be on a level with our Standard II.; the lowest grade of the New York grammar school would correspond with our Standard III. or IV. In America the pupils commence later, they move up by more gradual steps, and the grades cover a longer time than the English standards. Thus the elementary course in Boston commences at five, and extends through twelve grades and nine years. In New York it generally commences at six, and comprises fourteen grades, extending over eight years. In Cincinnati

P

it is eight years in length ; in Chicago it is ten. If the time spent in our infant schools (from three to seven) is taken into account, our elementary course is generally longer than the American ; and yet ours is nothing like so ambitious a course. There is another difference between the two courses. In England our attention is pretty much confined to the "three R's;" in America, what we call "special subjects" are taught all along the line. A foreign language is often commenced in the lowest grade of the primary school; and the reports of Cleveland and Cincinnati prove with what success the plan is attended. Grammar, geography, and natural science are commenced at very early ages. I remember when the study of physiology was introduced into the rural schools of New York State. In fact, nearly twenty years ago the programme of some district schools in Chemung County (New York) was more comprehensive than in any public elementary school in England which I have ever seen.

But the materials for a close comparison between the studies and results of English and American schools are wanting. The decentralization of the American system effectually prevents the collection of any reliable data.

There is no prescribed course of study in any State, and although examinations are everywhere held, there is no uniformity of method or test. By studying the admirable reports published by the Boards of the large cities, one may form a pretty correct idea of their comparative progress, and may also learn in what respect their systems are essentially different from that in operation in the large towns of England. But outside the cities the American reports furnish no information by means of which the attainments of the scholars can be measured.

It is worthy of remark that American educationists do not appear to recognize that the absence of uniformity in study and examination weakens their system. The nearest approach to a uniform course of study which has ever been attempted by any State is to prescribe the text-books which shall be used, and where this has been done it has been sometimes resented, and the cry of centralization has been raised. It is obvious that it would be a great advantage to statesmen and statisticians, and to the nation at large, if there were some test by which the progress of scholars in each State could be definitely ascertained. But the municipalities are loth to surrender any part of their discretion, and it is certainly better that each district should be able to fix its own standard of education than that the State should have power to prescribe a low standard for the whole country. The results of the exercise of such a power are manifest in England to-day. Experience has proved that elementary education flourishes most where the provision for higher education is most ample. If the elementary schools of Germany are the best in the world, it is owing in a great measure to the fact that the higher schools are accessible to all classes. In England not only have the aims of the elementary schools been educationally low and narrow, but an impassable gulf has separated the people's schools from the higher schools of the country. In the United States the common schools have always produced the best results where the means of higher education have been most plentiful. "The common school is always feeble and inefficient where high schools, academies, and colleges are wanting. Educational science teaches that educational improvement works from the top downward, and not from the bottom upward. It was, therefore, with the wisest foresight that the Prussian Government, in undertaking the regeneration of the State through education, after the crushing defeat of Jena, began by the establishment of the great Frederick William University at Berlin. Since Sadowa, Austria is following this example of developing, strengthening, and liberalizing the higher education, not only for its own sake, but as a means of promoting general intelligence through the common schools. Our own history affords a striking illustration of this principle. Harvard College was, for a long period, the mainspring of the success of the common schools of Massachusetts." ([1])

The step from the common school to the high school or academy, and thence to the college or university, is generally an easy one in the States. The programme of the elementary school is usually framed in anticipation that scholars in considerable numbers will pass on to the high school.

The cardinal studies of the common school are reading and writing, grammar, arithmetic, and geography. Drawing and vocal music are also generally taught. ([2]) In the upper grades, history, book-keeping, natural science, and composition form part of the usual course.

In the Western schools, notably in those of Cincinnati, Cleveland, St. Louis, and Chicago, the teaching of German forms a prominent feature of the elementary course. In New York, also, German is taught in all grades of the grammar schools. The study of a foreign language promises to become much more general in the elementary course. Experience teaches that it facilitates advancement in English branches. The reports of the St. Louis, Cleveland, Cincinnati, and New York schools contain very valuable information under this head.

To obtain a complete view of the course of study in the chief cities, the reader must refer to the reports themselves; but as few will have that opportunity I have thought it desirable to print in Appendix B the Grammar course in New York and Boston, and the complete course (district and intermediate) in Cincinnati.

The schools of Boston have long been famous, not only

---

[1] Boston Report, 1874, p. 398. [2] Statement of Theory, p. 15.

in America, but throughout the world. There are signs that the supremacy of this city in educational matters is to be disputed by some of the Western cities, but for the present, at any rate, it is entitled to the first place. It has been already explained that the grammar schools are intended to complete the elementary course, begun in the primary schools. Of the new programme of study, Mr. Philbrick, the late superintendent, writes: "Since the adoption of this programme, I have studied the most approved courses of study in foreign countries, where the science is vastly more advanced than it is in this country, and I am gratified to find that our programme for elementary instruction is so nearly up to the standard of best existing models, both in respect to the subjects of study and the aims proposed in each." ([1])

The complete Grammar course will be found in Appendix B. The average age in the lowest class is nine or ten, and each class is supposed to require a year's study.

Let the reader compare this course with the code which up to the present has been in use in English schools. Of course, without the text-books before one, it is impossible to estimate exactly the range of the grade, but the attainments of the scholars may be partly measured by what they do in the primary schools. "Even in the third class," says the Superintendent, "it is not uncommon to find fluent reading, with distinct articulation, and a pleasant modulation of the voice." ([2]) The class referred to is in the primary schools, and would comprise the scholars in the first half of the second year of their attendance at school.

An important matter to consider is the gradation of the scholars according to age and acquirements.

In the Boston primary schools in 1874, the classes stood as follows:—

---

[1] Boston Report, 1874, p. 293. [2] Ibid, p. 379.

	No. of Scholars.	Per Cent.
First Class	2,985	16
Second Class	2,942	15
Third Class	2,949	15
Fourth Class	2,763	15
Fifth Class	3,293	17
Sixth Class	4,176	22 ([1])

"This table," says the Superintendent (referring to the report for 1873), "contains the most important information respecting the condition of these schools that can be presented in one statistical view. The eye of the expert will at once perceive its significance. It shows how well the pupils are advanced from class to class. The point to be arrived at is to make the percentage in the three upper classes equal that of the three lower classes." ([2])

In his Report for 1869 the Superintendent says: "The number promoted was 29·6 per cent. of the average whole number belonging. This is a high percentage; higher, I think, than has heretofore been obtained. If the promotions during the year amount to 33·3 per cent. of the number belonging, it is evident the pupils will average only three years in the primary school course, which is the time assigned in the programme. ([3]) So near an approach in practice to the theory of the system must be gratifying to its administrators. That the system of grading adopted works well is apparent. The Superintendent says: "If a child of the proper age enters the primary school at the right time, the chances are fifty to one that if his health is good and his attendance is regular he will get through the course and enter a grammar school in three years." ([4]) Under our English system the chances are reversed, and the odds are fifty to one against a child getting through the earlier standards in the proper time.

---

[1] Boston Report, 1874, p. 380. [2] Boston Report, 1873, p. 120.
[3] Boston Report, 1869, p. 225. [4] Ibid, p. 209.

The ages of the pupils in the primary classes in 1873 were as follows:—Five, 17 per cent.; six, 23 per cent.; seven, 20 per cent.; eight, 20 per cent.; nine, 17 per cent. As the pupils are supposed to have finished the primary classes at eight, here are 17 per cent. out of their proper grade—far too many, according to the opinion of the Boston school authorities. ([1]) How does this compare with the standing of English scholars?

In 1873 for England and Wales there were present at inspection 1,847,216 scholars. Out of this number only 752,268 were presented in standards at all, leaving over a million of whose standing or attainments no account was taken. Of the 752,268 selected scholars, the Education Department estimate that the number who ought, according to their ages, to have been examined in the first three standards was 388,178. The number actually examined in these standards was 621,172, of whom 233,535 were over ten years of age. Taking the whole number present at inspection, no enquiry is made respecting the progress of 59 per cent. of them. Of the remainder it is ascertained that $37\frac{1}{2}$ per cent. over ten years of age are still in standards suited for children of seven, eight, and nine years.

Of the rank of the Boston primary schools, Mr. Philbrick says: "In my address to the Committee on Teachers, last autumn, on foreign education, I was made, by some of the newspaper reports to say that our primary schools were very inferior to what was found abroad. I meant to say no such thing. I have never seen a better set of primary schools, take them together. What I did mean to say was, that I saw a trained master instruct a class of young children in a model school in Vienna more skilfully than I had ever

---

[1] Boston Report, 1873, p. 121.

seen any other teacher handle one. But, as a whole, the primary classes of pupils there, cannot bear a comparison with our own." [1]

The gradation of the grammar schools is not so regular as that of the primary schools, the withdrawal of scholars beginning to tell after the third year. Of the grammar schools the Superintendent says: "There is now generally a fair gradation in respect both to the age and attainments of the pupils from the lowest class to the highest."[2]

The following table shows the numbers in the different classes in July, 1874:—

Classes.	No. of Pupils.	Per Cent.
First Class	1,532	7
Second Class	2,365	10
Third Class	3,084	14
Fourth Class	3,941	18
Fifth Class	5,077	23
Sixth Class	6,181	28 [3]

Dividing the elementary course into three periods of three years each, we have the following results:—

	No. of Pupils.	Per Cent.
First three years	19,108	46·2
Second three years	15,199	36·8
Third three years	6,981	16·9

Considering that the schools embrace all classes, this must be acknowledged to be a very admirable result, although the Superintendent complains of the unequal numbers in the last six grades. There are too few pupils in the upper classes, and too many in the lower. For many years, however, the

---

[1] Boston Report, 1874, p. 380.
[2] Ibid, p. 386.   [3] Ibid, p. 390.

percentage of scholars in the upper grades has been steadily increasing, and at the same time the standard of instruction has been greatly raised. During the administration of Mr. Philbrick, extending over eighteen years, the proportion of increase in the high schools was 300 per cent.; in the grammar schools, 123 per cent.; and in the primary schools, 50 per cent. [1]

In the elementary schools of New York city, the average attendance in the primary grades in 1874 was 61,016; in the grammar grades, 35,233. [2] The difference between this showing and that of Boston is more apparent than real, since the primary grades in New York are supposed to embrace four years, while in Boston they only cover three years. The percentage of pupils in each grade was as follows:—

Primary Schools.		Grammar Schools (Male.)	
1st grade	11·8 per cent.	1st grade	4·8 per cent.
2nd „	13·4 „	2nd „	6·8 „
3rd „	14·7 „	3rd „	9·0 „
4th „	16·7 „	4th „	11·4 „
5th „	17·6 „	5th „	10·7 „
6th „	25·8 „	6th „	15·3 „
		7th „	20·0 „
		8th „	22·0 [3] „

The percentage of scholars in attendance during the first four years was 63·3; in the second four years, 36·6.

The Superintendent says: "All the classes in every school under the care of the Board have been examined at least once during the past year, and many of them several times, so that the work of every teacher employed in the schools has been brought under the minute supervision of the

---

[1] Boston Report, 1874, p. 278.
[2] New York Report, 1874, p. 4.   [3] Ibid, p. 30.

Superintendent's department and its character carefully ascertained and recorded." . . . " Of 2,112 classes thus examined, the instruction in 1,041 was found to have been excellent, in 901 good, 149 fair, in 20 indifferent, and in 1 bad." ([1]) . . . " Both as to instruction and discipline these results are exceedingly creditable to the schools in general, inasmuch as in more than 90 per cent. of all the classes examined the results were found to be deserving of commendation." ([2])

Comparing the course of instruction in the six primary grades in New York, extending over four years, with our English standards, taking arithmetic as the test subject, the complete primary course answers very nearly to our Standards I.-IV. The arithmetic of the last year in the primary course is much on a par with that of our fourth standard.

The mental arithmetic and drawing, and the object lessons, embracing instruction upon all common objects, such as colour, the human body, and familiar animals, parts and uses of limbs, geometric forms, plants, qualities in physical and natural science, &c., which are pursued through the whole of the primary grades, and which act as a powerful influence in stimulating the minds of children and inducing them to think, are almost wholly foreign to our ordinary English elementary schools.

The seventh grade of the grammar schools, which in point of time occupies the last half of the fifth year in the elementary course, is rather beyond our fifth standard, but not quite equal to our sixth. Above this there are six grades in the elementary (grammar) course. Through all of them pupils are instructed in reading, spelling, definitions, penmanship, arithmetic, mental and written. Geography, local and

---

[1] New York Report, 1874, p. 12.   [2] Ibid, p. 14.

descriptive, is taught in the five lowest grammar grades. It is omitted in the third and first, but the outlines of physical geography are taught in the second. Great attention is given to physical science. Oral instruction in elementary science is given through the five lowest grammar grades. By this means the pupil is instructed in the outlines of zoology, botany, mineralogy, physiology, and hygiene. In the third grade natural philosophy is taught, and continued through the course, with the outlines of astronomy and chemistry in the two highest grades. The history of the United States is taught in the fourth, third, and second grades. In the highest grade, ancient is added to modern history. Grammar, with the analysis, parsing, and construction of simple sentences, commences with the fourth grade, and continues and enlarges through the following grades to the highest, in which the pupil is practised in composition and impromptu exercises. Etymology, including the analysis and formation of words, receives special attention in the two highest grades. In the highest grade, algebra through simple equations, and the first book of geometry are taught. Some instruction in the principles of the Constitution of the United States is also given in the last grade. Phonography and book-keeping, architectural and mechanical drawing and designing are permissory in the highest grades of the course. There are also about twenty thousand pupils in the German classes of the Grammar schools. For the complete course in the Grammar schools see Appendix.

Leaving the comparatively long-established systems of New York and Boston, we come to the cities of the West, whose schools have developed with marvellous rapidity, although they do not yet approach the standard which it is the ambition of their citizens to reach.

The elementary schools of Cleveland (Ohio) show the following percentages of pupils in each grade :—

Grammar.		Per cent.	Primary.		Per Cent.
1st grade A	311	2·1	5th grade A	1,628	10·9
2nd „ B	576	3·9	6th „ B	2,495	16·9
3rd „ C	937	6·3	7th „ C	3,070	20·8
4th „ D	1,271	8·6	8th „ D	4,393	29·9
Total Grammar...		20·9	Total Primary...		78·5 [1]

As each of these grades is arranged for a year, we are able to compare the numbers under instruction at different stages with the Boston schools, with this result—

First three years	67·6 per cent.
Second three years	25·8 „
Last two years	6·0 „

A careful examination of the course of study leads to the conclusion that after the fifth grade ("A" Primary) all are higher than the English sixth standard. The written arithmetic in the primary grades does not, however, ascend so rapidly as under our code.

The questions submitted to Class C in the grammar grade (the third grade from the top and the sixth from the bottom, containing pupils in the sixth year of the course) at the examination in June, 1873, were as follow :—

"*Arithmetic.*—1. What is the cost of 372½ pounds of prunes, at 37½ cents a pound?

"2. If I spend $45·52½ for cocoa nuts, at 7½ cents a-piece, how many do I buy?

"3. Reduce ¼ of ⅜ to a simple fraction, and analyse the process. (No credit given without analysis.)

"4. Multiply ¼ by ⅜, and give complete analysis. (No credit given without analysis).

"6. Reduce 14 bushels, 3 pecks, 3 quarts to pints, and give complete analysis. (No credit given without analysis.)

"7. Find the g.c.d. of 362, 296, 312.

"8. Divide ½ of ⅔ of ¾ by $\frac{99}{11}$.

"9. How much cotton, at 15½ cents a pound, can be bought for $13¼?

---

[1] Cleveland Report, 1873, p. 38.

"10. A merchant owns $\frac{3}{8}$ of a stock of goods. If he sell $\frac{3}{7}$ of his share what part of the whole stock will he retain?

"11. If from a cask containing $31\frac{1}{2}$ gallons, $\frac{3}{8}$ of a gallon leak out per day, in how many days will one half the cask be lost?

"12. How does it affect the value of a fraction to divide the denominator by a whole number? Why? (No credit if the reason be not given.)

"13. From the sum of $2\frac{1}{2}$, $7\frac{5}{8}$, $2\frac{3}{8}$, take the sum of $1\frac{1}{2}$, $5\frac{1}{4}$, $2\frac{3}{8}$.

"14. Define subtrahend, minuend.

"15. How far will a locomotive run in 11 hours, at the rate of 16 miles, 25 rods, 2 yards an hour?

"16. How many cords of wood in a lumber yard, there being 17 piles, each of which is 11 feet long, 4 feet wide, and 6 feet high?

"17. If $4\frac{7}{8}$ yards of calico cost $5\frac{1}{4}$ shillings, what is the price per yard?

"18. A grocer bought $19\frac{3}{4}$ cwt. of sugar at $5\frac{1}{4}$ cents a pound, and sold the whole for $156·75; how much did he gain by the sale?

"19. A friend has $15\frac{3}{4}$ bushels of choice apples, and offers $\frac{3}{4}$ of them to me for $11\frac{1}{4}$ dollars. How much is that per bushel?

"20. What is meant by the least common multiple of two or more numbers?

"21. Reduce 5 yards, 2 feet, 3 inches to inches, and give complete analysis.

"22. If I have in different banks 141\frac{3}{8}$, 467\frac{3}{4}$, 417\frac{1}{10}$, and 348\frac{1}{11}$, how many dollars have I in all the banks?"

"*Grammar.*—1. Write the plural of chief, shelf, pony, monkey, molasses.

"2. Compare gentle, skilful, conscientious.

"3. Write the opposite gender of nephew, aunt, lad, belle, bride.

"4. Write five sentences, each one containing an irregular verb.

"5. Write five sentences, each one containing a transitive verb.

"6. Write sentences containing the possessive plural of I, he, she.

"7. Write two sentences, each of which shall contain the word 'mountain' as the subject. In the first sentence represent the subject as being acted upon, in the other as acting.

"8. Write a letter to your teacher, telling her what you think of the examination; whether you expect to pass or not; whether you wish to go to the higher grade next year, and if you have been in this grade more than a year you may urge that as a consideration. Make out as good a case for yourself as you can.

"9. Name two or three books you have read this year; or, if you have not read any, you may give the names of two of your school books, and state what part of each you have studied.

"10. When is a noun in the nominative case? Objective case?"

"*Geography.*—Locate the following: 1, Caspian; 2, Tigris; 3, Mont Blanc; 4, Rhine; 5, Teneriffe; 6, Siam; 7, Ceylon; 8, Sahara; 9, Tahiti; 10, Metz; 11, Liverpool; 12, Munich; 13, Bombay.

"14. What are the three principal rivers in France? 17. In South America. 20. In Africa. State in what general direction and into what does each one flow?

"23. What states or countries border on the Mediterranean Sea?

"24. What rivers flow into the Black Sea?

"25. In what longitude would a man be who had travelled 200° directly east from Greenwich?

"26. How many miles would he travel in going 180° on the Equator?

"27. Draw an outline sketch of the State of Texas.

"28. Describe the surface of Europe.

"29. What important city of the Atlantic plain a little further north than San Francisco?

"30. Through what countries of South America does the tropic of Capricorn pass?

"31. If you were to go directly north from Charleston, South Carolina, what great lake would you reach?

"32. What do the tropics mark?

"33. Through what countries, seas, and large islands does the Equator pass?"

"*Physics.*—1. What is the direction of the force of gravity? How may this direction be shown?

"2. What is meant by specific gravity? When does a body float on water?

"3. What is the direction of magnetic force? What magnetic instrument is based on this direction?

"4. How many kinds of electricity are there? How do the two kinds behave towards each other?

"5. What force is it that causes a body to appear as ice, or as water, or as steam?

"6. What is adhesion? What is capillary attraction?

"7. Give two examples of malleable bodies. Give two examples of ductile bodies. Give two examples of brittle bodies.

"8. How would you prove that air is elastic?

"9. What is a lever? The long arm of a lever is two feet, the short arm is one foot, at the end of the short arm is a weight of 100 pounds, what power must be applied at the end of the long arm in order to lift that weight?

"10. Explain how it is that water-pipes carry water to the upper storeys of houses in our city. What causes the water in a common pump to rise?

"*Spelling.*—Inaudible, Physician, Bureau, Precious, Vehicle, Subtile, Electrical, Strewn, Granaries, Roseate, Maniac, Labyrinth, Avalanche, Revenues, Soliloquies, Peril, Thraldom, Sceptre, Penitentiary, Annihilated, Inadequate, Presumptuous, Germinate, Balance, Separate." [1]

In addition to the foregoing examples are the questions in German. Over a third of all the pupils in the public schools studied German in 1873, or a monthly average of 3,572.

---

[1] Cleveland Report, 1873, pp. 177, 180.

The per cent. promoted to the next higher grade at the annual examination in 1872 was as follows :—

Grammar Grades.			Primary Grades.		
1st	A.	92·2	5th	A.	84·2
2nd	B.	82·5	6th	B.	80·8
3rd	C.	80·9	7th	C.	78·6
4th	D.	75·2	8th	D.	50·1 [1]

The average ages of children in the respective grades was as follows :—

Grammar	A.	14·4	Primary	A.	10·9
„	B.	13·7	„	B.	10·1
„	C.	12·9	„	C.	8·4
„	D.	12·2	„	D.	6·7 [2]

The reports of Mr. Rickoff, the Superintendent of the Cleveland Schools, would amply repay a careful study by English school officers; I regret that I cannot give them more attention.

The course of study in the famous schools of St. Louis is divided into seven grades, each grade including as near as may be an average year's work. The following was the classification of pupils in 1872:—

Normal	·39 per cent.
High School	2·60 „
1st grade (7th year)	2·65 „
2nd „ (6th „)	4·10 „
3rd „ (5th „)	6·83 „
4th „ (4th „)	11·45 „
5th „ (3rd „)	19·98 „
6th „ (2nd „)	18·66 „
[3] 7th „ (1st „)	33·32 „
or,	

---

[1] Cleveland Report, 1872, p. 43. [2] Ibid, Table vii., 1873.
[3] St. Louis Report, 1872, p. 25.

First three years .... 71·96 per cent.
Second three years .... 22·38 ,,
Last period .... 5·64 ,,

The elementary grades are intended to comprise a thorough course in "reading, spelling, writing, vocal music, geography, mental and written arithmetic, English grammar, history and Constitution of the United States, composition, and outlines of physics and natural history." [1]

German is taught in all the grades. In 1872 there were 10,244 pupils in German. Of these 7,827 were in the three lowest grades. [2]

The Cincinnati elementary schools, divided into "district" and "intermediate" departments, comprise eight grades, each grade arranged for a year. The classification of scholars in 1872 was as follows:—

Intermediate grades A. .... 3·0 per cent.
,, B. .... 5·5 ,,
,, C. .... 7·3 ,,
District grades D. .... 11·1 ,,
,, E. .... 12·8 ,,
,, F. .... 15·1 ,,
,, G. .... 15·4 ,,
,, H. .... 29·8 ,,

Reduced to periods of three years we have—

First three years .... 60·3 per cent.
Second three years .... 31·2 ,,
Last two years .... 8·5 ,,

---

[1] St. Louis Report, 1872, p. L.
[2] Ibid, 1872, p. 28.

The average ages of scholars in the different grades is as follows :—

Grade			Grade		
Grade A.	...	13·7	Grade E.	...	10·5
,, B.	...	13·1	,, F.	...	9·4
,, C.	...	12·3	,, G.	...	8·3
,, D.	...	11·4	,, H.	...	6·7

Seventy-five per cent. of the whole number were under twelve, and twenty-five per cent. over twelve years of age. This estimate does not include the pupils of the high school.

Upon the examinations for promotion in the district schools—that is, the five lower grades—the per cent. of passes was as follows :—

Grade D.	{ For promotion to intermediate grade }	...... 90·2 per cent.
,, E.	... For promotion to D.	...... 91·6 ,,
,, F.	,, E.	...... 87·4 ,,
,, G.	,, F.	...... 77·3 ,,
,, H.	,, G.	...... 68·1 ,,

Out of the twenty-two thousand pupils in the district schools only 166 were in the same grade two years, and only twelve in the same grade three years.

The report issued by the Board for 1873 contains the examination questions set at the annual examinations for that year in grades A to G. Grade G corresponds in respect to age with our Standard I, grade F with Standard II, and so upwards.

The written arithmetic in grade G is about equal to that set in Standard II. In grade F the written arithmetic is nearly equal to our Standard III, the money sums not being quite so difficult. In grade E the written arithmetic is about on a par with our Standard III. In grade D the written arithmetic partly answers to that of Standard V, and partly to that of Standard IV. In grade C the sums are more nearly equal to our Standard VI as far as the fractions go ; the other sums equal our Standard V. In grade B the arithmetical questions are harder than those set in Standard VI. Upon the whole, the conclusion is, that, so far as *written* arithmetic is concerned, our standards are a little above the corresponding grades, age for age, of the Cincinnati schools ; but, taken as a whole, our arithmetic is not anything like so exacting. In American schools the chief attention is given to mental arithmetic, and in these examinations the children are called upon to answer questions and solve mental problems which are not often attempted in English schools.

It is only in respect to arithmetic that any comparison is possible between the Cincinnati grades and our standards. In all other respects their course of study outruns ours. Commencing with grade G, grammar, object lessons, and German are taught over and above the ordinary requirements of our code; in the next grade (F) music is added; in grade E, geography is taken up; and in grade C, physics becomes a part of the course. We thus have in the elementary grades as ordinary parts of the course, besides reading, writing, and arithmetic—grammar, history, geography, physics, mental arithmetic, music, object lessons, spelling, and German. For the complete elementary course see Appendix B.

The Chicago schools, which have been rebuilt since the great fire, are divided into ten elementary grades—the first five (from one to five) constituting the grammar department, and the remaining five grades (from six to ten) the primary department.

The proportion of pupils in each grade, in 1873, was as follows :—

		Per Cent.				Per Cent.
1st grade	431 or	1·63	...	6th grade	2,401 or	9·1
2nd „	733 „	2·72	...	7th „	3,512 „	13·3
3rd „	1,137 „	4·27	...	8th „	4,236 „	16·06
4th „	1,752 „	6·59	...	9th „	4,187 „	15·9
5th „	2,324 „	8·75	...	10th „	5,649 „	21·43([1])

Supposing each grade to represent a year, the proportion of scholars at different periods would be as follows:—

First three years	53·39 per cent.
Second three years	31·15 „
Last four years	15·21 „

Of these scholars, about 73 per cent. were under twelve, and about 27 per cent. over twelve years of age.

The percentage of promotions in the various grades was according to the following table:—

Grammar Grades.		Primary Grades.	
1st.........	94·6	6th.........	85·5
2nd	76·9	7th.........	89·1
3rd	75·2	8th.........	77·02
·4th	78·2	9th.........	91·1
5th	72·07	10th	81·7 ([2])

In arithmetic, the grades below the third are not equal to those of Cincinnati, or to our English standards. In other respects the grades below the sixth are about on a par with our standards. The studies in the remaining grades are higher than our standards, those studies which are "special subjects" in our schools, being taught as part of the ordinary course in the upper grades of the elementary schools. of Chicago.

In 1873, 5,152 scholars were promoted in grades higher

---

[1] Chicago Report, 1873, p. 243.   [2] Ibid, p. 59.

than our Standard VI; more than half the number who passed the sixth standard in England and Wales during the same year. (¹)

In 1873 there were 3,724 pupils in the German classes in the Chicago district schools. Of these 1,525 were of German parentage, and 2,199 the children of Americans.

A passing word must be said of the night schools in the large cities, which are on a scale of real magnificence.

New York city has thirty-seven night schools, thirty-six of which are elementary and one is a high school. The average attendance in 1874 was 10,162. (²) The branches taught are English grammar and composition, arithmetic, book-keeping, penmanship, drawing, and German.

There are seventeen night schools in St. Louis, having over 4,000 pupils, whose average age is sixteen. A special feature of these schools is that one room in each school is set apart for the instruction of foreigners in English. (³)

In Boston there are eleven evening elementary schools, one evening high school, and four evening drawing schools. The average attendance in 1874 was 1658. (⁴)

The average attendance in the Cincinnati night schools in 1872 was 1,686. Besides the elementary night schools there is a high school, and a night school of arts and sciences. (⁵) The report of the Superintendent refers in high terms to the thorough organisation and unusual excellence of these schools.

In Philadelphia there are twenty-nine night schools, having over 8,000 scholars. (⁶)

Besides these large cities there are many others with famous night schools, amongst them being Baltimore, Lowell (Massachusetts), Lynn (Massachusetts), Jersey City, Newark

---

¹ Chicago Report, 1873, p. 59. ² New York Report, 1874, p. 4.
³ St. Louis Report, 1872, p. 101. ⁴ Boston Report, 1874, p. 360.
⁵ Cincinnati Report, 1873, p. 51. ⁶ Philadelphia Report, 1872, p. 11.

(New Jersey), Buffalo and Cohoes (New York), Pittsburg. (Pennsylvania), and Providence (Rhode Island).

(c) *Practical Outcome.*

The precise product of the common school is not to be learnt from the State reports, nor perhaps from any source ; but respecting the general result, guides are accessible which, if not altogether unerring, are sufficient for practical purposes.

By some means the natives of those States where the free school is well established have got the reputation of being a fairly-educated people. Either they have received a decent modicum of instruction, or they have a remarkable facility of concealing their ignorance, which is not written in characters that all who run may read; nor patent to the most casual observer, like that of the English labourer. Either, then, the American system has produced a satisfactory result, or else a conspiracy on a grand scale has been entered into by travellers from all nations, including such observers as De Tocqueville and Fraser, to deceive the world as to the measure of intelligence and information in the United States.

The simple ability to read and write, and that perhaps not well, is a very inadequate test of the acquirements of any people; yet it is often the best to be had. In this country the number of signatures to "marriage lines" supplies the only guide as to the proportion of illiterates. In the United States an attempt is made in taking the census to obtain precise information on the subject. This is not the kind of proof which one would choose if a choice were to be had. Though one appears sometimes to detect a modest pride in the declaration of the English peasant that he is "no scholard," yet it seems certain that most persons would hesitate to "write themselves down" as illiterate if they could help it. As a matter of fact, the returns of illiteracy in the census taken in 1850 and 1860 in the United States are said to be considerably under the mark. The accuracy of the returns for 1870 has not been, so far as I am aware, impugned. However this may be, no other information than that contained in the periodical census is supplied from official sources, and it must be taken for what it is worth.

Moreover, the figures from the census have been appealed to, though never actually adduced, to prove that the common school is a failure. It has actually been alleged that the census returns for 1840, 1850, and 1860 show a gradual increase in the proportion of "home-born white Americans" who are unable to read or write. Since there are vast numbers of children who are natives of the United States, but of foreign and illiterate parentage, and who do not inherit a love for education, even if this charge were true it would not amount to crushing evidence against the efficiency of the free school system. But it is easy to show that there is no atom of truth in the charge.

The census returns for 1840 do not distinguish between natives and foreigners. They give but one result—the number of adult white illiterates.[1] There is no basis, therefore, for a comparison between these and the later returns, in order to show either an increase or decrease in the proportion of illiterate natives.

In the census for 1850, and again in that for 1860, natives and foreigners were separated. The following table shows the comparative percentage of white native illiterate adults ("aged twenty and over") in 1850 and 1860:—

---

[1] Commissioner's Report, 1870, p. 470.

State.	Per cent. 1850.	Per cent. 1860.	Increase of Native Illiterates.	Decrease of Native Illiterates.
Alabama	20.35	17·73	—	2·62
Arkansas	27·77	18·93	—	8·84
California	3·55	6·76	3·21	—
Connecticut	·41	·28	—	·13
Delaware	13·91	13·42	—	·49
Florida	19·13	16·19	—	2·94
Georgia	20·08	17·97	—	2·11
Illinois	11·89	6·66	—	5·23
Indiana	18·70	10·81	—	7·89
Iowa	10·79	5·61	—	5·18
Kansas	—	6·32	—	—
Kentucky	21·60	17·60	—	4·00
Louisiana	17·05	11·46	—	5·59
Maine	·77	·78	·01	—
Maryland	10·19	5·97	—	4·22
Massachusetts	·24	·26	·02	—
Michigan	3·40	2·73	—	·67
Minnesota	12·57	2·26	—	10·31
Mississippi	11·67	10·44	—	1·23
Missouri	17·20	13·67	—	3·53
New Hampshire	·54	·61	·07	—
New Jersey	4·42	3·63	—	·79
New York	2·01	1·45	—	·56
North Carolina	30·68	24·29	—	6·39
Ohio	7·19	4·89	—	2·30
Oregon	1·70	5·59	3·89	—
Pennsylvania	4·82	3·26	—	1·56
Rhode Island	1·53	1·30	—	·23
South Carolina	13·62	11·50	—	2·12
Tennessee	25·92	20·05	—	5·87
Texas	14·74	7·65	—	7·09
Vermont	·40	·60	·20	—
Virginia	19·91	15·84	—	4·07
Wisconsin	1·86	1·35	—	·51

[For verification of Table, see p. 474 of Commissioner's Report, 1870.]

But not only was there a relative decrease in the proportion of native white illiterates between 1850 and 1860, but in many of the States there was an actual decrease in the numbers of native illiterates, including both white and coloured.

In Connecticut they decreased from 1,293 to 925, in Indiana from 69,445 to 55,903, in New York from 30,670 to 26,163, in Ohio from 56,958 to 48,015, in Pennsylvania from 51,283 to 44,930, and in Rhode Island from 1,248 to 1,202. [1] Therefore, whatever increase there was in the number of illiterates in these States during this period—and there was an increase in most of them—it must have been owing to immigration.

While there was the large decrease which has been noted in the proportion of native white illiterates between 1860 and 1870, there was, on the other hand, an increase during the same period in the proportion of foreign illiterates in the following States: Alabama, Arkansas, Delaware, Illinois, Iowa, Maine, Massachusetts, Michigan, Mississippi, Missouri, New Hampshire, Ohio, Pennsylvania, Rhode Island, South Carolina, Tennessee, Texas, Vermont, Virginia, and Wisconsin. [2]

By this means the general percentage of illiteracy was kept up. The total illiteracy of the white population (native and foreign) is given as 9 per cent. in 1840, 11 per cent. in 1850, and 9 per cent. in 1860. Including the coloured population, it was in 1850, 23 per cent., and in 1860, 20 per cent.

Comparing the returns of 1840, 1850, and 1860, illustrated by maps or "views," the report of the Commissioner for 1870 says: "View 10 shows us that the per cent. of illiteracy increased from 1840 to 1850, not only in the whole country, but especially in New England (chiefly from foreign sources), and in some of the Western and Southern States. View 11, on the contrary, shows how it was diminished in

---

[1] Report of Commissioner, 1870, p. 472.   [2] Ibid, p. 474.

the next decade, not only in the whole country, but in most of the Southern and Western States, though still increasing in New England, in Mississippi, and on the Pacific slope. View 12 shows that during the whole twenty years there was some improvement in respect to the per cent. of total illiteracy in the whole country, and in what States and parts of the country it was most marked. But a great increase of the evil is seen in New England and the Middle States, as also in Michigan and in one or two other States, for the main causes of which we need not go beyond the fact of ignorant immigration from Canada and Europe, and of slave migration towards the extreme south and south-west." [1]

And, again, in reference to the causes of illiteracy: "But already the maps we have been looking at and studying, point to several important causes—the influx of ignorance from Canada, and through Canada and to the great Atlantic ports, by immigration; the influence of slavery in the plantation States, and even more among the poorer farming population flowing westward from the older and wealthier portions of Virginia and North Carolina to the mountain valleys and to the newly-settled parts of those States, and of Kentucky and Tennessee, and even beyond the northern banks of the Ohio; the peonage and other adverse causes bearing upon the untaught population of New Mexico; the influences which have come down from some of the early settlers and immigrants of New York, Pennsylvania, and some other States, as compared with the school influences inherited in New England; and unfavourable circumstances and difficulties in new and sparse settlements in the pioneer Western States." [2]

The census returns for 1870, so far as they are given in the latest reports of the Commissioner, do not enable us to

---

[1] Commissioner's Report, 1870, p. 501. [2] Ibid, p. 502.

make a comparison with the results of 1850 and 1860, since the figures and calculations do not refer to the same ages.

The lessons of the last census are anything but cheering to patriotic Americans. The per cent. of adult illiterates for the whole country (States and Territories), including the native and foreign, white and coloured population, is enormously high—17 per cent. for males, and 23 per cent. for women. This is nearly as high as the English percentage, which, according to the report of the Registrar-General in 1872, stood at 19 for males, and 26 for women. ([1])

But this sad condition cannot be justly laid at the door of the free school system. In those States where the free school has penetrated, and had time for development, very different results are found.

The following table shows the percentage of adult illiterates, native and foreign, white and coloured, in the principal free school States:—

STATE.	Percentage of Illiteracy.	
	Male Adult.	Female Adult.
Connecticut	6·40	9·12
California	6·70	11·14
Illinois	7·16	11·16
Indiana	10·09	16·77
Iowa	5·30	8·37
Maine	3·38	3·91
Massachusetts	7·97	12·27
Michigan	6·04	7·22
New Hampshire	3·73	4·29
New Jersey	7·50	10·70
New York	6·91	10·18
Ohio	7·64	12·10
Pennsylvania	7·75	14·26
Rhode Island	10·58	16·13
Vermont	7·61	7·03
Wisconsin	7·01	10·17 ([2])

[1] 35th Report of Registrar-General, p. XIV.
[2] Commissioner's Report, 1872, p. 962.

It is sometimes said that immigration is an insignificant element in the production of illiteracy. The reverse is capable of the most complete demonstration.

If Indiana is excepted from the States named in the preceding table, the actual numbers of foreign illiterates (ten years old and over) are greater than the numbers of native illiterates (white and coloured) of the same age.

The figures are as follow :—

State.	Native.	Foreign.
Connecticut	5,078	23,938
California	9,520	22,196
Illinois	90,595	42,989
Iowa	24,979	20,692
Maine	7,986	11,066
Massachusetts	7,912	89,830
Michigan	22,547	30,580
New Hampshire	1,992	7,934
New Jersey	29,726	24,961
New York	70,702	168,569
Ohio	134,102	39,070
Pennsylvania	126,803	95,553
Rhode Island	4,444	17,477
Vermont	3,902	13,804
Wisconsin	14,113	41,328
Total	555,001	649,887 [1]

Going a step further, it will be found that in these States the proportion of illiterates amongst foreigners enormously exceeds the proportion of native illiterates.

The next table shows the proportion of native illiterates, ten years old and over, to the whole native population in the States named, in comparison with the proportion of

---

[1] Commissioner's Report, 1872, p. 956.

foreign illiterates, of the same age, to the whole foreign population :—

States.	Proportion of Native Illiterates.	Proportion of Foreign Illiterates.
Connecticut	1·33	21·06
Illinois	4·47	8·34
Indiana	7·35	9·85
Iowa	2·52	10·10
Maine	1·38	22·63
Massachusetts	0·71	25·42
Michigan	2·46	11·41
New Hampshire	0·69	26·76
New Jersey	4·14	13·21
New York	2·17	14·80
Ohio	5·84	10·48
Pennsylvania	4·25	17·52
Rhode Island	2·74	31·54
Vermont	1·37	29·27
Wisconsin	2·04	11·33 ([1])

But these figures do not fully explain the whole extent of the obstruction caused by immigration, since amongst those who are classed as native illiterates are large numbers of children of foreign parentage, who do not immediately come under free school influences.

It has been alleged that the foreign population in the States is drawn from countries where more attention is devoted to popular education than in America. This is only partially true. The last census shows that of the foreign population 3,115,583 (including only 140,835 Scotchmen) were born in Great Britain, Ireland, and British America, as

---

[1] Note.—The above percentages are calculated from statistics contained in the Commissioner's Report for 1872, pp. 942, 956.

against 1,690,533 born in the German Empire, and 316,219 in Austria, Bohemia, Hungary, Denmark, Norway, and Sweden. ([1])

The truth, then, is that the free school system has had a double mill-stone round its neck, and it may be taken as proof of its vitality that the combined influence of slavery and illiterate immigration has not been able to destroy it. How greatly its efforts have been paralysed by these opposing forces history will show; but, notwithstanding the incubus it has been forced to carry, it has still kept the percentage of illiteracy lower in the States than it is in England, where the State Church has taken education under her wing.

But it is well for America that her educationists are not content to glorify themselves for what has been done. One of the healthiest signs in the country is the apprehension and alarm which the census statistics of illiteracy have caused, and the widespread conviction that the common school must not only be extended, but must be made more efficient than it has been. There is no blinking, on the part of statesmen or school officials, of the task which lies before the nation—a task which must strain to the utmost the capacity and efficiency of the common school system. But if the work to be done is mighty, there is a mighty energy at the heart of the system, as those who love America best are glad to know.

The results of the common school are apparent to every traveller in the free States. No one ventures to deny that the Americans of the North and North-West are an educated people. But it is said that their intelligence and education are due to other agencies—the press, for example. No doubt, the press exercises a most powerful influence in stimulating intelligence, but it must have a basis of instruction for its work. Have we not a press in England as powerful and as

---

[1] Commissioner's Report, 1872, p. vi.

intelligent as the press of the United States? The churches then, it is said, do the work. But we also have churches, which, alas! for education, have taken it under their protection.

Englishmen are not likely to be led off the trail by such controversial subterfuges as these. In whatever land they find schools in abundance, full of energy and enthusiasm, even if frequently rude in organisation and imperfect in detail, and find also an instructed population, they will be pretty sure to connect the education with the schools. For the share of the common school in the work of national education, I refer, in conclusion, to the report of Bishop Fraser, to whose work I have been greatly indebted. He says of the system, that, "if not accomplishing all of which it is theoretically capable, if lacking some elements which we justly deem primary, and of which Americans themselves feel and regret the loss, it is still contributing powerfully to the development of a nation of which it is no flattery or exaggeration to say that it is, if not the most highly educated, yet certainly the most generally educated and intelligent people on the earth." [1]

With this testimony Americans may well be content.

---

[1] Fraser's Report, p. 203.

VII.

REVIEW.

To sum up, it is not pretended by Americans—it never has been advanced by the section of Englishmen who are attracted by American institutions, and especially by the common school—that their system is even theoretically perfect, much less that it produces in practice the utmost measure of success. It is the habit of American educationists, ungrudgingly, and with sincere admiration, to give the palm to Germany. Nor is this a mere complimentary recognition of excellence. It is shown to be genuine by the manner in which they are accepting from Germany, not only lessons in the details of educational science, but vital principles like compulsion.

But while the German system is mature, and has probably reached, or nearly reached, the highest point of excellence, that of the United States is still in its infancy. Therefore, the most important consideration for Americans is whether they have started upon the right lines. The process of undoing, as we find in England, is sometimes more difficult and laborious than that of constructing.

That which impresses us most in regard to America is the grasp which the schools have upon the sympathy and intelligence of the people. Those of the cities are the lions of America. The intelligent foreigner, and also, as it would appear from some recent criticisms, the unintelligent foreigner who visits the States, into whatever town he goes, is taken to the schools as the first objects of interest. Amongst public questions education occupies the foremost place, and of all topics it is that upon which the American speaker is most ready and most willing to enlarge. Public intelligence has recognised the fact that the highest and best interests of the nation are indissolubly bound up with the question. Thus every American feels not only a personal but a patriotic interest in the welfare of the schools. Owing to this popular feeling their organisation possesses a spring and force and energy which are in strong contrast with the sluggish instincts of the parochial system.

This widespread popular regard which constitutes the propelling power, appears to be chiefly due to two features—government by the people, and ownership by the people. It is a vast proprietary scheme, in which every citizen has a share. While it is undoubtedly true that all do not set the same value on school rights, it is also certain that their existence immensely stimulates public interest and diffuses a sense of responsibility through the entire community.

For no reason is the principle of local government more dearly prized, than because of the control which it gives the people over the schools. They would be as ready to surrender all municipal powers and privileges as to transfer their management to a sect or to any other private organisation. This recognition of responsibility is the mainspring of the system, and the cause of its best results. In another generation the same feeling will prevail in England. It would undoubtedly create surprise and opposition if, in this country, an unrepresentative body were to claim the right to control the municipal government of a town. Yet such a city as Gloucester still acquiesces in the important work of education being transacted by voluntary societies. It might with equal or even greater discretion, transfer to the Dean and Chapter the functions of the Corporation.

That the decentralisation of the American system is excessive, and leads to inefficiency in certain cases, has already been explained. That any radical change will be made is highly improbable. The advocates of a federal law under which large powers would be vested in the National Bureau of Education, are at present in a hopeless minority. The principle of State sovereignty is too firmly rooted in the public mind, and has worked too well, to be easily shaken. Of late years, however, a disposition has been manifested to increase the powers of State Superintendents and State Boards of Education; and, in the view of Englishmen, this is a movement in the right direction. The principle of local government should be supplemented by adequate power in the Executive of the State to meet those cases in which, from public apathy or other causes, the local authorities fail to perform their duties. It is also worthy of the consideration of American educationists whether the State taxes, which now provide a very considerable portion of the school income, could not be administered by a State department under some such scheme as our English plan of "payment by results." Under such an arrangement a minimum standard might be fixed for each State, which would ensure the performance of certain definite work in a year. The danger that School Boards would limit their efforts to earning the State grant would not be great in a country where public emulation is so general. New York would still compete with Boston, and Chicago with Cincinnati, in the development of the best methods and the attainment of the highest results; and the example of all the great cities would

R

still have its due effect upon the country towns and districts. The powers of the State Executive would then, as now, be subject to the will of the people, whose voice would determine the general policy of education. It appears to be extremely improbable that, in a country where the best intelligence circulates so commonly through all ranks of society, the schools would fall into a narrow groove, or lose the energy and independence which now characterise them. While such a scheme would incalculably benefit the backward districts, it need not, in any appreciable degree, hamper the more advanced and energetic localities.

A Ministerial department at the head of the school system in each State need not be inconsistent with the most ample exercise of local discretion; and there would be no reason to fear that in America such a department would be permitted to usurp the functions of School Boards. It is difficult to see how compulsion can be effectively carried out otherwise.

The advantages of the establishment of the National Bureau of Education cannot be over-estimated. By bringing together the results in each State educational thought and enterprise have been greatly quickened. Even with its present limited powers, the action of the Bureau is full of promise for the future.

The means provided for local inspection or supervision are very ample, the rule, subject to a few exceptions, being an inspector or superintendent for each county. The benefits of the plan are apparent from the State reports The duties of the County Superintendent are largely consultative; he is more the friend and adviser of the local school managers than their superior officer. In some respects he possesses advantages over English inspectors. The latter is an officer whose visits are generally looked forward to with apprehension, and back upon with relief.

The unexpressed but well-understood rule is, that he is not to be afforded too much insight into the exact condition of the schools. The most popular inspector is the one whose duties sit most easily upon his shoulders, and who is content with the most brief and cursory inspection.

In some of the States it is the duty of the County Superintendents to examine the scholars. The State Reports give very little information respecting the examinations in the country districts, but in the towns they appear to be of the most thorough and searching description.

The popularity of the schools is attested by the large aggregate attendance. It is evident from the number of scholars enrolled annually, that, practically, all American children, and a large percentage of the children of foreign parentage, attend school at some period. In the cities a large number attend with great regularity, but a very considerable percentage are also very irregular in their attendance. In the country districts irregular attendance is the greatest bane of the schools. For this there is but one remedy—compulsion.

It cannot be denied that compulsion of any kind is repugnant to American ideas of government. In a country where individual freedom is a passion, to force children into school, even for their own good, appears at first sight to be an arbitrary proceeding, and opposed to popular government. Nevertheless, so strong is the determination to have efficient schools, that Americans have, to a large extent, overcome their natural repugnance to compulsory school laws, and in every State the question is being urged upon the consideration of the several Legislatures.

Indirect compulsion, in various forms, has been tried, and has failed under circumstances which afforded the most favourable conditions for the experiment. The co-operation of employers in Connecticut and Rhode Island, and other

States to carry out the law, afforded an excellent opportunity for testing its value. The result of the experiment has proved that there is a class of parents who cannot be reached except by direct compulsion. The experience of England and the United States on this subject points to exactly the same conclusion.

The laws providing for direct compulsion which have been passed in seven or eight States are regarded as tentative. The evidence as to their operation is at present incomplete. In Michigan, it must be admitted that the result has not been satisfactory. That is owing, however, not to any strenuous opposition to the law, but to the want of proper means of administration. It only indicates the necessity of a vigorous State department to superintend the action of the local authorities.

The period of school attendance is being gradually lengthened throughout the Union. In this respect the laws are behind the spirit of the people. The school terms in many of the States are considerably longer than the periods required by law. The present compulsory laws only aim at securing from 200 to 140 attendances during the year, half of which must be consecutive. With the gradual increase of the school term, and as the idea of compulsion becomes familiar, it will no doubt be possible to increase the number of compulsory attendances.

Hitherto the work of American educationists has not, except in some of the large cities, been greatly obstructed by a "religious difficulty." The first aim of the schools has been to provide a good secular education, leaving religious instruction mainly to the Churches and the Sunday schools. The schools have generally been opened by some short religious exercise—the reading of the Bible, prayer, or singing of a hymn. A very large measure of success has attended this practice. With it the great majority of Americans are well content, and were it not for the Catholic element in the population the custom would probably continue unchallenged, at any rate for the present. As it is, however, there are indications that the peace which has hitherto so generally prevailed is about to be disturbed. The conflicts which have already taken place in New York, Cincinnati, and other cities, afford sufficient evidence that the common school will not be permitted to continue on its present basis without a contest. Either it must be abandoned, and the parochial school substituted for it, or the teaching given in it must be purely secular. Of these alternatives, there can be little doubt that the overwhelming majority of Americans would prefer the latter. The parochial or denominational system is opposed to the whole current of American feeling. The sentiment of the country must undergo the most radical change before it will be possible for it to obtain national recognition. No such revolution is probable. The Roman Catholic element consists chiefly of the Irish population. The American is not readily inoculated with Irish ideas. On the contrary, the Irishman who seeks a home in the United States becomes an American. The conversion of the Roman Catholics to the common school, as a national institution, is more likely than the conversion of Americans to a denominational system.

But it does appear probable that the common school will, in time, be made purely secular. Large numbers of schools, including all those of such cities as Cincinnati and St. Louis, are wholly secular already. And the same movement has commenced in Chicago. The idea that the secular school is godless or infidel does not exist outside the Roman Catholic communion. There is nothing horrifying to the Protestant American in teaching secular subjects at one time and place, and leaving religion to be taught at another time and place. The fact that these secular schools do exist and find favour with the American people is noteworthy, especially when it is remembered that religious feeling is much more general, and has taken a far stronger hold upon the masses, than in this country.

It has been seen that the profession of teaching in America labours under some serious disadvantages. The want of a sufficient number of normal training schools to supply the requisite staff of trained teachers is the most marked deficiency. How to surmount this obstacle is one of the most important problems of discussion at the present time. The energy and resources of American educationists will be severely tasked in providing adequate means of training, and it must necessarily be a work of considerable time. In the interval, the deficiency of training is much less observable than in other countries, on account of the great natural aptitude of Americans, and especially of American women, for the work of teaching.

The shortness of the school term and the low rate of salaries also combine to keep the profession of the teacher below its proper level. In both these particulars considerable progress has been made within the last few years, and the improvement still continues.

As a set-off to the disadvantages which have been noted, the standing of the teachers is socially high. In this respect the contrast with England is remarkable.

The extensive employment of women as teachers has been due partly to natural causes, but more to the conviction, which experience has confirmed, that women are better qualified for the work of elementary teaching than men.

In all the discussions upon the means of supplying trained teachers, the English method of employing pupil teachers finds no support. The universal opinion is that the age when teaching may begin must be raised rather than lowered. The example of Germany in regard to this point is accepted as of higher authority than that of England.

The reports issued by the School Boards of the great cities—Boston, New York, Philadelphia, Cincinnati, St. Louis, Chicago, Cleveland, Washington, and many others—afford the fullest information respecting the studies of the schools, the ages of the scholars, and the results attained. A study of these reports, which American officials are always glad to supply, will satisfy any English reader how far the elementary schools of the cities of the United States are in advance of our own. If the elementary schools of England were free, and the course of study were raised above its present pauper level, a large proportion of the middle classes would be glad to send their children to them, in preference to inefficient private schools. There would then be no reason why the elementary schools of our large towns should not rival those of the great American cities, the results of which, in the absence of compulsion, must be regarded as very admirable.

Outside the larger cities it is not possible to ascertain the definite results of the schools. Much depends upon their size, much upon the public spirit of each locality, and much more upon the skill and energy of the teacher. There may be a great want of thoroughness, but there is sufficient evidence that these schools supply to the children generally, that invaluable and indispensable primary instruction which gives the start, and places the tools in the hand of every child, to be used afterwards as capacity or opportunity may determine. To use Mr. Morley's words, they are " not so absolutely illusory as to turn out the majority of their workers in the numb ignorance of an English boy to whom the Third Standard is an impassable bridge." (¹) This is faint praise. To

---

[1] "The Struggle for National Education," p. 105.

those who have observed the working of hundreds of district schools in the small towns of Massachusetts, New York, Pennsylvania, and Ohio, it will seem to be absolute injustice.

The great popularity of the American system, which is manifest from the large enrolment and the amount of taxation contributed for its support, and which indeed no one disputes, is due mainly to one cause—that the schools are free. In sending a child to school no leave has to be asked, no patron has to be consulted, no charity has to be sued for or accepted. The schools belong to the people. They are proprietary schools.

Hundreds of parents in the school districts visit the schools every year—and not only the schools of the great cities, which have been called "show" schools.

In 1872, in Southbridge (Mass.), the registers recorded 907 visits, an average of over 47 to a school. As the schools averaged about 300 sessions annually, the visitors averaged one to every six sessions. [1] The visits to the schools of Port Huron (Mich.), in 1872, numbered 734. [2] These were the visits of parents and others interested in the work, and do not include those of superintendents or officials.

The amount which is expended upon public education in the United States is greater than in any European nation, except, perhaps, Portugal. In his work upon popular education, M. Emile de Laveleye tabulated the amount of public school expenditure in different countries. In Upper Canada it amounted, in 1863, to 4 francs 16 centimes per head of the population; in Lower Canada (1863) it was 4fr. 40c.; in Denmark (1867), 5fr. 28c.; Saxony (1867), 2fr. 17c.; Sweden (1867), 1fr. 23c.; Norway (1863), 1fr. 50c.; Luxembourg (1867), 3fr. 10c.; Netherlands (1868), 2fr. 72c.; Bavaria

---

[1] Mass. Report, 1873, p. 212.   [2] Mich. Report, 1873, p. 355.

(1864), 1fr. 50c.; Belgium (1869), 2fr. 60c.; France (1864), 1fr. 56c.; England (1870), 2fr.; Spain (1866), 1fr.; Portugal (1864), 32fr. ([1]) In the Cantons of Switzerland, the expenditure varied considerably. In Neuchatel it was 4fr. 62c.; in Zurich, 5fr. 37c.; in Lucerne, 2fr. 60c.; in Basle (Ville), 7fr. 50c.; in Geneva, 2fr. 30c. ([2])

The above figures include the total expenditure upon public education. A reference to the table on page 71 *ante*, will show that *the amount raised by taxation only*, for public education in twenty-six of the United States, averages six shillings and ninepence, or eight francs, per head of the population.

And yet the most intelligent Americans consider that their system is cheap, and all look upon the free schools as a good investment. The reasons for this are not far to seek. The prosperity of a district is often determined by the character of its schools. The reports show that the rapidity with which a district is settled is frequently decided by their reputation. ([3])

Again, it is well known that an average of the estimates made by many large manufacturers, employing many thousands of hands, gives, as a result, that a knowledge of the elements of a primary education, reading and writing only, adds 25 per cent. to the value of a simple labourer. ([4])

The wealth of a State is found to be in proportion to the amount of education within its borders, and it will generally be seen that the average wealth per head of the population is in the inverse ratio to its illiteracy. In Connecticut, the average wealth is $1,141 per capita; in Illinois, $835; in Massachusetts, $1,463; in New Jersey, $1,038; in New York, $1,483; in Ohio, $838; in Pennsyl-

---
[1] "L'Instruction du Peuple," p. 483.   [2] Ibid, p. 334.
[3] See New York Report, 1872, p. 62; West Virginia Report, 1872, p. 76.
[4] Commissioner's Report, 1871.

vania, $1,081; in Rhode Island, $1,366. In States where the free school system has not been in operation it sinks to between $200 and $400 per capita. And this notwithstanding that they may be States of superior natural resources. ([1])

On the other hand, it is not difficult to show that ignorance and crime, and ignorance and pauperism, are intimately allied. The proportion of criminals totally illiterate varies, in the different countries of Europe, from 35 to 95 per cent. In the United States the percentage of prisoners "totally ignorant" or "very deficient" varies, in New York and Pennsylvania, from 33 to 60 per cent.; in the Central North-West, from 46 to 75 per cent.; in the West and Pacific, from 31 to 50 per cent.; and in the South from 60 to 85 per cent. ([2]) Ignorance amongst criminals is the rule, and education the exception.

In Pennsylvania, Ohio, and Illinois, the proportion of paupers among the illiterates is sixteen times as great as among those of common education. "Although the effect of ignorance in producing crime is very great, yet its effect in producing pauperism is greater. If, then, society has to pay so heavily for keeping a part of its people in ignorance, would it not be wise and prudent to educate them?" ([3])

The last extract sums up the whole matter. The people of the United States have come to the conclusion that it is cheaper to pay for schools than gaols and poorhouses. Public intelligence has accepted the fact that education is the best investment for the community; therefore it is that education taxes are paid cheerfully. What is spent in this direction returns many fold in increased national power and wealth. The people seem to have taken to heart the wise words

---

[1] Commissioner's Report, 1872, p. 945. [2] Ibid, p. 589.
[3] Ibid, p. 601.

of Wm. Penn respecting the education of his children: "Let their learning be liberal; spare no cost, for by much parsimony all is lost that is saved."

For the benefit of some timid people in this country, it may be well to remark that free schools have not yet sapped the independence of the American character. Mr. Dawson found in Ohio that the man who looked after the buggy would do so on no other condition than that he should sit down at his master's table. The truth is that the free school encourages and stimulates independence. Mr. Mill said: "Instruction does not enervate, but strengthens and enlarges the active faculties; in whatever manner acquired, its effect on the mind is favourable to the spirit of independence. Help in this form has the opposite tendency to that which, in so many other cases, makes it objectionable; it is help towards doing without help." If it may be said without offence, the majority of the persons who urge that the independence of the working classes would be destroyed by free schools are not anxious to promote the kind of independence which education encourages. It clashes with the Catechism, or with that part of it which teaches a child to "order himself reverently and lowly to all his betters."

Another cry against free schools has been provided by Professor Fawcett, who expressed an opinion in the House of Commons, that if the "demand for free education were not resisted, encouragement would be given to socialism in its most baneful form."

Men who regard Professor Fawcett himself as a revolutionist, are grateful to him for this warning. They have taken up his cry, and free education has been denounced as the first step towards communism. In this light it is important to consider what has been its effect in the United States. There for a hundred years the free school has been growing in power, and obtaining a stronger and stronger hold upon the people. Can it be said, even by those who hold American institutions in most horror, that socialism has been developed to an alarming extent?

The advocates of free schools have had no *arrière pensée*—the demand for free food has not followed the cession of free education. The theory of communism has had attractions for a few enthusiasts, amongst them some of the best intellects of America. But the attempt to reduce the theory to practice has had no success. The communistic societies of the United States no more represent the American people, than the New Forest Shakers represent England. This is the best practical reply to Professor Fawcett's dismal apprehensions.

The free school controversy in the States is at an end, and reformers and educationists are now united in devoting their attention to points of detail in which imperfections are admitted. That there is room for improvement no one denies, but there is nothing sluggish in action, nothing retrogressive in principle. Every movement is forward. In the ultimate accomplishment of the destiny of the Republic, the usefulness and success of its education system and its influence as a first measure in the development of national power and prosperity are unlimited.

APPENDIX.

APPENDIX

APPENDIX A.

That a considerable amount of misconception respecting popular education in our own and other countries should exist in the public mind is not astonishing. At first sight, the education of the people would appear to be a question about which there could be no great difference of sentiment, at all events as to principle. This is the view which strikes the mind of the layman. But then steps in the priest, bringing confusion with him; and education becomes good so far only as it can be cast in a Roman Catholic, or Episcopal, or Methodist mould. Thus it is made a "burning" question, and all sorts of prejudices and passions are enlisted. The road, apparently free enough at first, becomes blocked. In the struggle of rival creeds and factions, facts become distorted, and different views are often taken of precisely the same phenomena. This is the reason that there has been and is a great deal of loose writing and more loose talk respecting educational systems.

The Rev. Dr. Rigg, who has laid a heavy indictment against the American system, complains that this has been the case, especially respecting education in the United States. As to the main fact, I am inclined to think that he is right, but I cannot admit that the misrepresentation has proceeded from the League side of the controversy. In the end that will be determined by public judgment. That much error and misconception have gone abroad no one doubts. Consequently, the most opposite views of the educational experiment in the United States are now held by different sections of the English public.

To put the people right, "to set forth the general outline of the case truly," "to dissipate radical and altogether misleading misconceptions," is a task to which Dr. Rigg felt himself called. Accordingly, he devoted a chapter of his book on National Education to "School Education in the United States." He has since contributed an article on the same subject to the *Quarterly Review*, and has addressed a series of letters to one of the daily papers on the question. I have no special authority for stating that he is the author of the article in the April number of the *Quarterly*, but the style, and certain peculiar methods of dealing with evidence, stamp it as his work unmistakably. The reviewer confirms the opinions of Dr. Rigg, and Dr. Rigg, in his letters to the *Hour*, endorses those of the reviewer. Not only so, but, like the gentleman in "Pelham" who sent billets-doux to himself, Dr. Rigg, under his own sign-manual, quotes the reviewer as an authority. In this manner it is sought to give cumulative force to very scanty and untrustworthy evidence.

As, upon Dr. Rigg's own showing, his great object in writing is to correct the errors and misrepresentation which he says have been diligently propagated, the public has a right to expect that he himself will be accurate. As he strongly condemns certain methods of deduction in other people, he cannot be excused if he follows the same methods himself.

There are two charges to which Dr. Rigg has laid himself open. In the first place, he has not taken sufficient pains to see that his "facts" are facts. Wherever he makes a particular statement, the chances are that he is mistaken. Wherever he speaks generally—"generally and broadly," as he phrases it—he is almost certain to be wrong. And secondly, he has drawn wholesale inferences, most unfairly, from particular cases which are altogether insufficient to establish a general conclusion.

He complains that—

"It has been customary for persons to take the model schools of Boston, or of New York, as examples of the United States' National system ; whereas they are quite exceptional, and only serve to illustrate the enlightenment and liberality of public educationists in these two cities." (P. 100, "National Education.")

Also that—

"The ideas and projects of Massachusetts theorists have been accepted as if they were the facts of universal American law and life ; whereas they have never become realities even in New England, and have found no place whatever in the States generally." (P. 459, *Quarterly*.)

Dr. Rigg does not tell us by whom and when these mistakes have been made, and I do not know where to look for the particulars. It would certainly be a grave mistake, and one which no person having American experience would make, to assume that Slabtown can compete with Boston, or Texas with Massachusetts, in the matter of public education. Massachusetts has set the pattern which other States have tried, with more or less success, to imitate, and Boston and New York have supplied the types for other cities.

The advocates of free common schools for England have done precisely what the States severally have done—they have chosen for their example the State where the system has been most highly developed and produced the best results. It is a very different thing to say that the pattern represents the condition of affairs throughout the Union. It is probable that speakers and writers for the League have more often referred to the schools of Boston than those of any other city. The reason for this has been that in this city only have been found in practice three of the most essential features of the scheme advocated by the League—representative government, free admission, and compulsory school attendance. But I am not aware that anyone has said that the Boston type was universal.

Dr. Rigg has fallen into just the opposite error. He has selected the schools of some of the smallest and most primitive States in the Union, and presented them as affording a favourable comparison with the more populous and advanced free school States. Thus he instances Vermont "as affording a favourable sample of what is done in the way both of teaching and training, when compared with the generality of States, especially North-Western and Western." (P. 111.) An old report of Vermont supplies the stock on which he chiefly trades, both in his book and the *Quarterly*.

Again, from such facts as he has collected he draws most unwarrantable inferences. He enlarges, for example, upon the admitted deficiency of normal training in the States, and he says that this means that the teachers "have received, for the most part, no thorough instruction at all, even as scholars."

But Dr. Rigg will probably admit that in making deductions it is first of all desirable to be sure about your premises.

I propose to make some extracts from his articles, and by a reference to authentic reports to show how far his work can be accepted as a true statement of the case. It will be quite impossible for me, in the space at my disposal, to indicate all his errors or to trace their source; I shall content myself with correcting some of his principal mistakes. So much I feel called upon to do as a duty to the system to which I am not without obligations.

The italics throughout are my own.

The following extracts explain Dr. Rigg's ideas of the manner in which the funds to support the free schools are provided.

On page 93 he says:—

"Nor is the 'common school' the creation of the several States. These States, as well as Congress, do indeed in many instances require the township, or district, or county to provide 'a requisite supply of common schools,' and also furnish some quota of aid, *chiefly, I believe, from the revenue of land appropriations, towards the support of the schools.*"

And in another place—

"An *easy* and *costless* method of maintaining the school and the teacher was also plain enough to all; it was to *assign* land out of the common possessions of the town or township for such maintenance." (P. 95.)

A reference to the table on page 62 *ante*, will show how erroneous is the idea that the revenue derived from land appropriations constitutes a large proportion of the school moneys. The revenue arising from permanent funds is there compared with the income raised by taxation.

Respecting the relative proportion of the State tax and the income derived from endowments, the following figures will be instructive. The first column represents the interest on the permanent school fund (chiefly, but by no means wholly, accumulated from land grants), and the second the amount of the State tax (corresponding to our Government grant).

S

State.	Interest on Endowment.	State Tax.	Report.
	$	$	
Maine	19,558	386,166	1874; p. 9
Rhode Island	28,899	90,000	1874, p. 49
Connecticut	132,848	199,272	1874, p. 24
Massachusetts	87,356	nil.	1873, p. 151
New Jersey	35,363	1,307,331	1873, p. 8
New York	335,000	2,500,032	1874, p. 21
Pennsylvania	nil.	700,000	1873, p. xlvi.
Ohio	231,276	1,486,793	1873, p. 4
Michigan	194,479	465,912	1873, p. 59
Indiana	420,519	1,190,626	1874, p. 4
Illinois	528,811	900,000	1872, p. 13
Iowa	275,789	605,353	1873, p. 11

Again, referring to the power of the State, Dr. Rigg says : " Its grants of money are altogether trivial." (P. 99.) And also: "The large State grant would be the lever, the only possible lever, by means of which any such change in the actual condition of the schools, and of school administration in the States, might be brought about. Of such a consummation there would seem to be no prospect whatever at present." (P. 131.)

These extracts reveal the most complete ignorance of the finances of the American system. By comparing the annual State tax, as given in the last table, with the average attendance, we can get at the precise amount of the State grant per child in average attendance in each State. The following table explains itself. The State tax is taken from the reports of each State, and the average attendance from the Commissioner's Report, 1873 (p. 511).

State.	State Tax.	Average Attendance.	Amount per Scholar.
	$		$ ct.
Maine	386,166	103,548	3.75
Rhode Island	90,000	22,435	4.00
Connecticut	199,272	67,599	2.94
New Jersey	1,307,331	87,840	14.89
New York	2,500,032	503,240	4.96
Pennsylvania	700,000	511,418	1.36
Ohio	1,486,793	407,917	3.64
Michigan	465,912	170,000	2.75
Indiana	1,190,626	286,301	4.15
Illinois	900,000	329,799	2.72
Iowa	605,353	204,204	2.96

From this table it will be seen that in the free school States, the State tax, or Government grant, is often larger than in England.

One extract from the *Quarterly Review* will show how extremely incorrect are Dr. Rigg's ideas respecting American currency.

He says—

"In New York the requisite funds are derived from (1) *a State school tax of one and a quarter million on the taxable value of real and personal property;* (2) an equal amount from the city and county; (3) one twentieth of one per cent. on the taxable property of the city and county of New York; (4) the balance derived from the municipal taxes and revenue of the city of New York, but not to exceed $10 per capita on the whole number of children taught. *The total cost last year was not less than $2,800,000*, the entire average number of children taught being not quite 108,000; that is to say, the cost per head for each scholar was $26." (P. 458, *Quarterly*.)

The items numbered 1 and 2 would give Dr. Rigg two and a half million dollars. He has estimated the rest, and put the whole cost for last year at "not less" than $2,800,000. But in 1872 the expenditure was $3,196,117, and in 1873 it had risen to $3,537,730. Last year, I have no doubt it was more. Dr. Rigg evidently does not comprehend the terms of the United States currency. The State raises a tax of *one and a quarter mills* on the value of real and personal property, and out of this the city receives a share, and the city and county furnishes an equal amount.

Dr. Rigg has taken *mills* to be a contraction for millions!

Upon the subject of free schools Dr. Rigg, writing in 1873, more than two years after the entire disuse of rate-bills, says: "It is a mistake to suppose that the American common schools are universally free. In a considerable number of the States 'rate-bills' are still in general use." (P. 95.)

The dates of the abolition of rate-bills will be found on page 75 *ante*.

Respecting graded schools, Dr. Rigg makes the following statement:—

"Graded schools are not the rule in the States; they are the rare exception. They are far from universal even in Massachusetts, although they may be nearly so in the city of Boston. Such schools, indeed, could hardly be the prevalent type of public elementary schools, except for large towns." (P. 100.)

Let us see. In the school statistics contained in the Commissioner's Report for 1872, the cities are classed under three heads—class A, containing 10,000 inhabitants or more; class B, containing over 5,000 and less than 10,000 inhabitants; and class C, containing less than 5,000 inhabitants. There were 153 cities in class A, 108 in class B, and 131 in class C. Reports had been received from 141 in class A, 82 in class B, and 103 in class C. Of those cities from which reports had been received, it appears that 130 in class A, 81 in class B, and 97 in class C reported that their schools were graded. (See p. 614—683, Commissioner's Report, 1872.)

Again, he says, of high schools—

"Very few of the towns of the States indeed, outside of Massachusetts, except the very largest, have 'high schools,' a sort of school which corresponds with our superior grammar school, organised on a comprehensive modern basis. Many have not even a grammar school in addition to the primary school." (P. 102.)

Of the cities above referred to, 123 in class A, 77 in class B, and 88 in class C report high schools (v. Commissioner's Report, 1872, p. 624). In Illinois there were, in 1872, 34 towns having high schools; in Indiana, 24; in Iowa, 22; in Maine, 10; in Massachusetts, 15; in Michigan, 23; in New York, 16; in Ohio, 29; in Pennsylvania, 17; and in Wisconsin, 15. These were the numbers three years ago. Without doubt they have largely multiplied in the interval.

Of the scholars in the Boston schools Dr. Rigg makes the following evidently random statement :—

"Even in Boston, undoubtedly the best educated city in the Union, the number who never pass beyond the primary stage—that is, who leave school at eight or nine—is very considerable, amounting, indeed, to one fifth of the whole number year by year, only four out of five passing forward into the grammar school." (P. 103.)

The complete answer is contained in the Superintendent's Report for 1871, p. 132. He says: "All the pupils of the primary schools are expected to pass into the grammar schools, and this expectation is practically realised."

Mr. Philbrick also says, in the Boston Report for 1872 (p. 229), that the primary schools "during the year receive upwards of 4,000 new pupils, who enter school for the first time, and transfer about the same number to the grammar schools."

On page 102 Dr. Rigg says—

"Nor even in New York and Boston do more than a small fraction of the children pass onward through the grammar and high schools, or even through the grammar school."

One is led to wonder what Dr. Rigg considers a small fraction. In Boston, it appears from the Superintendent's Report for 1874 (p. 189), that the returns (which, however, were admitted to contain some slight inaccuracies) show that forty-two per cent. of the pupils go into the highest class of the grammar schools. The Boston school officials do not think so highly of this result, but when in England we are able to pass forty-two per cent. of the pupils into even the sixth standard, we shall not call it a small fraction.

Dr. Rigg, writing in 1873, gives the training colleges in the chief States as follows :—

"Massachusetts is the best supplied; it has four training colleges. Pennsylvania has three. New York State, with four or five millions of population, and some 17,000 teachers, had, till lately, only one training college; within the last three years a second, for the city and county of New York, has been established. The great State of Ohio has no training college." (P. 113.)

The Commissioner's Report for 1873 contains a list of training colleges in the States, from which it appears that Massachusetts had six, Pennsylvania ten, New York nine, and Ohio ten. (See p. xxxi.)

Dr. Rigg impeaches the public spirit and educational zeal of the citizens of Maine. He says—

"It is evident that some of the Maine schools cannot be open more than three or four weeks in the year—just so long, probably, as the 'district' share in the State school fund will serve, without any local tax, to pay an amateur teacher who happens to be out of a situation." (P. 118.)

The best answer to this may be given by quoting an extract from a recent report. The State Superintendent for Maine says, in his report for 1872 (p. 30) :—

"The sixth source of school revenue consists in the voluntary contributions by towns, voted in the annual town meeting, additional to the amount required by law; also additional sums voted by school districts to prolong the regular term. As these additional sums are merely voluntary, their amount will depend upon various conditions—the general educational interest, the activity of one or two individual citizens, the good or poor school work, the enthusiasm awakened by teachers, &c. This revenue has generally been from twenty to thirty per cent. of the amount required by law. The total excess reported this year is $232,406."

On the subject of compulsion Dr. Rigg assumes that he is exceptionally well informed, and he proceeds, according to his lights, to instruct the English Public, but he makes blunders at every step.

He says (we quote from his "National Education," p. 117)—

"It is often said that school attendance in the States is compulsory. This is so, as respects the letter of the law, in some few of the States, chiefly the New England States and New York ; and some attempt is made in Rhode Island, and also, I believe, though not so strenuously, in Boston, and one or two other towns of Massachusetts, to carry out the law."

When this was written there was no compulsory law in the State of New York, the truant law in Rhode Island had never been put in operation, and Boston was the only city in the Union in which compulsion was thoroughly enforced. In the article in the *Quarterly* he contradicts his book, so far as New York is concerned. "The first legislative attempt in the State of New York to carry out 'compulsory education' was passed into law on the 11th of last May" (p. 424). In Rhode Island, he says, "a law of compulsion has of late been enforced with some strictness" (p. 438, *Quarterly*). The facts in regard to Rhode Island are these : Previous to 1870, Town Councils were authorised "to make all needful provisions and arrangements concerning habitual truants" (School Laws, chap. 70, sec. 1). In his report for the year ending April 30, 1871, the School Commissioner says : "Chapter 70, relating to truant children and absentees from school, is wholly ineffective, inasmuch as no penalty follows a neglect to fulfil its requirements. Not a city or town in the State has taken action as authorised and required by this section" (Report, 1872, p. 27). Upon the recommendation of the Board of Education, the Act was amended, by making it obligatory upon the towns to take action under the section here referred to. The first section of the amended law runs as follows : "Town Councils shall make needful provisions and arrangements concerning habitual truants and children not attending school, or without any regular and lawful occupation, or growing up in ignorance, between the ages of 6 and 16 years" (p. 129 of Report for 1874). I have read the reports from 1870 to the end of 1873, and I cannot find that a single town had carried out the law up to that date. The Town Council of North Providence passed an ordinance in accordance with the requirement of the Act, and it was sent to the State Commissioner for approval in 1873. While his sympathies were in favour of the regulations, he was unable to approve them, as being legally invalid. (¹) The reports of the Town Superintendents abound with complaints of the evils arising from irregular attendance. The law prohibiting the employment of children in factories, has long been wholly inoperative (vide p. xiii, Rhode Island Report, 1872).

In a note on page 425, *Quarterly Review*, Dr. Rigg discusses with an air of much legal learning, the difference between English and American compulsion. He says—

"But direct compulsion in the United States assumes a totally different form from what is found in any other country, and such as would by no means agree either with the ideas or the needs of this country. The truant officer is a kind of educational policeman, and is not an officer of the School Board, but of the State. He is appointed to deal directly with the boy as an offender against the State law, being neither at school nor at work. The offender is sent, on a sentence of a magistrate, to a penal school, sometimes called a truant school, sometimes a house of industry or a place of detention, sometimes a reformatory school. The parent is not proceeded against, and no account is taken of mere irregularity of school attendance as such."

This Dr. Rigg considers of so much importance that he quotes it in the *Hour*. He evidently confounds compulsory laws and truant laws—between which, as so great an authority ought to have known, there is a wide distinction. Nearly every State which has a direct compulsory school law makes provision to enforce the law against the parent. By the law of Massachusetts parents are required to send their children to school under a penalty of $20 for each offence against the law (Fraser's Report, p. 36). In Texas parents are liable to a penalty of $25 for not sending children to school (sec. 6, Free School Law, 1871). By the law of Michigan parents are liable to a fine of not less than $5 nor more than $10 for the first offence, and not less than $10 nor more than $20 for every subsequent offence (sec. 3, Compulsory School Law). By the law of New Hampshire parents are liable to a penalty of $10 for first offence, and $20 for second and every subsequent offence. (²) The compulsory law for the district of Columbia, passed in 1864, requires parents to send their children to school under a penalty of $20 (Washington Report, 1872-3, p. 137). By section 4 of the compulsory law of Connecticut it is provided that parents and others violating the Act may be punished by a fine of $5 for every week during which they fail to comply with its provisions.

Dr. Rigg appears to be quite ignorant that compulsory laws have been passed in Connecticut, New Hampshire, Texas, Nevada, district of Columbia, and Michigan.

In dealing with statistics Dr. Rigg displays a carelessness, to say the least of it, highly censurable. On page 440 *(Quarterly)* he gives the following statistics, taken from the Report of the Commissioner, 1872 :—

"In the State of New York the population which is regarded as of school age is returned as 1,502,684, the 'number enrolled' as 1,028,110, the

---

[1] R. I. Report, 1874, p. 95.
[2] See 3, Compulsory School Law, New Hampshire.

'average attendance' as 493,648, the 'average absence' as 534,462. In Massachusetts the returns are as follow: School population, 282,485; enrolled, 276,602; average attendance, 205,252; average absence, 71,350. In Pennsylvania the returns are: School population, 975,753; enrolled, 834,313; average attendance, 536,221; average absence, 298,092. In Illinois: School population, 882,693; enrolled, 662,049; average attendance, 329,799; average absence, 332,250. In Indiana: School population, 631,549; enrolled, 459,451; average attendance, 286,301; average absence, 173,150. In Connecticut (one of the best educated States in the Union): School population, 128,468; enrolled, 113,588; average attendance, 79,511; average absence, 34,077. In Ohio: School population, 1,073,274; enrolled, 1,028,110; average attendance, 493,648; average absence, 534,462."

It is a small matter that for the correct Ohio figures he substitutes, no doubt by accident, the "enrolment," "average attendance," and "average absence" in New York State. What follows, however, strikes me as of some consequence. He says—

"These statistics show that, even during the brief school year, which, except in cities, varies from three or four months to six or seven, the attendance is very unsatisfactory. *It must be remembered, too, that this is the return for the school population of all classes.*"

It is hardly credible that Dr. Rigg should omit to include the column showing the attendance at private schools; but it is nevertheless true. He thus leaves out nearly a quarter of a million scholars for these seven States, while he represents that they are included. This is a fair illustration of his ordinary habit of writing. To ascertain the numbers in private schools he was not required to examine and analyse the State reports. The information was supplied for him in the same table from which his other figures were gathered.

A correspondent of the *Schoolmaster* complains that Dr. Rigg's method of dealing with these figures is not fair. He says: "The fact that the scholars are reckoned to reach twenty-five per cent. of the population is never brought out, but the consequent necessary fact that the attendance is irregular is made prominent over and over again."

Upon the subject of private schools it is noticeable that Dr. Rigg is exceedingly disingenuous. When it helps his immediate contention he represents that the public schools include all classes of the population; in another place, and in order to support another argument, he dwells upon the large numbers of the higher classes educated in private schools; and, again, he states that the very lowest classes are not found in the public schools. Here are three statements in reference to New York city, each of which is used in its turn to illustrate the particular point for which Dr. Rigg is immediately contending:—

"The New York schools are for all classes, and include not only 'primary' but 'grammar' departments." (P. 441.)

This is intended to show that, the attendance at the public schools being small, education in the city is anything but general.

"Private schools are still in use in the States, especially for the children of the more refined and highly educated classes . . . . They abound in such cities as Boston, Philadelphia, and New York." (P. 444.)

Here he endeavours to prove that private schools are undermining public schools.

"Such being the complete scheme and provision of public education in New York, for all classes of its citizens, except, indeed, the very lowest, of which the children are not found in these public schools." (P. 448.)

This is intended to convey the idea that low results cannot be accounted for by the presence of a low class of pupils.

In reference to the decentralisation of the system Dr. Rigg says (p. 435, *Quarterly*)—

"The entire absence of central authority appears in every part of the Commissioner's Reports . . . Although the Bureau was established in 1868, the Commissioner in 1872, had to report that seven States, headed by Kentucky, made no return of the number of scholars in the State, and that sixteen did not give the 'enrolment' during the year, nor the average attendance."

Then in a note he adds: "No statistical summary as to these points is given in the report for 1873."

Dr. Rigg appears to have read the report with his usual care. He may find the summary he requires on page 511.

Amongst the perpetual surprises which Dr. Rigg prepares for his readers, nothing is more startling than the following extract :—

"In the great State of Missouri, with St. Louis for its capital, the intelligent and vigorous State Superintendent seems to have a hard fight. There is a great, and it would seem a growing, dislike to the school tax and to the principle of 'free schools.'"

It is not too much to say that no mind, except one warped out of all shape by prejudice, could find colourable evidence in the recent Missouri reports to support such a conclusion.

In the seventh report—that to which Dr. Rigg refers—the Superintendent says of the general spirit of the State—

"A desire to read and gain information has been quickened as if by some magic inspiration ; and the monthly periodical, the weekly and daily newspapers, have been more eagerly sought for, and more widely distributed than ever before. The miscellaneous book trade receives so powerful an impetus as to astonish the most hopeful." (P. 10.)

The schools "have shared in the general boon of progress. They have increased in number ; they have increased in power and efficiency. They find to-day a largely increased circle of friends and supporters." (P. 10.)

Later on, the same report says—

"The public school system needs to be kept no longer on trial in Missouri. With us it is no more an experiment. It has already demonstrated its adaptation, efficiency, and necessity." (P. 126.)

There are complaints about taxation, it is true, both numerous and urgent ; but it is the unequal incidence and distribution of the taxes which make the grievance. There is not a line in the report to justify the statement that there is a growing dislike to the principle of free schools. I have read the reports of the County Superintendents with great care, and can affirm that the evidence of a growing feeling in favour of free schools is overwhelming. There are only 16 counties that report dissatisfaction, while there are 56 that report an increasing public sentiment in favour of the system. Even in those counties where the enemies of free schools are found, the reports do not show that there is a growing dislike to the principle. Reading the reports for 1872 and 1873, I have found but one county where it is distinctly stated that the free schools are decreasing in popular favour. The evidence in the report for 1873 is even more emphatic than that in the preceding report. While only 9 counties report that there is dissatisfaction respecting the school taxes, 67 report that public sentiment increases in favour of the schools and the system.

The length of the school term and school life is another subject upon which Dr. Rigg is habitually incorrect. In his book (p. 119) he says—

"The school age throughout the States begins several years later, and is continued *correspondingly* later than in this country."

There are only three States where the school age is of the same length (10 years) as in England—viz., Massachusetts, South Carolina, and California. In the other States it extends over 11, 12, 15, 16, or 17 years. (See Commissioner's Report 1873, p. 510.)

In the *Quarterly Review* (p. 438), Dr. Rigg says the schools of Missouri "are open, on an average, four and a half months." He adds: "The schools still further South are open, on an average, for yet a shorter time than in Missouri."

An examination of the school terms in the States south of Missouri shows that the average is over $4\frac{1}{2}$ months. (See Commissioner's Report 1873, p. 511; Commissioner's Report, 1872, p. 609.)

"Florida," says Dr. Rigg, "reports 2 months 15 days" (p. 439, *Quarterly*.) In the Commissioner's Report for 1872 (p. 609), the school year in Florida is stated to be $4\frac{2}{3}$ months; in the Commissioner's Report for 1873 (p. 511) it is given as 102 days.

On p. 445 *(Quarterly)* Dr. Rigg attempts to show that the common schools in New York are being undermined by corporate schools and denominational schools :—

"In New York city, what are called the corporate schools, and, with these, the 'denominational schools,' do no inconsiderable share of the work of primary education. The Report of the Board of Public Instruction for 1872 shows that the percentage of increase in the average attendance at the common schools has steadily diminished since 1862, having been 61 per cent. increase for the period 1857 to 1862, 21 per cent. increase from 1862 to 1867 (inclusive), and no more than 9 per cent. from 1867 to 1872; whereas during the same intervals the average attendance at the corporate schools had increased successively 34 per cent., 47 per cent., and 36 per cent."

This statement looks alarming in its nude form. When the proper explanation is given it is found to be without importance. Dr. Rigg omits to state that the corporate schools are included in the New York statistics as common schools, and that they participate in the school fund. They are in reality children's aid societies, where young pupils are fed and clothed as well as taught. That such schools should be found necessary in a city of the size and character of New York is not wonderful, and the idea that they threaten the public school system, of which they are a part, is simply ridiculous. The New York Report for 1871, says that "the movement has been greatly stimulated within the last few years by liberal donations from the State." Dr. Rigg is also careful not to state the reason why the attendance at the city ward schools has not of late increased in the same proportion as formerly. During the last period to which he refers, the laws relating to the children of non-residents have been enforced, thus preventing the children of Brooklyn, Westchester county, and Jersey city from attending the New York city schools. Several thousand pupils were removed from the schools in 1871 under these regulations. (New York Report, 1871, p. 14.)

Another of Dr. Rigg's "facts" which needs correcting relates to the term for which teachers are engaged. In his book (p. 123) he refers to the schools as taught "not often by the same teacher for two terms together, very rarely for three, scarcely ever for all the four terms of the year."

Again, in the *Quarterly* (p. 422), he says—

"The teacher, throughout the States, except in a few of the largest cities, is paid by the month and engaged by the term."

Upon this Dr. Rigg lays great stress, referring to it again and again. The truth is bad enough, but let us have it. At the meeting of the National Education Association held at Boston in 1872, attended by teachers and school officials from all parts of the Union, the Hon. John Swett, of California, formerly a New England teacher, read a paper on the engagement and examination of teachers. In it he referred to the rule throughout the Union— "A teacher holds the office only one year." "This annual election system was handed down to us from the primitive New England 'town meetings.' I believe that here in Boston, and in all New England cities and villages, and, in fact, in most parts of the United States, it is still kept up." (Proceedings of National Education Association, 1872, p. 73.) In the discussion which followed, a general assent was given to this statement, and it was determined to wage a war of independence "against the outrageous system of the *annual* election of teachers."

This brings me to the consideration of Dr. Rigg's strictures upon American teachers. It is very difficult to account on any charitable supposition for the feeling he displays, especially towards women.

The animus with which he writes on this subject is one of the most conspicuous features of his work. That he should deplore the want of training, admitted by all Americans to be a grave defect, is natural enough; but he goes beyond this, and speaks of them as a class in terms of contumely and contempt—which come with a very bad grace from one who is himself a teacher. He says their labour is not "skilled labour;" they are "more often smart" than able; they are "teaching casuals." He even descends to question their devotion to their duty: "Their teachers are not to be compared to those of our own country in respect of fitness for their office and devotion to their work" (p. 141). Their fitness being the question, why "devotion to their work"?

Upon women he is especially severe. Referring to certain small schools in Vermont, he says—

"No wonder that such schools are left in charge of women" (p. 439). "Young women may commonly be seen teaching scholars of the other sex little younger than themselves. This has sometimes been lauded as one of the admirable points in what is spoken of as the American school system. In simple truth, however, it is the result, not of theory or of choice, but of necessity." (P. 426, *Quarterly*.)

The necessity he explains in three ways—first, because men are not to be had on account of the low salaries; secondly, by reason of the excess of females over males in the Eastern States; and, thirdly—save the mark!—because the "reputable and energetic daughters of New England freehold farmers," who formerly devoted themselves to factory employment, have "found school teaching to offer better and more congenial attractions to them than the mills." (P. 428, *Quarterly*.)

Massachusetts is an Eastern State, having an excess of female population, and a large excess of female teachers—the proportion being seven eighths females, and one eighth males. Let us see how far this has been the result of theory or necessity. The report of the Board of Education (1873, p. 14) says—

"For upwards of thirty years this process of diminution in the number of male teachers and increase in the number of female teachers has been going on. During past years the Board and their secretaries have frequently referred with approbation to the substitution of female for male teachers in our schools as a movement in the direction of progress. But the time must come, if it has not actually arrived, when it will be necessary to consider seriously whether the best interests of education do not require some limitation of this movement. If it be true, as most persons will probably admit, that females have superior aptitude for certain departments and situations in teaching and disciplining, is it not equally true that males have superior aptitude for other departments and situations?"

That the excess of female population is not sufficient to explain the preponderance of female teachers is evident from the fact that in many States where there is an excess of males, female teachers are the more numerous. In Ohio the excess of male population is about 10,000; in Illinois, 90,000; in Kansas, 40,000; in Iowa, 50,000; in Missouri, 70,000. The percentage of female teachers in these States is as follows:—Ohio, 56 per cent.; Illinois, 56 per cent.; Kansas, 54 per cent.; Iowa, 61 per cent.; Missouri, 35 per cent. (See Missouri Report, 1873, p. 43.)

The Superintendent for Missouri says on this subject—

"The figures I have quoted demonstrate that where the public school system is in its best estate the percentage of female teachers is greatest. The mere fact of a preponderating female population, as we have seen, does not account for the fact. The only conclusion is that, for the majority of these schools, women make the best teachers. It is also true that the same amount of money will produce better teaching talent among women than among men. That women should receive less than men for the same work, simply because they are women, no right-minded person can admit. But that women of equal qualifications with men can be obtained for less wages may be accounted for by a reference to other causes. The pursuits open to self-dependent women are fewer than those which men may enter. Pre-eminently among these, and strikingly adapted to the constitution and peculiarities of the sex, stands the business of teaching. The market supply, therefore, of men, is not so great as that of women; and when for any reason a good male teacher is demanded, he is harder to be found than a good female teacher. Hence the higher price paid for him. If the inferences I have drawn respecting the excellence of women for teachers appear shadowy, let us come nearer home for our facts. The schools of our large cities, St. Joseph, Kansas city, and St. Louis, it will be admitted, are better schools than can be found, as a rule, elsewhere in the State. In the schools of St. Joseph forty-one teachers are employed, of whom seven only are males ; in the schools of Kansas city thirty-five teachers, of whom twelve only are males ; and in St. Louis 613 teachers, of whom seventy-one only are males. In the last-named city women are employed as principals in some of the district schools—schools which contain ten or twelve rooms—and when so engaged they receive the same salaries as would be given to men in the same situation." (Missouri Report, 1873, p. 44.)

Here is another shaft which Dr. Rigg aims at female teachers :—

"It would, beyond question, be better on all accounts if the young women were in much larger proportion destined to be given in marriage, and to devote themselves to family cares and child-training at home, and if public school teaching were far more largely in the hands of trained and able masters." (P. 430, *Quarterly.*)

How thoroughly he misses the mark is evident when it is remembered how brief the school life of female teachers is, and how great a difficulty it entails upon the American system.

If this book should fall into the hands of any American teachers, they may be consoled for Dr. Rigg's criticisms by reading, in the extract which I have quoted from Bishop Fraser's report (*ante,* p. 194), the judgment of an English gentleman upon their class, and one eminently qualified to give a reliable opinion.

Dr. Rigg discusses the question of illiteracy at considerable length, and besides much that he charges "generally and broadly," he makes certain definite allegations which can be seized and examined.

On page 135 of his book he says—

"Indeed, the amount of actual illiteracy in the States is far larger than appears to be generally known in this country. As is intimated by Mr. Barnard, the Commissioner of Education, in the extract from his report quoted by me at the beginning of this chapter, the successive censuses of the States in 1840, 1850, 1860, showed a gradual increase in the proportion of *home-born white* Americans who can neither read nor write."

The extract from Dr. Barnard to which he calls attention, is as follows :—

"Startling and humiliating statistics of the national census of 1840, 1850, and 1860, as to the number of the *white adult population* unable to read and write in certain States, and for the whole country."

Readers must judge for themselves whether Dr. Barnard's reference to the "white adult population" can be twisted into an intimation that the censuses show a gradual increase in the proportion of "*home-born white* Americans" unable to read and write.

In the article in the *Quarterly* Dr. Rigg slightly modifies the statement in his book. He says (page 432)—

"During the decade 1850-1860, the number of illiterates largely increased, but the proportion appears to have diminished, especially among the native-born illiterates."

It will be seen, however, that he still leaves on record his statement respecting the increase of "home-born white" illiterates. The particulars respecting each State will be found in the table on page 231 *ante*. The proportion of native white illiterates in all the States decreased, between 1850 and 1860, from 10 per cent. to 7·57 per cent. Nor was there any large increase in actual numbers. In 1850 they were returned as 808,024—in 1860, as 819,541; an increase of 11,517. (Commissioner's Report, 1870, p. 478.)

In support of his charges in regard to illiteracy, Dr. Rigg quotes from a pamphlet written by Dr. Leigh, a writer apparently after Dr. Rigg's own heart. Dr. Rigg has succeeded in extracting from Dr. Leigh's book a paragraph which gives colour to his statements. But Dr. Leigh is bound by the tables and statistics which he uses, and these establish beyond question that there was a relative decrease in native illiteracy between 1840 and 1860. Any reader can satisfy himself by referring to the Commissioner's Report for 1870.

On page 430 *(Quarterly)* Dr. Rigg says—

"There is more illiteracy in the States than has generally been supposed in England. There were altogether in the United States, according to the census of 1870, of the population ten years old and upwards—unable to read, 4,528,084; unable to write, 5,658,144; of whom 4,880,271 were native-born Americans."

This is an imposing array of figures. It is not strictly accurate, because Dr. Rigg has included the Territories. Many of the illiterates are native-born Americans in the purest sense, since the aborigines are embraced in the figures. Nearly three millions also of these "native-born Americans" are of the African race.

Dr. Rigg goes on to say—

"It is not surprising to find that in the Southern States illiteracy greatly prevails; that in Alabama, for instance, more than half the population over ten years are unable to write. But it will surprise many to learn that so large a proportion of the population of the Northern and Central States—'enlightened free States'—are illiterate. In Massachusetts, 8·42 per cent. are unable to write; in Vermont, 6·84; in New York State, 7·08 per cent., being a total of 239,271 illiterates over ten years old; in Ohio, 8·86 per cent., being a total of 173,172 illiterates; in Indiana, 10·61 per cent., being a total of 127,124; in Illinois, 7·38 per cent., or 133,584; in Pennsylvania, where, however, there is a considerable sprinkling of coloured people, where, also, are the chief seats of heavy manufacturing labour, the percentage is 8·56, and the total number 222,356; in Rhode Island we find the high average of 12·62 per cent., or 21,921 illiterates. In these States, speaking generally, the vast majority of the illiterates must belong to the white population." . . . . "In New Hampshire the percentage is 3·81; in Maine, 3·86."

The above figures refer to illiterates ten years old and over, and they include all races and colours. As the report from which they are taken (Commissioner's Report, 1872) does not distinguish the native and foreign population of ten years and over, we have no means of ascertaining separately the exact proportion of native illiterates compared to native population of ten and over. We can, however, determine the number of native illiterates compared to native population of all ages, and the number of foreign illiterates compared to foreign population of all ages.

On this basis the percentages are as follow in the States which Dr. Rigg mentions :—

State.	Native.	Foreign.
Massachusetts	0·71	25·42
Vermont	1·37	29·27
New York	2·17	14·80
Ohio	5·84	10·48
Indiana	7·35	9·85
Illinois	4·47	8·34
Pennsylvania	4·25	17·52
Rhode Island	2·74	31·54
New Hampshire	0·69	26·76
Maine	1·38	22·63

Indeed, when the actual numbers of the foreign and coloured illiterates ten years of age and over are added together in these States, they largely exceed in number the native white illiterates of the same ages.

The statistics which establish these conclusions Dr. Rigg has had before him, but he does not bring them forward. His comment on the long roll of illiteracy, which he attempts to lay at the door of the free school system, and which is enormously augmented by blacks and foreigners, is: "This condition of things is too manifestly a national evil. Foreign immigration scarcely enters into it as an appreciable element." (P. 433.)

What, then, are the appreciable elements in Dr. Rigg's estimation? He says—

"To anyone who will realise the actual situation of thousands of American settlers, buried and sequestered many and many a mile away from any town or any railway, in the depths of vast regions, only inhabited at very distant intervals by lonely settlers like themselves, it will be easy to understand how such settlers may become utterly ignorant, and almost savage." (P. 434, *Quarterly.*)

Having laid stress upon the illiteracy in the "enlightened free States," he accounts for it by going into the "desolate mountain ranges," "between West Virginia, Ohio, and Kentucky," and in Eastern Tennessee, where "common schools are few and far between, and whatever may have been learnt at school is very likely to be lost in after life, for want of any accessible literature."

There are districts, also, in New York, "completely shut out from the life-current of the world." "It is largely, no doubt, to this condition of things that the illiteracy of the United States is owing." (P. 434, *Quarterly.*)

In his blind haste to depreciate the results of the American schools, Dr. Rigg fixes the seat of illiteracy, not where the most ignorant population of Europe and British America congregate, but in districts inhabited "at very distant intervals by lonely settlers."

The last and chief topic discussed by Dr. Rigg is the standard of education and the age of scholars in American schools. He examines with some minuteness the school systems of New York, Cincinnati, and Boston, describes the course of study, states the ages of the scholars, and makes a general comparison between them and the standards of education and status of children in the schools of this country.

As the result of his enquiry, he arrives at the remarkable conclusion, restated in various forms, that the public schools of America are vastly inferior to the public elementary schools of England. (P. 447.)

"The range of education in the States, age for age, is decidedly lower in the graded public schools than in good English schools." (P. 455, *Quarterly*.)

Again : "Enough will then have been said in regard to the public schools of New York, to show how very low throughout is the graded instruction given in these schools, as compared with that given, age for age, in our English public schools, whether elementary or higher. (P. 450.)

Again, he says that it will not be allowed by any who know what a good English elementary school is and does, that the Cincinnati district schools "are superior to our good English schools for corresponding ages." (P. 452, *Quarterly*.)

Whether it is reasonable to compare the schools of a whole city to picked English schools, the public must decide ; but at any rate there should be no mistake respecting the facts which form the basis of comparison. It will be seen that, for the purpose of Dr. Rigg's contention, the ages of the scholars at particular stages, and the length and scope of the various grades, are of the essence of the whole controversy. If his premises are altogether wrong the deductions he has made must be wholly fallacious. Of New York he says—

"The legal school age in New York ranges from six to twenty-one ; but the theory here, as elsewhere in the States, is that children should enter school late rather than early, and few enter school so young as six years." (P. 447.)

From what follows this would appear to apply to the State and not the city, it being described as a "middle-class nation which is predominantly agricultural, a nation of freehold farmers," &c. But, applied to either State or city, the statement is incorrect. The legal school age in the State is from five to twenty-one (p. 10, New York State Report, 1871). It is true that the theory is that children should enter school late rather than early ; but six is considered late. The assertion that "few enter school so young as six years" has no foundation in fact. The number of scholars under six years of age for the whole State is not given in the report, but I find that in 1873 there were under that age, in the schools of Brooklyn, 4,800 children ; in Buffalo, 1,500 ; in Fulton, 275 ; in Peekskill, 450 ; in Poughkeepsie, 420 ; in Rochester, 987 ; in Syracuse, 373 ; in Troy, 954. (See Commissioner's Report, 1873, p. 523.)

In the city of New York the legal school age is from four to twenty-one (Commissioner's Report, 1873, p. 523). That many children do not enter school till six is certain ; that many enter before is equally certain. The New York City Report for 1874 (p. 83) says—

"The largest increase in the attendance is to be found in the lower classes, which are constantly crowded with very young children, from four to six years of age."

Dr. Rigg proceeds to describe the system in New York city :—

"The New York system of free education embraces four gradations of school or college provision. First, there are the primary schools or departments, in which the ages of the children vary in general from *seven to twelve*, though sometimes, as we have ourselves learnt on the spot, children of thirteen are found in these primary departments. These schools include six grades, and their course for a good scholar should include three years, although for a slow or dull scholar it may extend to four years, or even more. Next come the grammar schools, in which the ages of the scholars range, in general, *from ten or eleven to seventeen*, and which are organised in eight 'grades,' implying for a good scholar a course of four years." (P. 448, *Quarterly*.)

It will be seen that Dr. Rigg overstates the ages of the scholars in the primary schools by three years, and those in the grammar school by three years. The New York City Report, 1871 (p. 25) says—

"The average ages of those in the primary school grades range from *six years (the average of the lowest) to ten years*, that of the highest grade. Grammar school pupils average from *ten and a half years in the lowest to fourteen and a half* in the highest grade."

Respecting the schools of Boston, Dr. Rigg makes the following extraordinary statement :—

"In Boston we find the remarkable fact that the total number of children in the primary schools is less than the number of those in the grammar schools, *although the course for each school is a three years course*, and although many of those who have been scholars in the primary schools never pass into the grammar schools. The explanation, no doubt, is that many of the citizens of Boston prefer to have their young children taught at home, or to send them to private schools, rather than to send them to the common primary schools. Boston is a refined city, and parents in Boston have often, and naturally, the same objection to their young children attending promiscuous public schools that is felt among parents of a similar class and character in England. These same children, however, are very often sent to the grammar schools, the children attending which are already disciplined, and from which already the children of the lowest classes have been almost entirely eliminated." (P. 443, *Quarterly*.)

We have already seen, on the authority of Superintendent Philbrick, that all the children of the primary schools pass into the grammar schools. The explanation, therefore, falls to the ground. But no explanation is needed when the real facts are given—the truth being that the primary course is a three years course, and the grammar course a *six* years course.

The Boston Report for 1873 (p. 147) says—

"Pupils are admitted to the primary grade at five years of age. The course is arranged for six classes and three years."

"The grammar schools are designed to receive the pupils from the primary schools at eight years of age and upwards, and carry them on through a thorough course of practical clementary instruction. The course is arranged for six classes and six years."

This blunder runs all through Dr. Rigg's review of the grammar course in Boston, and makes positive nonsense of his deductions.

Again, in regard to age in the Boston schools, he is altogether abroad. The Superintendent says that "the aim should be to transfer the pupils from the primary to the grammar school grade at the age of eight years—that is, before the completion of the ninth year." (Boston Report, 1872, p. 170.) Writing of the schools in 1872, Dr. Rigg says—

"Of the scholars in the grammar schools, twenty-six per cent. are in the lowest class *(age about ten or eleven)*, and afterwards the numbers in the different classes gradually run down, the proportions being 23 per cent., 17; 15, 12, and 7 respectively. From which it is evident that even in Boston many children leave school at twelve, and many more at thirteen." (P. 443, *Quarterly.*)

In the year to which Dr. Rigg refers there were 5,075 pupils in the sixth (lowest) class of the grammar schools (p. 123, Report, 1872). The average age in this class is not given, but 4,059 pupils in the grammar schools were nine years of age and under, and 3,419 were ten years of age (p. 252, Report, 1872). It is evident, therefore, that all, except a very small fraction of the primary pupils, are promoted between eight and nine years of age, and the average age of the lowest class in the grammar schools must be under ten years.

In writing of the Cincinnati schools, Dr. Rigg is nearer the mark as to age, though even here he is not accurate. He says: "The average age of the children in the first or highest grade of the district schools is twelve, in the second eleven, and in the third ten" (p. 451, *Quarterly*). The Superintendent gives the exact ages as follow: Grade D (the highest in the district schools), 11·4; grade E, 10·5; grade F, 9·4; grade G, 8·3; grade H, 6·7. (See Cincinnati Report, 1874, p. 99.)

This mistake of Dr. Rigg's would make a difference of nearly a grade in the standing of the pupils.

Having advanced the ages in the New York city schools in the manner indicated, Dr. Rigg proceeds to discuss the course. Of this he gives a most garbled and unintelligible account, marked also by the gravest mistakes. In order to place the matter in the clearest light before the English public, I have appended the complete course in the New York and Boston grammar schools and in the Cincinnati district and intermediate schools; adding, for purposes of comparison, our English standards.

Respecting the studies in the New York grammar schools Dr. Rigg says—

"It will be noted that no foreign language is included; indeed, the rudiments of English grammar and composition have scarcely been mastered." (P. 449, *Quarterly*.)

Two things call for attention here. First, German was included in the grammar course at least five years ago (see the complete course, Appendix B). Last year there were in the grammar schools 19,842 pupils in German (see New York Report, 1874, p. 26 and 115). Secondly, Dr. Rigg, who writes glibly of educational science, seems to be ignorant of the fact that in American schools foreign languages are taught all along the course.

By a reference to the course it will also be seen that he is mistaken as to the arithmetic taught in the first year, and as to the time when grammar is commenced.

The mistake which Dr. Rigg makes as to the length of the Boston grammar school course is against his own contention that, age for age, the standards of our English elementary schools are more exacting than the requirements of American schools. On the other hand his summary or description of the subjects taught in the grades is most incomplete, and wholly fails to convey any adequate idea of the thoroughness of the programme. He, moreover, assigns to the first or highest class subjects which are taught in the third class, and omits from the course of the first class other subjects which are taught.

T

For instance, he says the oral instruction prescribed for the first class "recognises, for the first time, some slight elements of science, under the heads of air, water, respiration" (p. 454). By a reference to the course itself it will be found that these studies are introduced in the third class. He omits from the list of subjects in the first class, "natural philosophy," "physiology," and "book-keeping."

As far as it goes, his description of the Cincinnati course appears to be correct, but when he says that it "presents a theory, an ideal standard, not a legal minimum examination standard," a wholly wrong impression is conveyed. The course represents the standard actually required at the examinations, as a comparison with the examination questions conclusively proves.

Of the specific subjects in our English schools Dr. Rigg says that they "may be regarded as representing not only the aspirations, but, in a fair measure, also the actual achievements and performances of English teachers in spite of difficulty and discouragement" (p. 450, *Quarterly*). Of the difficulty and discouragement no one will entertain the slightest doubt, but that the list of specific subjects represents "in a fair measure the achievements and performances of English teachers" is at least questionable.

In the year ending August, 1873, 131,096 children were presented in standards IV-VI. Of these, 77,896 were examined in one or more specific subjects. Of this number 55,941 passed successfully, 23,488 of them in two subjects. 61,361 children were examined in geography; 20,388 in grammar; 19,817 in English literature; 16,762 in history; 3,681 in algebra; 725 in physiology; 658 in physical geography (which Dr. Rigg says is always taught in good inspected elementary schools); 600 in domestic economy; 174 in French; 46 in Latin; 62 in natural science; 53 in mensuration; 17 in mental arithmetic; 14 in chemistry; 8 in electricity; and 7 in telegraphy. (See p. 15, Appendix, Report of Committee of Council, 1873-74.)

Dr. Rigg is much given to patronising American educational officials. One is "candid and well-informed," another "intelligent and vigorous," another "very competent," another of "grave responsibility" and "long and intimate acquaintance with facts." If he can find a sentence in a report which can be used to support his indictment against the American system, he proceeds to eulogise the author. I regret being precluded from giving the public the benefit of American opinion upon Dr. Rigg's work, conveyed to me in letters from several State Superintendents; but there is one official who has published his view of Dr. Rigg's book—whose competence has been thoroughly proved, whose acquaintance with American education has been long and intimate, whose candour Dr. Rigg will not impeach. I refer to Mr. Philbrick, who retired last year from the office of Superintendent of the Boston Schools, a post which he occupied for eighteen years. He says of the reverend and learned author's chapter on education in the United States, that it "is made up, for the most part, of a wonderful conglomeration of erroneous statements and wrong inferences."[1] I venture to add that every person acquainted with the American system, who examines his work, will be compelled to arrive at the same conclusion.

---

[1] Boston Report, 1874, p. 355.

APPENDIX B.

NEW YORK.

COURSE OF INSTRUCTION PRESCRIBED FOR GRAMMAR SCHOOLS.

EIGHTH GRADE.

Reading.—Of the grade of a Third Reader (first half), with a review of punctuation, Roman numbers, and elementary sounds; and with exercises on the subject-matter of the lessons.

Spelling.—From the reading lessons, with miscellaneous words, and words derived therefrom; also exercises in writing words and short sentences from dictation. Particular attention to be given to the use of capitals.

Definitions.—From the reading lessons, to teach the meaning of the words, with illustrations by forming sentences; in no case to be committed to memory and mechanically recited.

Mental Arithmetic.—As far as in written arithmetic, to include exercises in the analysis of operations and examples, and in rapid calculation without analysis.

Written Arithmetic.—Through the simple rules and Federal money, with practical examples.

Tables of weights, measures, &c., reviewed, with practical illustrations and simple applications.

Geography.—Primary geography, including the general outlines, with definitions and illustrations, by means of the globe, of the form, magnitude, and motions of the earth, zones, &c.

Elementary Science.—By oral instruction in the qualities and uses of familiar objects, such as articles of clothing, food, materials for building, &c.;

also a knowledge of geometrical forms, with illustrations on the blackboard and by models.

SEVENTH GRADE.

Reading.—Of the grade of a Third Reader (latter half), with exercises as in the eighth grade.

Spelling and Definitions.—From the reading lessons, with exercises in miscellaneous words and sentences, as in the previous grade.

Mental Arithmetic.—As far as in written arithmetic, with exercises in analysis and calculation.

Written Arithmetic.—A review of Federal money; common fractions commenced; simple operations to be taught, with practical applications, avoiding difficult or complex examples.

Tables of weights and measures reviewed and applied.

Geography.—Outlines of North America, including the United States and West Indies, with the descriptive geography of those countries; only conspicuous or important localities to be taught; elementary definitions and illustrations continued, with the addition of latitude and longitude.

Elementary Science.—By oral instruction. The qualities and uses of familiar objects; also an outline knowledge of zoology.

SIXTH GRADE.

Reading.—Of the grade of a Third Reader, with the exercises of the preceding grade; particular attention to be given to clearness of articulation and naturalness of intonations and general style.

Spelling.—Oral and written, as in preceding grades.

Definitions.—As in the preceding grades, with easy exercises on the prefixes and suffixes, and their applications.

Mental Arithmetic.—As far as in written arithmetic, with exercises as in the preceding grades; also practice in the application of the arithmetical tables.

Written Arithmetic.—Through common fractions, with their simple applications; including also a review of Federal money, and practice in the simple rules to secure rapidity and accuracy.

Geography.—Of the United States in detail; localities as in the preceding grades, with a brief description of each State and Territory.

Elementary Science.—By oral instruction. The uses and qualities of familiar objects continued; also an outline knowledge of botany, including the general structure and common uses of plants.

FIFTH GRADE.

Reading.—Of the grade of a Fourth Reader (first half), with the exercises of the preceding grades.

Spelling and Definitions.—From the reading lessons, as in the preceding grades.

Mental Arithmetic.—As far as in written arithmetic, with exercises as in the sixth grade.

Written Arithmetic.—Through decimals, with practical applications in both common and decimal fractions, and their conversion one into the other.

Geography.—Local and descriptive, through South America and Europe; the topics of the preceding grades to be occasionally reviewed in outline.

Elementary Science.—By oral instruction. The uses and qualities of familiar objects; also an outline of mineralogy, illustrated by specimens.

FOURTH GRADE.

Reading.—Of the grade of a Fourth Reader (latter half), with particular attention to emphasis, intonations, and naturalness of expression.

Spelling and Definitions.—As in the preceding grade.

Mental Arithmetic.—A review of the preceding grades, with exercises in calculation and analysis.

Written Arithmetic.—Through denominate numbers and fractions, with practical applications.

Geography.—Local and descriptive, through Asia, Africa and Oceanica; localities as in the preceding grades.

English Grammar.—To include the analysis, parsing, and construction of simple sentences, and with such definitions *only* as pertain to the parts of the subject studied.

History of the United States.—The early discoveries and the outlines of Colonial History to 1753; important events only to be taught, with such dates as are specially requisite for a complete understanding of the subject.

Elementary Science.—By oral instruction. The topics of the preceding grades continued and reviewed, and, in addition, the simple outlines of physiology and hygiene.

THIRD GRADE.

Reading.—Of the grade of a Fourth Reader, continued, with exercises as in the preceding grades.

Spelling.—From the reading lessons, with exercises in writing miscellaneous words and sentences, and in the analysis and construction of words, according to the rules of spelling.

Definitions.—From the reading lessons.

Mental and Written Arithmetic.—Commercial, through percentage, interest, profit and loss. Problems to be chiefly such as involve the ordinary business transactions.

English Grammar.—Continued, with the analysis, parsing, and construction of easy, complex, and compound sentences; also, writing short compositions, under the inspection of the teacher.

History of the United States.—From 1753 to 1789; the outlines of the Revolutionary War to be taught, and the events which led to the adoption of the Constitution.

Natural Philosophy.—Including mechanics, hydrostatics, and pneumatics. A simple text-book to be used.

SECOND GRADE.

Reading.—Of the grade of a Fifth Reader, with spelling and definitions, as in the third grade.

Etymology.—With the analysis of words and their formation from given roots.

Mental and Written Arithmetic.—Through square root and its simple applications; problems as in the preceding grade.

Outlines of Physical Geography.

English Grammar.—Continued, with analysis, parsing and construction, and the correction of false syntax; also, composition. The exercises in analysis to be such only as are required to show the general structure of sentences.

History of the United States.—Outlines completed; events and dates as in the preceding grades.

Astronomy, Elementary.—The solar system, with an explanation of the ordinary phenomena. A simple text-book to be used.

Natural Philosophy.—Simple outlines completed, to include acoustics, pyronomics, optics, magnetism, and electricity.

FIRST GRADE.

Reading, Spelling, and Etymology.—Continued.

Arithmetic.—Mental and written continued, with mensuration.

English Grammar.—Continued, with composition, the latter to include impromptu exercises. Practice to be afforded in letter-writing, with instruction as to folding, directing, &c.

Astronomy.—Outlines continued.

Algebra.—Through simple equations.

General History.—The outlines of ancient and modern.

Book-keeping.

Constitution of the United States.

The Rudiments of Plane Geometry.—(First book of Legendre, or an equivalent.)

Chemistry.—Elementary principles and facts, without text-book.

GENERAL DIRECTIONS.

Such pupils as are making preparation for admission into the introductory or lowest class of the Normal College, or the College of the City of New York, shall be permitted to pursue the first grade, with such modifications as may be necessary for that purpose.

Penmanship and Drawing shall be taught in each grade of the above course.

Instruction in *Sewing* may be given to the pupils of the female schools.

Exercises in writing sentences, paragraphs, &c., from dictation, shall be given in each grade; and the pupils in all the grades shall be trained in the correction of language, and taught to avoid common errors of speech.

The oral lessons in the different departments of science prescribed for the several grades shall be given with especial thoroughness and regularity, and daily if practicable, the number of lessons in each week being in no case less than three. These lessons shall be such as will train the pupils in habits of observation and reflection, as well as impart useful knowledge.

COURSE OF INSTRUCTION IN THE GERMAN LANGUAGE.

The following shall be the course of instruction in the German language, to be pursued in connection with the several grades of the grammar school course, in the schools in which the study of the said language may be introduced; and whenever said course shall be pursued, such additional time shall be given to each grade as may be required to enable the pupils thoroughly to complete the progress prescribed for that grade.

SEVENTH AND EIGHTH GRADES.

The *Alphabet*, both printed and script, with simple exercises in reading and writing, by dictation and by copying; *oral translation* of simple sentences in German and English, including subjects and predicates of various forms, with instruction in the use of the *article*, and the *present tense* of *regular verbs*, and of the verb *sein*.

Colloquial Exercises in the same.

SIXTH GRADE.

Reading and *Writing*, by dictation and copying, continued; *oral* and *written translation* of simple sentences, in German and English, including subject, predicate, object and simple adjuncts, with instruction in the *gender, number,* and *case* of *nouns* and *pronouns*, the present and past tense of regular verbs, and of the verbs *sein* and *haben*.

Colloquial Exercises, by the use of similar sentences.

FIFTH GRADE.

Reading and *writing* continued, as in the preceding grades; *oral* and *written translation* of simple sentences in German and English, including phrases and the use of the preposition; also of easy compound sentences, with instruction in the declension and comparison of adjectives, the declension of pronouns, and the conjugation of the indicative mood of regular verbs, and of the verbs *sien* and *haben*.

Colloquial Exercises adapted to the progress of the pupil.

FOURTH GRADE.

Reading and *writing* continued, as before; *oral* and *written translation* of simple and compound sentences in English and German, affording practice in the cases of nouns and pronouns, the tenses of the indicative and imperative moods of regular verbs in both voices, and the use of adjectives and adverbs, with instruction in grammar, as applicable to such sentences.

Colloquial Exercises in the same.

THIRD GRADE.

Reading from a German reader, with translation into English; *writing*, by copying and dictation; *oral* and *written translation* of sentences, in German and English, affording practice in the regular and irregular verbs (indicative mood), with instruction in grammar continued.

Colloquial Exercises.

SECOND GRADE.

Reading and *translation* from the German Reader continued; *memorising* and *recitation* of select passages; *writing*, by dictation and copying, continued;

oral and *written translation* of sentences, in German and English, affording practice in the indicative and subjunctive moods of regular and irregular verbs ; *grammar* continued ; German composition commenced.

Colloquial Exercises in all the topics of the previous grades.

FIRST GRADE.

Reading and *translation* of select passages; elocution ; *oral* and *written translation* of miscellaneous passages in German and English ; the *Grammar* completed and reviewed ; *German composition* continued, including epistolary and business forms.

Colloquial Exercises and conversations on promiscuous topics.

BOSTON.

GRAMMAR SCHOOLS.

SIXTH CLASS.—BOOKS.

Hillard's Fourth Reader ; Worcester's Spelling Book ; Payson, Dunton and Scribner's, or A. R. Dunton's Writing Books ; Warren's Primary Geography ; Eaton's Intellectual Arithmetic ; Swinton's Language Lessons and Introductory Grammar and Composition ; Second National Music Reader ; The American Text-books of Art Education ; Bartholomew's Drawing Books, new series ; Hooker's Child's Book of Nature, *permitted* as a reading or lesson book.

STUDIES.

Reading.—The Fourth Reader, all the pieces; special attention to fluency of utterance, distinctness of articulation, correctness of pronunciation, and the points and marks of punctuation ; practice on the exercises in the introduction ; the spelling and defining lessons to be omitted.

Spelling.—Through the spelling book, omitting the exercises for writing, each lesson being *read* by the class before it is given out for study ; a sentence from the reading lesson written daily from dictation.

Writing.—Three writing books—numbers one, two, and three—with analysis of letters.

Arithmetic.—Written arithmetic through the operations of the ground rules and reduction, with simple practical questions involving small numbers ; mental arithmetic carried along in connection with written, the same topic in both kinds being taught at the same time [sections first and second].

Geography.—Reading half through the primary text-book, with conversational illustrations ; rudiments of map-drawing, showing how geographical objects are represented by symbols, taking as subjects for practice the schoolroom, the schoolyard, the common, the public garden, and the outline map of the State ; the globe used to illustrate the form, magnitude, and rotation of the earth, the position of the axis, poles, zones, and principal circles.

Grammar.—Oral instruction in distinguishing the noun, the adjective, and articles ; exercises in correcting common grammatical errors ; practice in the use of capitals.

Composition.—Letter-writing on the slate once a week.

Morals and Manners.—By anecdotes, examples, and precepts, and by amplifying and applying the hints and suggestions relating to these topics contained in the reading lessons.

Vocal Music.—Musical notation, singing, and exercises on the music charts, fifteen minutes each day, under the general direction of the director of music for the class.

Vocal and Physical Culture.—Exercises as contained in Monroe's Manual, ten minutes each session.

Drawing.—Lines and angles, and plane geometrical figures.

Oral Instruction.—Weights and measures, and articles of clothing and food.

Conversations on the reading lessons as follows : Lessons 7, 11, 26, 42, 43, 44, 51, 52, and 58.

FIFTH CLASS.—BOOKS.

Hillard's Intermediate Reader ; Worcester's Spelling Book ; Payson, Dunton and Scribner's, or A. R. Dunton's Writing Books ; Eaton's Grammar School Arithmetic, and Eaton's Intellectual Arithmetic ; Warren's Primary Geography ; Swinton's Language Lessons and Introductory Grammar and Composition ; Second National Music Reader ; The American Text-books of Art Education ; Bartholomew's Drawing Books, new series ; Hooker's Child's Book of Nature, as in the sixth class.

STUDIES.

Reading.—The Intermediate Reader, all the pieces ; practice on the exercises in the introduction on articulation, pronunciation, accent, emphasis, and inflection, and attention to their application in the reading lessons ; the defining lessons to be omitted.

Spelling.—Through the spelling book, with definitions of words from page 109 to page 130, omitting the exercises for writing ; a sentence from the reading lesson written daily from dictation.

Writing.—Four writing books—numbers 1, 2, 3, and 4—with analysis of letters.

Arithmetic.—Written arithmetic, vulgar fractions and decimal fractions, with simple practical questions involving small numbers; mental arithmetic carried along in connection with written, the same topic in both kinds being taught at the same time [sections third and fourth.]

Geography.—Reading of the text-book, with conversational illustrations completed; drawing of outline maps, from memory, of each of the New England States; use of the globe continued.

Grammar.—Oral lessons on distinguishing the parts of speech, completed; correcting errors; sentence-making.

Composition.—Letter-writing on paper once in two weeks, with occasional abstracts of geography lessons.

Morals and Manners.—As in the preceding class.

Vocal Music.—Musical notation continued, singing and exercises on the music charts, fifteen minutes each day, as in the preceding class.

Vocal and Physical Culture.—As in the preceding class.

Drawing.—Lines and angles, and plane geometrical figures, as in Drawing Book No. 2.

Oral Instruction.—The national flag, the national and State [Mass.] coat of arms; the parts of a vessel, with the distinctions between the different kinds of sailing vessels and between the different kinds of steam vessels; biographical sketches of Washington and Franklin.

FOURTH CLASS.—BOOKS.

Hillard's Franklin Fifth Reader; Worcester's Spelling Book; Payson, Dunton and Scribner's, or A. R. Dunton's Writing Books; Eaton's Grammar School Arithmetic, and Eaton's Intellectual Arithmetic; Warren's Common School Geography; Swinton's Language Lessons and Introductory Grammar and Composition; Third Music Reader; the American Text-books for Art Education; Bartholomew's Drawing Books, new series.

STUDIES.

Reading.—Franklin Fifth Reader, through reading lessons, Part I., with special reference to their meaning and the information they contain; definition lessons at the end of the pieces, with exercises in introductory treatise.

Spelling.—Through the spelling book; in the exercises for writing, the words italicised to be written from dictation, the phrases and sentences in which they occur being read by the teacher in order to indicate their meaning and application; a sentence from the reading lesson written daily from dictation.

Writing.—Four writing books—numbers 2, 3, 4, and 5—with analysis of letters.

Arithmetic.—Written arithmetic, Federal money and compound numbers, with questions as in fifth class; mental arithmetic carried along in connection with written, the same topic in both kinds being taught at the same time [sections fifth and sixth].

Geography.—A general view of the geography of the world, with Mercator's map and the globe; the oceans, seas, and principal gulfs and bays;

the continents, grand divisions, and largest islands; the most important ranges of mountains, with the plateaus and low plains; the water-sheds, chief rivers and lakes, with their basins; map-drawing, from memory, of the map of the United States, as a whole, by progressive steps.

Grammar.—Oral lessons on modifications of nouns, pronouns, adjectives, verbs, and adverbs; correcting errors; sentence-making.

Composition.—On paper, once in two weeks, abstracts of oral lessons, alternating with letter-writing.

Drawing.—The course indicated for the sixth class to be repeated.

Morals and Manners, Vocal Music, Vocal and Physical Culture.—As in the preceding class.

Oral Instruction.—Rectangular and spherical solids; buildings, the different kinds, and the materials used in their construction; object lessons on ten metals, ten specimens of the most useful woods, and on ten kinds of rocks.

THIRD CLASS.—BOOKS.

Hillard's Franklin Fifth Reader; Worcester's Spelling Book; Payson, Dunton and Scribner's, or A. R. Dunton's Writing Books; Eaton's Grammar School Arithmetic, and Eaton's Intellectual Arithmetic; Warren's Common School Geography; Anderson's Grammar School History; Kerl's Common School Grammar; Third Music Reader; the American Text-books for Art Education; Bartholomew's Drawing Books, new series.

STUDIES.

Reading.—Hillard's Franklin Fifth Reader, reading lessons, Part II., completed in the manner prescribed for the preceding class.

Spelling.—Spelling book reviewed by selecting words to be written from dictation twice a week, no lesson being given out for study; a sentence from the reading lesson written daily from dictation.

Writing.—Four writing books, numbers 3, 4, 5, and 6, with analysis of letters, and practice while sitting in three different positions, viz.: right side at the desk, left side at the desk, and facing the desk.

Arithmetic.—Written arithmetic, percentage with its applications, the easier practical problems being performed; mental arithmetic in connection with written, the same topic in both kinds being taught at the same time [sections 8 and 9].

Geography.—The United States; the climate, physical features, and productions of the different sections; the thirty largest cities, their location, their natural advantages and disadvantages, and the peculiar characteristics of the business carried on in each; outline map of each State, drawn from memory.

History.—United States; first half of the text-book read, some dates and facts learned and recited.

Grammar.—Etymological parsing; inflections and definitions learned from the text-book; correcting errors, especially such as are violations of the principles of etymology; sentence-making.

Composition.—Once a month, on some topic embraced in oral instruction;

business papers, such as letters, orders, bills of purchase, receipts, promissory notes, drafts, advertisements, invitations, &c.

Drawing.—Drawing book; the course indicated for the fifth class to be repeated.

Morals and Manners, Vocal Music, and Vocal and Physical Culture.—As in the preceding class.

Oral Instruction.—Air, water, respiration; municipal and State governments; courts of justice; historical sketches of Pericles, Chatham, Jefferson, Samuel Adams, and Lincoln.

SECOND CLASS.—BOOKS.

Hillard's Sixth Reader; Payson, Dunton and Scribner's, or A. R. Dunton's Writing Books; Eaton's Grammar School Arithmetic, and Eaton's Intellectual Arithmetic; Warren's Common School Geography; Kerl's Common School Grammar; Anderson's Grammar School History; Hullah's Adaptation of Wilhem's Method of Teaching Vocal Music, with Additions by Sharland; the American Text-books of Art Education; Bartholomew's Drawing Books, new series.

STUDIES.

Reading.—Sixth Reader, to p. 200, with practice on the examples in the introduction. Expressive reading to be aimed at in connection with the study of the thought and emotion of the pieces.

Spelling.—In connection with the other studies, the new and difficult words that occur, to cultivate the habit of *observing the orthography of words;* instruction in the significance of prefixes and affixes; a weekly exercise in writing passages dictated from the Reader.

Writing.—One writing book—No. 7 of Payson, Dunton and Scribner's, or No. 8 of A. R. Dunton's.

Arithmetic.—Written arithmetic, proportion and square root, with a review of all the preceding subjects, performing a few selected examples *to illustrate the principles;* mental arithmetic, seventh section.

Geography.—The continents; map of each, drawn from memory, representing the boundaries of the countries; separate memory maps of the principal countries of Europe; problems on the globe.

History.—United States, completed in the manner prescribed for the preceding class.

Grammar.—Syntactical parsing, the rules learned in connection with their application; exercises in correcting errors, especially such as are violations of the principles of syntax; sentence-making.

Composition.—Once a month, the subject to be developed by conversation in connection with oral lessons; business papers as in class three; declamation for boys, twice each term.

Vocal Music.—To be taught one half-hour each week, by the director of music; and ten minutes each day, except Wednesday and Saturday, shall be devoted to musical instruction by the regular teachers.

Drawing.—Simple objects in outline, and elements of perspective.

Morals and Manners, Vocal and Physical Culture.—As in the preceding class.

Oral Instruction.—The solar system, the properties of matter, the mechanical powers; historical sketches of the Crusades, the discovery of Amercia, the Declaration of Independence.

FIRST CLASS.—BOOKS.

Hillard's Sixth Reader; Payson, Dunton and Scribner's, or A. R. Dunton's Writing Books; Eaton's Grammar School Arithmetic, and Eaton's Intellectual Arithmetic; Warren's Common School Geography, Kerl's Common School Grammar; Cooley's Elements of Natural Philosophy; Worcester's History, Hullah's Adaptation of Wilhem's Method of Teaching Vocal Music, with Addition by Sharland; The American Text-books of Art Education; Bartholomew's Drawing Books, new series; Worcester's Dictionary.

STUDIES.

Reading.—Sixth Reader, completed, as in the preceding class.

Spelling.—As in the preceding class.

Writing.—One writing book, No. 11 of Payson, Dunton and Scribner's, or No. 7 of A. R. Dunton's.

Arithmetic.—Written arithmetic, cube root; review, with special reference to *the discussion of the principles;* some review of mental arithmetic.

Geography.—A few lessons in review of the continents and the United States, with special reference to political geography and commercial relations; maps of the United States as a whole and in sections, and the countries of Europe, drawn from memory.

History.—Outline of the history of England, by topics.

Grammar.—Syntactical parsing and analysis of sentences; exercises in correcting false syntax.

Composition.—As in the preceding class.

Declamation for Boys.—Twice each term.

Natural Philosophy.—Outlines of the properties of matter, motion, mechanics, hydrostatics, pneumatics, sound, heat, optics, electricity and magnetism.

Physiology.—By oral instruction; circulation, respiration, digestion, and secretion, with practical hygiene.

Drawing.—Simple objects in outline, and elements of perspective, continued.

Morals and Manners, Vocal Music, and Vocal and Physical Culture.—As in the preceding class.

Book-keeping.—By single entry.

Constitution of the United States and the Constitution of the State read, with conversational explanations.

CINCINNATI.

COURSE OF STUDY.

DISTRICT SCHOOLS.—GRADE II.

Studies.—Elements of reading, writing, arithmetic, singing, grammar, object lessons, drawing; and German, when desired by parents.

Books.—Mason's Music Charts; Uniform Slates; Knell and Jones's Phonic Reader. This is a grade for oral and black-board instruction; and the teacher is expected to use the black-board and such cards for instruction in the elements of reading, and such charts for teaching object lessons, as are provided by the Board.

Spelling and Reading.—Pupils shall be taught to write at dictation, and to spell by sound any sentence in their Phonic Reader, as far as p. 29; or they may be required to write at dictation similar sentences.

Writing.—They shall be taught to write in a plain, legible hand, on their slates, any of the words which they are required to read in sentences.

Arithmetic.—They shall be taught, by means of objects, to perform mental and slate exercises in the four fundamental rules, to amounts not exceeding ten.

Grammar.—They shall be taught to speak correctly any sentence they may be required to use. The teacher shall converse with them frequently, in order to correct their language, individual recitation being practised as far as possible.

Object Lessons.—In this grade the names of objects are given, and the ideas of some of the most prominent properties developed, and terms given.

The cultivation of the observation is the main point here.

Objects are used at first, and properties developed, but after a number of qualities of the same class have become familiar, as colour, form, &c., these properties may be made the subject of the lesson, and other material may be introduced, as colour charts, artificial forms, &c.

The following list will furnish material from which the teacher *may select.* Similar familiar objects may also be taken:—

1. Objects in the school room—table, chair, slate, pencil, crayon, blackboard, bell, door, window.

2. Parts of the human body—head, face, eyes, nose, mouth, chin, cheeks, ears, hair, trunk, arms, shoulder, upper arm, elbow, lower arm, wrist, hand, fingers, thumb, fore finger, middle finger, ring finger, little finger, legs, hip, thigh, knee, ankle, foot, instep, heel, sole, toes, nails.

3. Clothing—hat, bonnet, shoe, boot, apron, jacket, dress.

4. Objects from the child's home—knife, fork, spoon, tumbler, plate, cup, ring, ball, cane, basket, bucket, broom, clock, candle, soap, sponge, coal.

5. Food—apple, peach, cherry, grape, potato, tomato, turnip, pea, bread, meat, butter, milk, water, vinegar, sugar, salt.

6. Some familiar flowers—rose, pink, lily.

7. Some familiar plant, with roots, stem, branches, leaves.

Drawing.—Attitude of the body in general. Exercises on slates with reference to dots and dashes in reference to position, direction, distance, and number, now and then interspersed with simple figures, representing objects composed of short straight lines.

The lessons in representing objects being more interesting, should be given as a reward for good work of a previous lesson. Pupils in this grade shall also be required to have uniform slates.

GRADE G.

Studies.—Spelling, reading, writing, arithmetic, grammar, drawing, singing, composition, object lessons; and German, when desired by parents.

Books.—Young Singer, Part I. (for teachers only); Mason's Music Charts; McGuffey's First Reader, or Knell and Jones's Phonic Reader; Uniform Slates; Bartholomew's Drawing.

Spelling.—Pupils shall be taught to write at dictation, and to spell by sound any sentence in their reading lessons, or similar familiar sentences, and to write sentences from their object lessons.

Reading.—They shall be taught to read fluently and distinctly any lesson in their Reader, and number each page by its figures.

Writing.—They shall be taught to write on their slates, at dictation, all the words they are required to spell.

Arithmetic.—They shall review the H grade course, and perform mental exercises in the four fundamental rules, no number used or produced in multiplication or division to exceed 20; shall count, with and without objects, as high as 100; shall learn to understand, read, and write the fractions, $\frac{1}{2}$, $\frac{1}{3}$, and $\frac{1}{4}$, add the 1's, 2's, and 3's as high as 100, and subtract them from 100; perform slate exercises in the four fundamental rules to amounts not exceeding 100, the divisors and multipliers being 2 and 3; and be taught, objectively, the denominations of our paper and specie currency, and the use of the dollar and cent marks; problems involving concrete numbers shall contain but one arithmetical operation.

MODEL EXAMPLES IN MENTAL ARITHMETIC.

Section II., Lesson 1; Section III., Lesson 1; and Section V., Lesson I., of Ray's Second Book.

Grammar.—They shall be taught to speak correctly any sentence they may be required to use ; particular reference shall be had to the proper use of *a* and *an*, *this* and *that* (singular and plural forms), the pronoun *I* as a capital letter ; the capital letters at the commencement, and the period and question mark at the termination, of sentences ; and the singular and plural of nouns and verbs.

Music.—They shall be taught to name the music characters, and write at dictation the exercises on p. 8 of the Young Singer.

Object Lessons.—In grade G (and also in the subsequent grades) the exercises are to be both oral and written. Comparison as to similarity and difference is the principal feature of the work in this grade.

I.—Besides treating more fully the objects given in H grade, the teacher may take the following objects :—

Book, desk, school-bag, ruler, pen, ink, stove, floor, ceiling, wall.

PROPERTIES, &C., OF OBJECTS FOR GRADE G.

1. Form and direction—four corners, three corners, sides, edges, round like a ring, round like a plate, round like a ball, round like a cane, straight, curved, vertical, horizontal, slanting, parallel.
2. Colour—white, black, red, yellow, blue, brown.
3. Size—long and short, longer and shorter, broad, narrow, high, low, large, small, larger, smaller.
4. Weights—heavy, light, heavier, lighter.
5. Place—position of objects in the schoolroom and of objects placed on the table, as right, left, &c., before, between, &c.
6. Parts—name of parts, number of parts, use of parts.
7. Material—wood, iron, stone, glass, paper, cloth.
8. Use of objects.
9. Care of things in school. Do not meddle with things of others.

II.—The human body ; principal parts named—head, trunk, arms, and legs.

Head { Top of the head,
Back of the head,
Sides, temple, ear.

Face { Forehead,
Eyes,
Nose,
Mouth,
Chin.

Arms { Shoulder,
Upper arm,
Elbows,
Lower arm,
Wrist.

Hand { Palm, Back, Finger.

{ Thumb,
Fore finger,
Middle finger,
Ring finger,
Little finger,
Knuckles,
Finger joints,
Nails.

Legs { Hip,
Thigh,
Knee (knee-pan),
Lower leg (shin and calf),
Ankle.

Foot { Instep,
Heel,
Sole,
Toes.

Add lessons on health, and also add :—

Actions.—Of the head : Raising, bowing, nodding, turning, shaking, rolling.

Of the arms : Hanging, bending, stretching, turning, twisting, twirling, folding, swinging, thrusting.

Of the legs : Stretching, bending, lifting, swinging, kicking, walking, running, hopping, skipping, jumping, dancing.

III.—Clothing. Besides the articles named in grade H, cap, shawl, coat, pants ; comparison.

1. Names of articles of clothing.
2. Names of parts of garments.
3. Colour. Add here, orange, green, purple, pink, gray ; for degrees of colour use light and dark.
4. Material—wool, cotton, silk straw, leather, fur, felt, paper.
5. Uses.
6. Lessons on cleanliness, neatness, order, and taste.

IV.—Covering of animals ; comparison with our clothing.

V.—Plants.

1.—Fruit { Names,
Names of parts—stem, peel, pulp, core, seeds, dimple, eye.
Colour,
Taste and other qualities, as juicy, hard, mellow, green, ripe, tough, rich.

VI.—Flowers—name, colour, odour ; flowers distinguished by odour.

VII.—Rose bush, currant, or quince bush ; name of parts—roots, stem buds, leaves, flowers, fruit, seeds.

Composition.—1. The pupils of this grade shall be required to describe orally the pictures in their reading books.

2. They shall be required to write *sentences* on objects named in their course in object lessons, and to begin every sentence with a capital letter, and end it with its appropriate mark. These sentences, in the beginning of the course, may be such as have been formed by the aid of the teacher, all the pupils of the class writing the same sentences.

3. Each pupil shall be required, after an object has been discussed orally in an object lesson, to write as many sentences about that object as he can possibly form, and without further aid from the teacher than has been given in the oral lesson.

4. As another step in advance, an object of marked characteristics shall be set before the pupils, and, without any other direction from the teacher than that they are to examine that object closely, they shall be encouraged to write as many sentences about it as they can think of—not only about its qualities, but its uses, where the latter are apparent.

5. Pupils studying German should have frequent exercises in translating the sentences, formed on the foregoing plan, from English into German, and also in translating in writing the easiest sentences from their Readers.

Drawing.—The instruction in this grade shall consist of the following exercises : Drawing of straight lines from one to two inches in length in different directions, such as vertical, horizontal, and slanting lines ; combination of such lines into figures ; divisions of lines into two and four equal parts. The terms horizontal, vertical, and slanting or oblique, in reference to direction, and right, acute, and obtuse, in reference to angles, triangles, and square, are to be taught.

Pupils are to be taught to make use of the inch as a unit of measure, the inch to be marked on the slate the same as in H grade. The pupils shall also be required to have uniform drawing slates.

GRADE F.

Studies.—Spelling, reading, punctuation, penmanship, drawing, arithmetic, grammar, composition, music, object lessons ; German, when desired by parents.

Books.—McGuffey's Second Reader ; Uniform Slates ; Young Singer, Part I. ; Mason's Music Charts ; Bartholomew's Drawing.

Spelling.—Pupils shall be taught to write at dictation any sentence which may be formed from words contained in their reading lessons, and also sentences from their object lessons.

Reading.—They shall be required to give a full and intelligent explanation of the subject of the lesson, and the words used ; to read the lesson with fluency, distinctness, and suitable modulation ; and to render an oral abstract of the same as a whole.

Punctuation.—They shall be taught to name all the punctuation marks in their reading lessons.

Penmanship.—They shall be taught to write the capitals and small letters, in words or sentences, on slates or paper.

Drawing.—They shall practise on vertical, horizontal, and oblique lines, and be taught to draw figures composed of squares, rectangles, parallelograms, and triangles, and such other figures as may be found in their text-book, and to divide lines and sides of figures into two, four, eight, sixteen, and more equal parts.

Arithmetic.—They shall review the G grade course, shall read and write numbers as high as 10,000, and the fractions $\frac{1}{2}, \frac{2}{3}, \frac{1}{3}, \frac{3}{4}, \frac{1}{4}, \frac{1}{5}, \frac{2}{5}, \frac{3}{5}$, and $\frac{4}{5}$.

They shall use numbers and figures as high as 5's, as follows :—

1. Mental addition and subtraction as high as 100.
2. Mental multiplication and division as high as 50.
3. Slate exercises in the four fundamental rules to amounts not exceeding 10,000.

Problems involving concrete numbers shall contain but one arithmetical operation. Object lessons shall also be given in this grade in the weights— ounce and pound ; the measure—bushel, peck, small measure, quart, pint, yard, foot, inch ; year, month, week, day, hour, minute, second. Pupils shall learn to use the different marks pertaining to each.

MODEL EXAMPLES IN MENTAL ARITHMETIC.

Section II., Lesson 1 ; Section III., Lesson 1 ; Section V., Lesson 1 ; Section VI., Lesson 1.

Grammar.—They shall be taught to speak and write correctly any sentence they may be required to use. They shall be given a correct idea of what a sentence is ; and of the distinction between a statement, an enquiry, a command, and an exclamation. Special attention shall be given to punctuation (period, question mark, comma, and exclamation point).

They shall also be taught to distinguish nouns, adjectives, verbs, adverbs, prepositions, conjunctions (as connectives of words), and interjections, by giving the principal uses of each.

Music.—They shall be taught to read and sing exercises in 2-4 time, consisting of half and quarter notes, and their corresponding rests, in the scale of C (G clef), embodying intervals of the 3rd and 4th.

Object Lessons.—The work in this grade has reference principally to the essential and accidental properties of objects preparatory to classification.

I.—Familiar animals.
1. Mammals—dog, cat, cattle, horse, sheep, pig, mouse.
2. Birds—hen, pigeon, goose, duck, turkey, canary.
3. Insects—fly, mosquito, bee.
   Motion, food, habitation, use.

II.—The surroundings of the house—yards, garden, street, objects found there.

1.—Plants.
- Stem, { bark, wood, pith, }
- Leaf, { Stalk, Blade, } { mid vein, veins, veinlets, pulp. }

2.—Flowers.
- Name,
- Parts, { stem, calyx, sepals, corolla, petals, stamen, pistils, pollen. }

III.—The different trades and occupations of men. Workshop—tailor, shoemaker, hatter, milliner, seamstress, mason, plasterer, whitewasher, paperhanger, carpenter, glazier, painter, blacksmith, cooper, butcher, baker, miller.

1. Name of occupation.
2. Articles produced.
3. Materials used.
4. Tools.

PROPERTIES OF OBJECTS FOR THIS GRADE.

1. Form—angular, triangular, square, oblong, circular, oval.
2. Colour—flesh colour, pale blue, indigo, buff, corn, crimson, scarlet, lemon, lilac, violet.
3. Size—inch, foot, yard, and their halves and fourths; judging distance and size, and measuring of objects, of room, of building, of school-yard, and of square. Representation of these measurements, as far as practicable, on the blackboard.
4. Weight—pound, half pound, quarter pound; two, three, &c., pounds. The children are required to judge of the weight by lifting.
5. Less obvious qualities—acid, fragrant, porous, elastic, brittle, transparent.
6. Material—lead, gold, silver, brass, steel, copper, tin, zinc, horn, bone, tallow, wax.

Composition.—1. Pupils of this grade shall be required to join the sentences formed from simple objects, according to the methods laid down for grade G, into a composition.

2. Pupils shall next take two objects for a composition, tracing their resemblances, and afterward their differences.

3. They shall write descriptions of the pictures found in their Readers, and of those furnished by the Board.

4. They shall be taught to use the comma, where required; also to turn declarative into interrogative sentences, and affirmative into negative ones.

5. The same rules in regard to translation are to be observed as in grade G.

The uses of objects should engage a larger share of attention in this than in the preceding grade.

GRADE E.

Studies.—Spelling, reading, punctuation, penmanship, drawing, arithmetic, geography, composition, music, grammar, object lessons; German, when desired by parents.

Books.—Syllabus of Geography (for teachers only); McGuffey's Third Reader; Young Singer, Part I.; Bartholomew's Drawing.

Spelling.—Pupils shall be taught to write at dictation sentences formed from words in their reading lessons, or lessons in geography; also sentences from their object lessons.

Reading.—They shall be required to give a full and intelligent explanation of the subject of the lesson, and the words used; they shall be taught to read the lessons with fluency, distinctness, and suitable modulation, and to render an oral abstract of the same as a whole. Seventy selected lessons shall be required for spelling.

Punctuation.—They shall be taught to name and give the use of all punctuation marks in their reading lessons.

Penmanship.—They shall be taught to write with a pen all the small letters and capitals in words and sentences.

Drawing.—They shall take the course laid down in their text-books, and have exercises in drawing and combining straight lines into figures representing objects.

Arithmetic.—They shall review F grade course, shall use numbers as high as 10's in mental exercises in the four fundamental rules to amounts not exceeding 100, and figures as high as 9's in slate exercises to amounts not exceeding 100,000.

MODEL EXAMPLES IN MENTAL ARITHMETIC.

Section IV., Lesson 1; Section V., Lesson 2; Section VI., Lesson 3.

GEOGRAPHY.

Items starred (*) to be described by Teacher.

I.

ITEMS TO BE DETERMINED BEFORE USING MAPS.

A. East, West, North, South, North-east, North-west, South-east, South-west.

B. Locate teacher's table, door, windows, ventilator, and corners of room; St. Peter's Cathedral, Court House, Suspension Bridge, St. Mary's College, Washington Park, Lincoln Park, First Presbyterian Church, the High School Buildings, Public Library Building, Tyler-Davidson Fountain, Eden Park, and ten other objects of local importance.

C. A map of the city having been placed on the board by the teacher, the pupils shall give the *names* and *directions* of the principal streets of the city; ditto of school districts; ditto of street and residence; *location* and *general course* of Ohio River, Mill Creek, Miami Canal; and take walks, *mentally*, from one point of the city to another, naming the streets pursued and the directions.

D. Definition of river, creek, canal, pond, lake, hill, mountain, valley, and any other geographical feature the neighbourhood may afford facilities for studying. Surface elements of the earth—land and water. Apparent form or shape of the surface.

II.
(Using the Globe.)

A. Real form of the earth, with one or more simple proofs of the same.

B. Definitions of North Pole, South Pole, Equator, Northern Hemisphere, Southern, Eastern, and Western.

III.
(Using the Maps of the Hemisphere.)

A. Point out, number, and name the principal land and water divisions of the globe; their relative positions, sizes, and shapes.

B. Definitions of ocean, sea, gulf, bay, sound, strait, archipelago, cape.

C. Climate of the grand divisions, as determined simply by their position with reference to the poles and equator; zones—general vegetation of same, animal life of the same; distribution and leading characteristics of races.

IV.

Local Geography.—The pupils are required to locate only the most important points and places, and to study the principal physical features, such as water-sheds, mountain ranges, valleys, plateaus, lakes, &c., of the United States and North America.

The geographical drawing of this grade shall include the *elements of map drawing*, as exhibited on p. 15 of Demcker's Course, Part IV.

Music.—After reviewing the F grade course, they shall be taught the extension of the scale to upper F, 3-4 and 4-4 time; whole note, eighth note, and dotted half; whole rest, the repeat, the slur, and the tie. Exercises in two-part songs involving the above shall be practised, as contained in the Young Singer, Part I.

Grammar.—They shall be taught to speak and write correctly any sentence they may be required to use. They shall review the work of F grade, adding the semicolon to the punctuation marks for that grade. They shall also be taught to distinguish the subject and the predicate of simple sentences; the distinction between transitive and intransitive verbs; the objects of verbs and prepositions; the kinds of nouns (common and proper); personal pronouns; the properties of nouns and personal pronouns (person, gender, number, and case); and the distinction of present, past, and future time, in the use of the verb.

Object Lessons.—In this grade classification into higher and lower orders is principally considered.

1. *Vegetable Productions.—Fruit, grain, cotton, grass, lumber*—where obtained, and for what used.

2. *Animal Productions.— Wool, leather,* butter, milk, cheese, lard—how obtained, and how used.

3. *Minerals.—Gold,* silver, *coal,* limestone, *marble, iron*—how obtained, and how used.

4. *The City.—Manufactories,* stores, *buildings*—name and describe varieties; comparison of *city* and *country.*

Animals.—Mammals : Most common specimens of canines compared with the dog ; of felines compared with the cat ; of gnawers compared with the rat ; of thick-skinned animals compared with the hog ; of cud-chewers compared with the cow.

Birds.—Most common specimens of scratchers compared with the hen ; of swimmers compared with the goose ; of perchers compared with the canary.

Fishes.—A few of the most familiar, for structure and habits.

Reptiles.—Snake, frog, or lizard, for structure and habits.

Plants.—Comparison of a few familiar fruit and forest trees.

Minerals.—Description of a few familiar stones and metals.

PROPERTIES OF OBJECTS FOR GRADE E.

Colour.—Standard colour, hues, tints, and shades ; harmony of colours.

General qualities. { Natural, artificial, pulverable, granular, adhesive, absorbent, liquid, solid, compressible, sparkling, opaque.

Teachers to select the material from which to give lessons on *colour* and *general qualities* of objects.

Composition.—1. Pupils of this grade shall continue the exercise of comparing, in writing, different objects, both as to qualities and uses.

2. They shall take for topics the subjects printed in italics in their course of object lessons, and such others in the same course as the teachers may select ; and after the pupils have gathered, through their own observation and the aid of their teachers, all necessary information about these subjects, they shall write their compositions without any assistance whatsoever.

3. Pupils of this grade shall be taught to change the form of the sentence without changing its meaning, and to point out the change of meaning produced by an additional word, phrase, or clause.

4. They shall continue the exercise of writing descriptions of the pictures in their reading books, and also of the pictures furnished by the Board.

5. They shall have exercises in translation similar to those prescribed for pupils studying German in the two lower grades.

GRADE D.

Studies.—Spelling, reading, punctuation, penmanship, drawing, arithmetic, geography, grammar, object lessons, composition, music ; German, when desired by parents.

Books.—McGuffey's Fourth Reader ; Ray's Second and Third Part Arithmetics ; Guyot's Elementary Geography ; Young Singer, Part I. ; Bartholomew's Drawing ; Johnson's Physiological Chart and Handbook (for teachers only).

DIRECTIONS TO TEACHERS.

Spelling.—Same as grade E.

Reading.—Pupils shall be required to give a full and intelligent explanation of the subject of the lesson, and the words used ; shall be taught to read the lesson with fluency, distinctness, and suitable modulation, and to render an oral abstract of the same as a whole. Forty selected lessons required for spelling.

Punctuation.—They shall be taught to name and explain the punctuation marks in their reading lessons.

Penmanship.—They shall be taught to write with a pen, neatly and legibly, words and sentences, from copy and at dictation.

Drawing.—They shall take the course laid down in their text-book; exercises in drawing curves of different kinds—the circle, oval ellipse, spiral or scroll, and application of these exercises in ornaments, leaves, fruit, and other objects.

Arithmetic.—They shall review E grade course, shall read and write numbers as high as 1,000,000, and shall complete long division and United States money. They shall have numerous *practical* mental exercises in the four fundamental rules and in United States money.

Geography.—Selected portion of the text-book.

Grammar.—They shall review the work of the previous grades, adding the quotation marks, the colon, and the dash to the punctuation marks previously taught. They shall also be taught the comparison of adjectives, the formation and comparison of adverbs, the distinction between regular and irregular verbs, and all the tenses of the indicative mode, active voice.

The following prefixes shall be used in this grade : *en, er, in, mis, out, pro, re, sub,* and *un.*

Music.—After reviewing the E grade course they shall be taught the extension of the scale to lower and upper G, 3-8 and 6-8 time; the dotted quarter note, dotted eighth note, and the sixteenth note; the eighth rest; the use of the sharp and flat as accidentals; the use of the natural; the use of *p, pp, f, ff, mf;* and to read by letter. Exercises and songs involving the above shall be practised, as contained in the Young Singer, Part I.

Object Lessons.—In this grade classification is carried forward, and the pupils are taught to form definitions. Adaptation to habitation and mode of living is principally considered.

Animals.—Mammals : 1. Two-handed—man.

2. Four-handed—ape, monkey.

3. Flesh-eaters, feline—cat, lion, leopard, tiger, panther; canine—dog, wolf, fox, jackal. Insect-eaters—bat, mole, hedgehog. Amphibious—seal, walrus.

4. Gnawers—rat, mouse, beaver, rabbit, squirrel.

5. Solid-hoofed animals—horse, zebra.

6. Cud-chewers—Cow, sheep, goat, deer, reindeer, camel.

7. Thick-skinned animals—elephant, hog, rhinoceros, hippopotamus.

Birds.—1. Raveners—eagle, owl, hawk, condor.

2. Perchers—canary, nightingale, skylark, humming bird, mocking bird, swallow, crow.

3. Scratchers—hen, turkey, dove, quail, pheasant, peacock, partridge.

4. Climbers—parrot, woodpecker.

5. Runners—ostrich.

6. Waders—heron, stork, ibis.

7. Swimmers—duck, goose, swan, pelican.

Human Physiology. —

Body,
- Skin
  - Use.
  - Qualities.
  - Adaptation of quality to use.
- Flesh
  - Fat
    - Qualities.
  - Muscles
    - Use.
- Blood.
- Bones
  - Head.
  - Trunk.
  - Limbs.
- Nerves.

Note.—Call especial attention to teeth and spinal column. Teach how to take care of them.

A short, concise statement of the processes of digestion, circulation, and respiration.

NOTE.—Let every opportunity be used to impress lessons on care of the body.

Composition.—1. Pupils of this grade shall write descriptions of some of the animals named in their object lesson course, comparing them with each other, giving their natural locations, and their habits and uses.

2. They shall be taught to write letters, simple forms of promissory notes, and bills of purchase and receipts.

3. They shall write descriptions of the pictures found in their text-books, and of those furnished by the Board, and of a series of actions performed for the purpose in their presence.

4. They shall, as often as once a month during the last half-year of their course, write a composition, on a subject of their own choosing, from such topics as flowers, fruits, the seasons, animals, places, sunlight, moonlight, &c. Subjects with which they are personally acquainted to be preferred, for the most part, to those they know about from reading and hearing only.

DIRECTIONS TO TEACHERS.

All full rooms in grade D shall be divided into two classes for study and recitation in arithmetic, grammar, and geography, and the time allotted for these branches shall be equally divided between the classes.

INTERMEDIATE SCHOOLS.

GRADE C.

Intermediate schools shall be composed of pupils received, upon examination, from grade D of the district schools, and no pupil shall be admitted or transferred into such schools unless he or she be proficient in the course of studies prescribed for the district schools. The principal of each school shall keep a record of all the pupils examined by him in each study, with the results of the examination, in a separate book, provided for that purpose by the Board.

Studies.—Spelling, reading, punctuation, penmanship, drawing, arithmetic, geography, composition, music, grammar, physics; German, when desired by parents or guardians.

Books.—McGuffey's Fifth Reader; Ray's Second and Third Part Arithmetics; Guyot's Common School Geography; Young Singer, Part I.;

Bartholomew's Drawing; Harvey's Grammar; Hotze's First Lessons in Physics (for teachers only).

Spelling.—Pupils shall be taught to write at dictation sentences formed from words in their reading lessons or lessons in geography; also sentences formed from words in their composition course.

Reading.—They shall be required to give a full and intelligent explanation of the subject of the lesson, and the words used, and shall be taught to read the lesson with fluency, distinctness, and suitable modulation, and to render an oral abstract of the same as a whole. Thirty-five selected lessons shall be required for spelling.

Punctuation.—They shall be taught to name and explain the marks of punctuation, and the rhetorical marks which occur in their reading lessons.

Penmanship.—They shall be taught to write with a pen, neatly and legibly, words and sentences, from copy and at dictation.

Drawing.—They shall practise as directed by the teachers of drawing.

Arithmetic.—They shall review D grade course; shall take all of simple reduction, except troy weight, apothecaries' weight, cloth measure, and circular measure, and shall finish common fractions of simple numbers, both mentally and on the slate; they shall solve, mentally, problems similar to to those in the first twenty-one sections of Ray's Arithmetic, Second Book.

Geography.—Selected portions of the text-book.

Composition.—1. Pupils of this grade shall be required to describe something made of, or requiring in its manufacture, iron, gold, silver, copper, tin, India-rubber, wood, glass, marble, leather, wool, cotton, silk, hair, paper.

2. They shall describe some object brought from or belonging to a farm, garden, forest, mill, store, ship, dwelling-house, school-house, river, cave, mountain, battle-field.

3. They shall write short compositions on vapour, fog, clouds, rain, hail, thunderstorm, dew, frost, snow, ice.

4. They shall write descriptions of pictures, and of actions performed in their presence.

5. They shall be taught to write letters, promissory notes, bills of purchase, and receipts.

6. They shall write short biographical and historical sketches.

7. And, in a few special exercises, the correct use in composition of capitals and italics, by underscore or otherwise; of parenthetical clauses, quotations, and interlineations, and the proper marks for the same; and of paragraphs and their uses.

Music.—They shall review the principles, as laid down in D grade course, and practise two-part exercises and songs in the keys of C, G, and F major, and A minor.

Grammar.—They shall review the work of previous grades. They shall also be taught the properties of verbs (voice, mode, number, and person), the relative and interrogative pronouns.

A text-book may be used in this grade; the text-book and subject to be completed in the next two higher grades. In all the grades, both of the district and intermediate schools, particular attention shall be given to the correction of false syntax, and to the construction of written sentences.

Physics.—

- Attraction
  - Cohesion
    - Solids.
    - Liquids.
  - Gravitation
    - Weight of solids.
    - Pressure of water.
    - Pressure of the atmosphere; suction pump; barometer.
  - Capillary
    - Ascent of liquids in tubes.
    - Sap in growing vegetables.
    - Illustrated in the sponge, lamp-wick, sugar, &c.

- Heat
  - Sources
    - Sun.
    - Combustion.
    - Friction.
  - Expansibility of bodies, illustrated in solids, liquids, and the air; Thermometer.
  - Change of the form of bodies by heat; solids into liquids, and liquids into gases.
  - Conducting power of bodies; radiation; clothing.
  - Application of principles; vapour, clouds, rain, thunder-storm, hail, fog, dew, frost, snow, and ice.

- Light
  - Sources
    - The heavenly bodies.
    - Combustion.
    - Friction.
  - Refraction; glass (prism), water, air.
  - Convex lens (burning glass); the eye; spectacles.
  - Reflection; looking-glass.
  - Necessary to the growth and health of vegetables and animals.

The lessons are to be given in the simplest form possible, and, as far as practicable, by the object method. They are not designed to be exhaustive of the different subjects, but to present only their most general and obvious features.

For recorded compositions teachers are to select their own topics from any of the above.

GRADE B.

Studies.—Reading, embracing spelling, defining, vocal culture, declamation, and analysis of words; object lessons; mental and written arithmetic; geography; English grammar, with exercises in the use of language; United States history (maps shall be drawn, either as a whole, or in groups, of the countries studied by the pupils); drawing; physics and composition; music and penmanship under the teachers of those branches; German, if desired by parents or guardians.

Books.—McGuffey's Sixth Reader and Spelling Book; Ray's Second and Third Arithmetic; Young Singer, Part II.; Young Singer's Manual; Harvey's Grammar; Guyot's Common School Geography and Wall Maps; Anderson's

Grammar School History of the United States; Wurst's German Grammar; Bartholomew's Drawing; Hotze's First Lessons in Physics (for teachers only).

Music.—Pupils in grade B shall carefully review the course of study in music in the district schools, and practise exercises and songs in the Young Singer's Manual, in the keys of C, G, F, D, and B flat. Singing in three parts shall commence in this grade.

Composition.—1. Pupils of this grade shall describe some article or object brought from England, France, China, South America, Greenland, Africa, &c.

2. The teacher shall form a list of objects, and require the pupils to describe the processes by which such objects have become what they are—such as a silk dress, a hat, a cup of coffee, a gold dollar, a book, &c.

3. They shall write compositions on their reading lessons, and on subjects selected from their course in physics, and in history.

4. They shall also write compositions on pictures found in their text-books, and on actions performed for the purpose in their presence.

5. They shall write short biographical and historical sketches. Pupils shall be taught the force and effects of particles and connectives, to state facts or truths in various ways—as general, specific, absolute or conditional, true or false.

6. They shall be taught to write letters, promissory notes, bills of purchase, and receipts. Teachers in the intermediate schools are allowed the use of Murray's Exercises, to accompany the authorised text-books on the subject of grammar.

Physics—

I.—Attraction { Electrical; lightning. Magnetic; magnetic needle.

II.—Motion, action and reaction, momentum, vibrations of water, of chords, of resonant bodies.

III.—Sound; musical sounds.

IV.—Mechanical powers { Lever, wheel and axle. Pulley. Inclined plane, wedge. Screw.

V.—Properties of Matter { Indestructibility. Inertia. Extension. Impenetrability. Divisibility. Density. Porosity. Compressibility. Elasticity.

Conditions of Transfer.—Pupils passing to grade A must pass an examination in spelling, in orthography and etymology, in grammar; on the history of the United States to the opening of the revolutionary war; on geography; on mental arithmetic to section 25, and to percentage in written arithmetic; on composition, drawing, music, and physics.

GRADE A.

Studies.—Reading, including spelling, defining, analysis of words, vocal culture, and declamation; object lessons; mental arithmetic, completed and reviewed; written arithmetic, completed and reviewed; geography, completed and reviewed; United States history; drawing; music; composition; German, if desired by parents or guardians.

Books.—McGuffey's Sixth Reader and Spelling Book; Ray's Second and Third Arithmetics; Metrical System of Weights and Measures; Young Singer, Part II.; Young Singer's Manual; Harvey's Grammar; Guyot's Common School Geography and Wall Maps; Anderson's Grammar School History of the United States; Quackenbos's Aid to English Composition.

Music.—Pupils in this grade shall review the course laid down in B grade; shall also study exercises and songs in the Young Singer's Manual, in all the keys there laid down.

Penmanship.—Principals may, at their discretion, use the time now given to penmanship, in whole or in part, for any other branch of study needing it,-taking care, however, that all written exercises shall be executed with due regard to improvement in this branch.

Composition.—1. Pupils of this grade shall be required to write compositions from their reading lessons, and to reproduce stories read to them or told them by the teachers.

2. They shall be required to write a sketch of what they heard, saw, read, or did yesterday, and of what they hope to do at some future time.

3. Pupils shall be required to translate the pictures and engravings exhibited to them, for the purpose, into a written composition.

4. Pupils shall write descriptions of actions performed in their presence; shall turn poetry into prose; shall be taught to write business letters, also letters descriptive of places they have visited; and they shall write short biographical sketches of some of the eminent men of our country.

5. They shall also write on subjects selected from their course in natural science.

Gymnastics.—Shall be optional for the girls of both grades, at the discretion of the principal of the school.

Spelling and Definitions, as a distinct branch of study, shall be omitted from the course.

DIRECTIONS FOR TEACHERS.

History.—The course of history in grades A or B shall be connected with the study of reading, and consist of the reading by the classes of the text-book in history in use, not to exceed two lessons per week. At each lesson the pupils shall be questioned in brief review of the previous lesson. Teachers are expected to make these lessons interesting, *and pupils are required to understand thoroughly what they read.* Examinations in this subject are to be of the most general character. The other reading lessons shall be in the regular text-books in reading, and shall not exceed two recitations per week.

Composition.—It is not designed that pupils shall write on *all* the objects named for the different grades in the foregoing course. Teachers are expected to exercise their own discretion in making selections from them. They will be at liberty to substitute objects outside the course for some of those named, whenever they may deem it to the advantage of their pupils to do so. They shall be careful to select such objects, particularly in the lower grades, as shall be attractive to pupils, and may be easily described.

In all the exercises the greatest care shall be taken to have all the words used correctly spelled and their meaning understood.

The correction of mistakes in orthography and syntax, in all the grades, shall be, as far as practicable, the work of the pupils themselves.

Teachers are especially to keep in mind that they are not, in any stage of the foregoing course, to do the work of their pupils; and that the object of the course is to train up thinkers, having forms of expression peculiarly their own—not mere copyists of the thoughts and language of others.

In grades D, E, F, and G, the amount of time given to instruction in this branch shall be so much as may be assigned it in the time-table. The time given to it in grades A, B, and C shall be at least one hour per week.

Every pupil in whose grade composition is required to be taught shall record neatly, uncorrected by others, and preserve for inspection at the annual examination, at least one composition for each month of the school year.

Grammar shall be taught practically in all the grades, in connection with composition.

Moral Instruction.—Moral instruction must be given in all the grades by the respective teachers, in such a manner as may be prescribed by the principals.

COURSE OF STUDY AND TEXT-BOOKS

IN THE

GERMAN DEPARTMENT.

DISTRICT SCHOOLS.

GRADE H.—Object lessons and exercises in language, reading by sound, spelling, writing, singing, and drawing.

GRADE G.—Object lessons and exercises in language, reading, spelling, writing, grammar, singing, drawing.

GRADES F AND E.—Object lessons, reading and declamation, spelling, writing, grammar, translation, composition, singing, and drawing.

GRADE D.—Reading and declamation, spelling, writing, grammar, translation, and composition.

BOOKS.

The Board to furnish moveable letters for grade H, pictures of animals, of tools, &c., for instruction in object lessons, and Mason's Music Charts. The teachers shall use the exercises in Plate's German Grammar (parts first and second), or similar ones. The pupils shall have uniform writing-books in each grade, and the following Readers, viz. :—

GRADE G.—Lesebuch fuer Amerikanische Volksschulen, Part First.
GRADE F.—The same, Part Second.
GRADE E.—New German Third Reader.
GRADE D.—Germanus's Third Reader.

OBJECT LESSONS.

Same as in English.

READING.

GRADE H.—Reading by sound, with moveable letters.
GRADE G.—Through the First Reader.
GRADE F.—Through the Second Reader.
GRADE E.—Thirty-six of the easiest lessons in the Third Reader.
GRADE D.—Twenty-four of the most difficult lessons in the Third Reader.

SPELLING.

GRADE H.—They shall be taught by sound, by letter, and at dictation, easy words and sentences, excluding words with silent letters.

GRADES F and G.—They shall be taught to spell any word, and to write at dictation any sentence in their Reader, and to use correctly the capitals, the period, and interrogation points. A gradual progress from easy to more difficult words shall be observed, and the most important rules for the use of silent letters in the long and short syllables shall be given.

GRADES E and D.—They shall review the rules for the use of silent letters, and they shall be taught to spell any word, and to write at dictation any sentence in their reading and object lessons, compositions, and translations, and to spell such words as are alike or similar in sound, but different in orthography and signification.

PENMANSHIP.

GRADES G and H.—They shall be taught to write, in neat and legible hand, on their slates, the letters and any of the words which they are required to spell.

The three higher grades shall be taught to write, with a pen and ink, all the small letters and capitals, and to combine them into words and sentences. The teachers shall rule the slates, and teach their pupils to write the letters according to the adopted system.

GRAMMAR.

GRADE G.—Exercises on the proper use of the definite and indefinite articles; singular and plural numbers of the nouns.

GRADE F.—Declension of nouns, with definite and indefinite articles, to be practised chiefly, in sentences; adjectives and their comparison; numerals; personal pronouns; conjugation of the verb in the present and imperfect tenses.

GRADE E.—Review; declension of nouns, with adjectives; pronouns complete; conjugation of the verb in all the tenses except pluperfect and future perfect tenses (active voice); exercises and verbs governing dative cases, likewise with transitive verbs governing accusative cases; all the prepositions except those governing the genitive case.

Formation of nouns (Plate II, pp. 5-9); formation of adjectives (*ibid*, pp. 15-19).

GRADE D.—Thorough review of all the parts of grammar taught in the lower grades; all the tenses in both voices, and all the modes except the subjunctive mode; the participles; prepositions governing the genitive case.

Formation of words, especially of verbs (Plate II, pp. 47-50), simple sentence, and simple sentence with its modifiers.

COMPOSITION.

GRADE F.—During the second half of the year they shall be taught to write, in short and easy sentences, descriptions of objects spoken of in their object lessons, and a number of short and pleasing stories told by the teacher.

GRADE E.—They shall be taught to write descriptions of things and animals spoken of in their object lessons, and a number of stories told by the teacher.

GRADE D.—They shall be taught to write a number of descriptions, stories, and letters, and to transform poems into prose.

TRANSLATION.

Translation in all the grades of the district schools is to be in constant connection with the course of grammar and object lessons in each grade.

A pupil cannot be expected to translate connected sentences, as has been the practice heretofore, before he has received instruction on the grammatical relation in which parts of speech may occur in sentences. This instruction is given in the lessons in grammar, and the lessons in translation will serve to practise the rules of grammar and to impress model sentences in the memory of the pupils.

It is most essential that the pupils should remember certain model sentences, with their correct translation, illustrating the rules of grammar of their course; for instance, in the use of the article (grade G): der Januar ist der erste, der Dezember ist der letzte Monat des Jahres— January is the first, December is the last month of the year; iron is a metal—bas Eisen ist ein Metall; &c.

The sentences are chiefly to be taken from Otto's German Grammar, and from object lessons in grades H to E inclusive.

In addition to this, the teacher will teach the pupils the correct use of the following words, which are so frequently used improperly by German-American children :—

GRADE G.—*Nouns:* Baby, barrel, brick, bottle, box, butcher, carpet, chimney, closet, dish, drawer, examination, example, frame, gas, gate, grocer, grocery (Krämer, Kramladen), hall, lesson, line, match, Mr., Mrs., Miss, note, pavement, pencil, pin, pitcher, poker, pork, position, railroad, rocking-chair, row, section, shop, slate, slipper, steam, street-car, store, string, teacher, tin-cup, vacation, yard.

Verbs: To call (nennen, heißen, rufen), to catch, cover, dress, fetch, fight, fix, hurt, jump, kick, like, lock, mix, pull, push, rock, rub, step, use (gebrauchen), whip.

Adjectives: Absent, clean, late, mad, nice, perfect, present, tardy.

GRADE F.—*Nouns:* Alley, band, bell, blacksmith, blot, blotting-paper, broom, brush, bucket, button, car, ceiling, change, Christmas, cistern, copy-book, cousin, cream, curl, curtain, furniture, harness, holiday, kindling, meal (breakfast, dinner, supper), monitor, niece, noise, pass, penholder, pig, rope, scarf, shutters, sponge, stairs, stove-pipe, umbrella.

Verbs: To ache, ask, beat, boil, care, change, copy, cure, hitch, hurry, load, march, pass, pinch, poke, prove, put, rest, ride, ring, rise, rule, rush, settle, shave, skate, show, shut, start, stitch, swing, tear, tease, touch, turn, watch, wear, whistle.

Adjectives: Crooked, cross, purple, slippery, smart, straight, tight, tough.

GRADE E.—*Nouns:* Addition (multiplication, &c.), awning, bale, ball, barber, barber-shop, blanket, boulder, carriage, cart, company, crossing, cupboard, curbstone, dray, factory, fair, friends (relatives), funeral, garbage, grate, gutter, labourer, linen, mantel-piece, mechanic, merchant, merit, picture, pistol, printer, race, race-track, reward, sewer, shelf, show, shower, sign, sum, suspension-bridge, warehouse.

Verbs: To add (subtract, multiply, divide), allow, cheat, coax, crush, dare, dry, dust, elect, erase, excuse, explain, finish, fool, fry, furnish, gain, grumble, handle, haul, hollow, hop, like, mark, match, meddle, order (out), pledge, pound, prepare, price, prove, punish, punch, quarrel, quit, save, spite, spread, starch, sting, stoop, store, stretch, strike, string, stumble.

Adjectives: hiefig, heutig, geftrig n. f. w., &c.—a gold ring, an iron fork.

GRADE D.—*Nouns:* Accident, agent, auction, auctioneer, bank, bargain, cash, complaint, college, counterfeit, dentist, depôt, election, engine, ferry, ferry-boat, festival, job, lease, officer, painting, partner, party, police, premium, prescription, press, procession, relations, relatives, rent, sale, society, surgeon, wages.

Verbs: To bail (out); to be able, aware, bound to, convinced, in a hurry, mistaken, obliged, opposed, ready, satisfied; to be (the child is to learn German, Otto's Grammar, p. 88), to bear in mind, beg, complain, enter, favour, gain, get, hand, happen; to have (to), hint, lecture, let (laffen), make (he made me do it), mind, offer, oblige, permit, please, propose, return, stay, turn (to), use (to).

Adjectives: Adjectives denoting nationality (Otto, pp. 73 and 108).

In each grade the list of words may be completed at the discretion of the teacher, who is expected to leave nothing undone to restrain and check the pernicious practice of mixing the two languages.

As the pupils will remember fixed examples of the usage of language much easier when they are given in the shape of poetry, it is desirable that the pupils of all grades should learn suitable pieces of poetry by heart, and that those parts of these pieces which have reference to the grammatical task of the respective grades should be translated, and the translation remembered as well as the original.

COURSE OF STUDY IN GERMAN DEPARTMENT.

INTERMEDIATE SCHOOLS.

STUDIES.

GRADES B AND C.—Reading, declamation, orthography, penmanship, grammar, composition, translation.

GRADE A.—Reading, declamation, orthography, grammar, composition, translation, an abstract of the History of German Literature.

BOOKS.

GRADE C.—Uniform writing books; Pagenstecher's Fourth Reader.

GRADES A AND B.—Grammar, Becker's Leitfaden (for teachers); Plate's Praktische Deutsche Sprachlehre, Part II (for pupils); Hailman's Literary Reader, also for Anglo-American pupils; Otto's Short Course in German and Hailman's Reader, for beginners.

DIRECTION TO TEACHERS.

GRADE C.—*Composition and Object Lessons.*—Pupils shall be taught to write a number of descriptions, stories, and letters, and to transform poems into prose.

Reading.—Twenty-four Lessons.—Pupils shall review the rules for the use of silent letters, and they shall be taught to spell any word, and to write at dictation any sentence in their reading and object lessons, compositions and translations, and to spell such words as are alike or similar in sound, but different in orthography and signification.

Grammar.—They shall review the course of the district schools, and shall be taught to analyse simple, compound, and complex sentences, and to parse the words therein. In their translation they shall be taught the similarities and differences of the English and German grammar.

Translation.—Lessons from their Reader.

GRADES A AND B.—Translations shall be made, in part, from the exercises in Plate's Grammar. After the compositions have been corrected, the model compositions prepared by the teachers are to be translated into English. In the same manner the English compositions, after being corrected, shall be translated into German from the model composition furnished by the English teachers.

NEW CODE (1874).

Standards of Examination in English Elementary Schools, 1874.

	Standard I.	Standard II.	Standard III.	Standard IV.	Standard V.	Standard VI.
Reading.	A short paragraph from a book used in the school, not confined to words of one syllable	A short paragraph from an elementary reading book.	A short paragraph from a more advanced reading book.	A few lines of poetry selected by the inspector.	A short ordinary paragraph in a newspaper, or other modern narrative.	To read with fluency and expression.
Writing.	Copy in manuscript character a line of print, and write from dictation a few common words.	A sentence from the same book, slowly read once, and then dictated in single words.	A sentence slowly dictated once by a few words at a time, from the same book.	A sentence slowly dictated once, by a few words at a time, from a reading book.	A short paragraph in a newspaper, or 10 lines of verse, slowly dictated once by a few words at a time.	A short theme or letter, or an easy paraphrase.
Arithmetic.	Simple addition and subtraction of numbers of not more than four figures, and the multiplication table, to 6 times 12.	Subtraction, multiplication, and short division.	Long division and compound rules (money).	Compound rules (common weights and measures). (¹)	Practice and bills of parcels.	Proportion and fractions (vulgar and decimal).

¹ The "weights and measures" taught in public elementary schools should be only such as are really useful;—such as Avoirdupois Weight, Long Measure, Liquid Measure, Time Table, Square and Cubical measures, and any measure which is connected with the industrial occupations of the district.

This note applies to the codes of 1874 and 1875.

NEW CODE (1875).

Standards of Examination in English Elementary Schools, 1875.

	Standard I.	Standard II.	Standard III.	Standard IV.	Standard V.	Standard VI.
Reading.	To read a short paragraph from a book not confined to words of one syllable	To read with intelligence a short paragraph from an elementary reading book.	To read with intelligence a short paragraph from a more advanced reading book.	To read with intelligence a few lines of poetry selected by the inspector, and to recite from memory 50 lines of poetry. N.B.—The passages for recitation may be taken from one or more standard authors previously approved by the inspector. Meaning and allusions to be known, and if well known to atone for deficiencies of memory.	Improved reading; and recitation of not less than 75 lines of poetry.	Reading with fluency and expression; and recitation of not less than 50 lines of prose, or 100 of poetry.
Writing.	Copy in manuscript character a line of print, on slates, or in copy books, at choice of managers; and write from dictation a few common words.	A sentence from the same book, slowly read once, and then dictated. Copy books (large or half-text) to be shown.	A sentence slowly dictated once from the same book. Copy books to be shown (smallhand, capital letters, and figures).	A sentence slowly dictated once from a reading book. Copy books to be shown (improved small hand).	Eight lines slowly dictated once from a reading book. Copy books to be shown.	Writing from memory the substance of a short story read out twice; spelling, grammar, and handwriting to be considered.	A short theme or letter; the composition, spelling, grammar, and handwriting to be considered.
Arithmetic.	Simple addition and subtraction of numbers of not more than four figures, and the multiplication table, to 6 times 12.	Subtraction, multiplication, and short division.	Long division and compound rules (money).	Compound rules (common weights and measures).	Practice, bills of parcels, and simple proportion.	Proportion, vulgar and decimal fractions.
Grammar, Geography, and History.		(1.) To point out the nouns in the passage read. (2.) Definitions, points of compass, form and motions of earth, the meaning of a map.	(1.) To point out the nouns, verbs, and adjectives. (2.) Outlines of geography of England, with special knowledge of the county in which the school is situated.	(1.) Parsing of a simple sentence. (2.) Outlines of geography of Great Britain, Ireland, and Colonies. (3.) Outlines of History of England to Norman Conquest.	(1.) Parsing, with analysis of a "simple" sentence. (2.) Outlines of geography of Europe—physical and political (3.) Outlines of History of England from Norman Conquest to accession of Henry VII.	(1.) Parsing and analysis of a short "complex" sentence. (2.) Outlines of geography of The World. (3.) Outlines of History of England from Henry VII. to death of George III.